Sir Ranulph Fiennes was the first man to reach both poles by surface travel and the first to cross the Antarctic Continent unsupported. In the 1960s he was removed from the SAS Regiment for misuse of explosives but, joining the army of the Sultan of Oman, received that country's Bravery Medal on active service in 1971. He is the only person yet to have been awarded two clasps to the Polar medal for both Antarctic and the Arctic regions. Fiennes has led over 30 expeditions including the first polar circumnavigation of the Earth, and in 2003 he ran seven marathons in seven days on seven continents in aid of the British Heart Foundation.

In 1993 Her Majesty the Queen awarded Fiennes the Order of the British Empire (OBE) because, on the way to breaking records, he has raised over £14 million for charity. He was named Best Sportsman in the 2007 ITV Great Briton Awards and in 2009 he became the oldest Briton to reach the summit of Everest.

RANULPH FIENNES

Fear

HODDER

First published in Great Britain in 2016 by Hodder & Stoughton
An Hachette UK company

First published in paperback in 2017

A CIP catalogue record for this title is available from the British Library

ISBN 978 1 473 61800 8

Typeset in Sabon by Palimpsest Book Production Limited, Falkirk, Stirlingshire

Printed and bound by Clays Ltd, St Ives plc

Hodder & Stoughton policy is to use papers that are natural, renewable and recyclable products and made from wood grown in sustainable forests. The logging and manufacturing processes are expected to conform to the environmental regulations of the country of origin.

Hodder & Stoughton Ltd
Carmelite House
50 Victoria Embankment
London EC4Y 0DZ

www.hodder.co.uk

For Simon and Fone, the very best of friends down the long years

Fear and Fearfulness
from the *Bloomsbury Thesaurus*

Fear: fright, terror, horror, horrification, affright, dread, awe, panic, phobia, aversion, mortal fear, fear and trembling, unholy terror, fit of terror, blind panic, icy fingers, cold sweat, blood running cold, hair standing on end, chattering teeth, knocking knees; *informal* funk, blue funk.

Fearfulness: nervousness, timorousness, apprehension, apprehensiveness, anxiety, uneasiness, tension, trepidation, consternation, perturbation, alarm, unease, disquiet, dismay, foreboding, misgivings, qualms, agitation, nerves, palpitations, shivers, quaking, shaking, trembling, goose flesh, goose bumps, butterflies in the stomach, sinking stomach, stage fright, shivers up and down the spine; *informal* the jitters, the jumps, the willies, the jimjams, the collywobbles, the heebie-jeebies, a flat spin.

Contents

1

The Fear Factor

If I were on the edge of a precipice and a large grass-hopper sprang on to me . . . I should prefer to fling myself over the edge.

Salvador Dali

Twelve years ago, in 2003, I had a sudden heart attack on an easyJet plane about to take off from Bristol airport. Over the next three days in an NHS intensive care unit, twelve unsuccessful attempts were made to start my heart again. On the thirteenth attempt it obliged. By then a brilliant Italian surgeon had removed one twelve-inch artery from my leg and another from my mammary system (not much use to men!) to replace the two furred-up arteries that had caused my collapse.

Five years later, when I was crawling up a rope some 300 metres below the summit of Everest, a massive angina attack reminded me that my body's engine was hovering around its sell-by date.

The original Bristol trauma occurred with no warning at all and I can still remember nothing about it. Although it nearly killed me, I felt no fear, whereas had I known what was about to happen I would, of course, have been extremely afraid.

The Everest trauma was preceded by extreme pain in my chest and I was immediately aware that, suspended from a rope on a near-vertical ice wall at almost 29,000 feet (8,800 metres) above sea level at midnight, I was about to have another heart attack. The result was immediate panic. I was more terrified at that moment than at any other time in my life and, as a result, failed to think and react sensibly. Initially, I quite forgot the glyceryl trinitrate pills in my jacket pocket, which I carried for the specific treatment of just such an angina attack. By the time I remembered the pills, ripped off my oxygen mask and located the bottle, the wire stitches that had held my rib cage together since the previous transplant operation felt as though they were being torn out of my chest.

Over the years I have experienced both apprehension and panic, and I learnt early on that to achieve success in my chosen career of breaking polar-travel world records, I would need to prevent fear from causing pessimism and negativity, both of which are powerful ingredients of failure.

Trained in the army to 'know your enemy', I studied all aspects of fear with meticulous care, as though it were the topic of an examination. From basic fight-or-flight responses to the multiple stresses and worries of modern life that are causing an ever-increasing number of anxiety-related suicides worldwide.

The mechanics of fear are still being studied in laboratories using rats, cockroaches, chimpanzees and medical students, but the basics were revealed by the American physiologist Walter Cannon early in the twentieth century when he discovered that all mammals' digestive systems are disrupted by stress. Other fear symptoms that he noted included the tensing of muscles in readiness for action, and raised heart rates and blood pressure to pump blood with speed into limbs in readiness to flee.

For millions of years our ancestors, whether monkeys or hominids, have been alerted and often saved by their inbuilt 'fight, flight or freeze' alarm system. Although the daily perils of prehistoric life are no longer with us, we have retained many of the once-useful and involuntary reactions of a caveman, such as nostril dilation and bristling of our hair follicles, which may once have made our ancestors look more scary to their enemies.

This fight-or-flight inherited impulse is strong enough, laboratory research has confirmed, so that even today we are more likely to fear events or aggressive creatures that provided frequent threats to our ancestors, instead of the potentially lethal dangers of our modern lives. Thus we are much more likely to fear snakes and cliff walks rather than guns and fast traffic.

Love and fear are important emotions that help humans reproduce and survive, and both come with differing levels of enthusiasm. We can feel friendly, loving or adoring just as we can experience anxiety, phobias, fear and outright panic. Fear comes from the Old English word *faer*, denoting calamity or danger. This changed in Middle English to mean alarm, dread and an intense desire to defend oneself by fight or flight. With fear, unlike mere anxiety, there is a clear danger located in space and time that must be dealt with. The danger is tangible, although the element of fear is not, since it merely arises and exists in the mind.

Over the last two decades various new instruments, including functional magnetic resonance imagery, have allowed neuroscientists to observe functions of the brain and so establish basic facts about fear, which were previously mere unproven theories. Also, by identifying some of the 2 per cent of human DNA that differs from that of chimpanzees, scientists have isolated a single gene which regulates the production of neurons.

We can produce 100 billion neurons, which give us far greater thinking powers than chimpanzees. This also means that our brains have grown in physical size so that our bigger skulls make human births more problematic and our necks are more easily broken. Evolution has clearly decided that increased brainpower makes these extra risks worthwhile. Monkeys evolved from crocodiles, whose thinking brain (or neocortex) is made up of thin single-cell sheaths. In monkeys these sheaths evolved into multicelled, onion-type objects with new capabilities, including clever use of tools.

Part of the further-evolved neocortex, which is only present in humans, is now identified as the prefrontal cortex and is the key to our uniquely capable thinking processes.

Returning to our definitions of the varying degrees of fear, most of us are *anxious* for much of our lives, for anxiety is an emotion similar to fear but without any objective source of danger. It is our ever-revolving radar scanner on the alert for trouble.

Most people have *phobias* without knowing it. They can be inherited or acquired and consist of exaggerated fear of a situation (say, a snake confrontation) that is out of proportion to the actual danger and is beyond the voluntary control of the afflicted phobic sufferer. The word 'phobia' stems from Phobos, a Greek god who provoked terror in his enemies. *Panic* involves an attack of intense fear when suddenly confronted with danger. The god Pan is usually known for his friendly rural music, but he was originally fabled for his ability to evoke terror out of thin air.

In my life I have found that *anxiety* is healthy if kept in its place, *panic* is to be avoided at all costs, and *fear* is a welcome mechanism that enables the body and brain to work at their best.

I do not claim to be an expert on Fear, and I am certainly no psychologist, but I do know that I have developed my own way of fighting my inner fears and in the following pages I will describe various situations that have made me anxious, other times when I was distinctly nervous and tempted to abandon the challenge of that moment, and quite a few memorable moments when I was scared stiff.

When I force myself to face up to such fears I concentrate on comparing myself with others who have stood up to far worse situations, and sometimes over many years. People, ordinary and not so ordinary, who through the twists and turns of fate have found themselves face-to-face with fear and terror in its various guises, from bullying, persecution and torture, to man-made massacres and natural disasters.

I say to myself, aloud, 'They did it and they survived. So don't be a wimp. Go for it . . . Now!'

* * *

In 1943 RAF fighters from 204 Squadron forced many German bombers to drop their bombs before they reached their London targets. Living in Surrey at the time, my mother witnessed the explosive results, including a blown-to-bits cow in the neighbouring field to our home. Another local peril at the time was the unpredictable arrival of V1 and V2 rockets, Hitler's latest hi-tech weaponry.

That August my father came home briefly from the war, my mother was pleased to see him and I was conceived. He was killed that November while leading his tank regiment, the Royal Scots Greys, to liberate Naples. His father, my grandad Eustace, died the same year, and my only other male paternal relative, Uncle Johnny, had been killed in the First World War.

Through the long months of 1944 whenever the sirens blared, my mother hustled me, then a baby, under the sturdy kitchen table with my three older sisters. Day-to-day life at that time, Mum later told me, was lived on the edge. Fear was never very far away, and nor were tales of horror.

The week that I was conceived, in June 1943, thousands of people were blown up or burnt to death during air raids on Coventry and London, with RAF revenge raids on Wuppertal and Hamburg, where a firestorm incinerated 31,000 citizens.

Three weeks before my first birthday, heavy RAF and USAF bombers flew over our house in a two-mile-wide formation on their way to the city of Dresden. There are old folk in Dresden care homes today who still remember the events of that night of terror in February 1945.

The city's old buildings, once hit, blazed and quickly linked together in an all-consuming inferno that in some areas of the city reached a temperature of over 1,000°C. The inferno created fire tornadoes of hurricane force that flung burning property, furniture and people with their clothes on fire into the air and over considerable distances. Many areas of the central city burned for three days, and a pall of smoke three-and-a-half miles high, containing paper, wood and other items, hung over the city.

Citizens, after cowering terrified in cellars and basements, died either from incineration while trying to escape amid huge curtains of flame, or by asphyxiation from smoke and fumes where they hid. In one basement ninety young girls were all found sitting as if still alive. For hours after the raids were over, the streets were full of the screams of the injured, and the death toll exceeded 23,000.

My grandmother Florrie, in her eighties with her husband dead and two sons killed, wanted to end her days back in her childhood home near Cape Town. So she took my mother and all of us children from war-torn Britain to the beautiful vineyard valley of Constantia, which had been farmed by her numerous Rathfelder ancestors for some three generations. I was still a baby at the time of our exodus to Africa. Whilst Granny supervised the building of our new home in the shadow of Table Mountain, we lived for a year beside the sea in a rented bungalow, and I gained a reputation there as the 'naughtiest boy on the beach', yelling at my nanny and tearing her stockings at a time when nylons were hard to come by.

I remember very little of those early days in Africa, other than various disconnected events that made me frightened, such as crossing the street between the beach and the bungalow when a bicyclist, struck head-on by a speeding car, shrieked as he splattered against the windscreen and was messily killed. I can still recall that image as though it happened yesterday.

According to my sister Gill, who is five years older than me, I was 'spoiled rotten', for Granny and my mother doted on me and I had no male relatives.

Aged four I was sent to the local Little People's School, where bullying was rife. My self-defence weapons were a piercing scream and the tactic of ingratiating myself with the main bullies by asking them home to tea, with an abundance of yummy cream cakes on offer.

My sister Gill loved her Anglo–Arab horse and often won showjumping competitions at gymkhanas, being beaten only from time to time by our cousin and near neighbour Gonda Butters who, as Gonda Betrix, later became South Africa's leading Olympic showjumper. I was given a Zulu pony but, after being kicked on the knee, tried to avoid all horsey activities whatsoever. Gill, after watching the movie *Ben Hur*, would, on horseback, tow me round and round the lawn on a piece of sacking and she gave me the name of Jockey Jelly John.

At the other end of our garden was a small, dark wood in which our gardener John made a grape-based drug with the local name of *dagga*. I was very frightened of that wood and never entered it. John disappeared one day and his successor, named Abner, fell out with a local witch doctor, who placed a spell on him. He begged for help from Granny, who told him that God would protect him. But Abner, who was from the Transkei, did not believe in God and he died for no apparent reason later that month.

At one end of our valley one of Granny's sisters owned a redundant swimming pool, which at that time was a slimy breeding ground for frogs and giant toads. One day, fishing for them with a butterfly net, I slipped and fell in. Being a non-swimmer, I cried out as I began to drown. Two of my sisters, who were sunbathing nearby, dived in and saved me, and for a while I stopped being rude to both of them. The fear of that brief moment of panic came back to me a year or so later during a beach outing to the Cape resort of Hermanus.

A white woman on the beach close to us fell asleep and her husband took his surfboard out into the breakers. After a while his wife awoke and, clearly worried about her missing husband, told the beach attendant. A rubber boat with an outboard was launched and I remember sharing a tiny part of the apprehension of that poor woman as she awaited the return of the lifeboat. I also recall her uncontrollable sobbing when her husband was brought back dead.

Some days after my sixth birthday, while my mother was away, Granny was ill and I wanted a slice of my birthday cake, which was locked in the larder. I asked Christine the cook, who held the key, for a slice, but she knew that this was forbidden until teatime and shook her head. I had recently come across a pistol (once owned by my father) while rummaging in my mother's bedroom, so I took advantage of her absence and, pointing the pistol at Christine's stomach, I told her, 'The cake or your life!' She screamed and fled. I was later beaten with a cane by my mother, who fixed a notice above my bed that read:

Never, never let your gun
Pointed be at anyone.

Granny kept fit in her early eighties by shuffling her way along the sandy trails between the vineyards that surrounded us. In those days the grape farms belonging to our relations covered an area of Constantia known as the Valley of the Vines and Granny would drop in for a cuppa with various cousins. On one occasion when I accompanied her, a pair of Rottweiler guard dogs, normally chained to their kennels, were loose and attacked us. Granny waved her walking-stick at them, so they took the easy option and went for me. I screeched in terror as one tore at my pullover and the other bit through my left hand. I retained the two round scars of its incisor teeth for many years.

In her mid-eighties Granny, the formidable driving force of our family for as long as I could remember, grew increasingly forgetful and quiet. So my mother, by nature a happy-go-lucky sort of person, had to make key decisions, one of which was whether or not to continue to bring up her four children in South Africa. Two factors helped her to decide that she would take us back to Britain. She was an active member of the Black Sash anti-apartheid movement and had heard, through local gossip, rumours of a 'petrol war' that the predecessors of the ANC were said to be planning, whereby the suborned household staff of well-off white people would set fire to their homes on a given night. Whether or not this plan was ever in danger of achieving fruition I have no idea, but to my mother and many of our friends it certainly created a background of fear and uncertainty.

One evening I heard my mother sobbing alone in the kitchen. I put my arms around her as she told me of two local men from the *vlei*, a collection of huts by the stream that flowed through our valley, who had severely beaten a stranger whom they believed to be a thief. They had dragged him, bleeding profusely and blinded in one eye, up our drive and demanded that my mother phone the police.

Their victim had apparently died by the time the police turned up, and my mother, who was badly shocked by the event, decided then that she would leave Africa as soon as Granny died.

That December, aged eight, I watched from our attic window as the seasonal *berg* winds caused great forest fires to race up the flanks of Table Mountain to the immediate north of Constantia. The following New Year's Eve our cousin and next-door neighbour, Googie Marais, sent a fusillade of bullets over our roof. My mother explained that this was a traditional and 'friendly' act, known as 'shooting the bounds'.

During my school holidays an historic event, known as the Van Riebeeck Festival, was celebrated in Cape Town. This event has taken place once every century since 1652 to celebrate the landing of Jan van Riebeeck, a Dutch colonial administrator who landed at Cape Town and established a way station there. Mum decided that I should visit the festival and enjoy the sideshows. At the last minute she could not go with me, so a family friend (who much later became my youngest sister's mother-in-law), a Scottish lady named Isobel, agreed to take me.

I was small for my age and timid. Isobel was keen that I should experience a chariot ride on a rickshaw hauled at a trot by a giant Zulu warrior with an ostrich-plumed headdress that must have made him seem huge and terrifying. I yelled, fled and ignored all Isobel's urgings and scornful comments. She reported my behaviour to my mother together with the dire warning that her only son was turning into a wimp, of whom his late, illustrious father would not be proud.

In 1950 Granny suffered a stroke and died. To please my mother, I made an effort to live up to my father's reputation. I would often look at the velvet-lined showcases of his medals and those of his father, and I dreamed that one day I would win my own medals. An early effort at 'being brave' was to join those macho boys at my school who could perform running somersaults into the school sandpit. Misjudging the distance on one occasion, I hit my head on the concrete edge of the pit and was taken to the local A&E unit where my neck was clicked back into its correct position; I felt proud.

Aged nine, I was sent to a boarding school where the headmaster, from time to time, beat me for very good reason. He also awarded me the School Divinity Prize, and for a month or two I decided to become a priest.

During my first term at the boarding school, there were two boys who had both been at my previous school. They were bigger and stronger than me and the three of us formed a close friendship, for which I was extremely grateful. However, during my second term a gang of three boys from a couple of classes senior to mine began to pick on the children in my class, especially during the seldom-supervised morning and afternoon breaktimes.

To my growing astonishment and dismay, my two special friends, instead of responding to my appeals to lead our own defensive grouping against the bullies, actually joined the three bullies by running errands for them, such as cutting and collecting bamboo canes with which to chase me and my classmates around the playground and the games fields.

To this day I can picture the faces of the two boys who betrayed the friendship that to me at the time was a life prop, a second family, an alliance which gave me self-confidence. It was my first seal of acceptance, like a child from a care home joining an urban gang.

Even now I think of them as the scum of the earth. They chose to sup with the Devil and betray their own best friend – me – out of cowardice, wanting to protect their own skins. It is a lesson I have never forgotten, and it helps that I still nurse the long-ago intense dislike I held for my two erstwhile school-friends, who dumped me and joined the school bullies to avoid being bullied themselves.

During the school holidays in South Africa, I would wake my mother every morning with a kiss and draw back her bedroom curtains. One day a dislodged spider landed on the back of my neck, bit me, then ran down the inside of my pyjamas. For some reason I felt numb with fear and sure that I was about to die in agony: maybe I had read too many deadly spider stories in my comics. Quite what the psychology may have been behind the resulting phobia I have never worked out, but I developed from that day and for many subsequent years a deep-rooted fear of all spiders, even harmless little English ones.

I was once badly bitten by a large, aggressive Rottweiler guard dog, but that never caused me to fear other dogs. And when I was nearly ten years old, my mother took all my sisters to the Kruger National Park in the summer holidays. I was considered too young and likely to do silly things near wild animals, so I was sent to Aunt Utcha's poultry farm in a desolate stretch of scrubland called Kommetie Sands.

I helped the only farmhand, Utcha's son Michael, to collect hundreds of eggs every dawn. There may not have been dangers at Kommetie, in comparison with the wild animals of the Kruger, but there was an abundance of snakes, mostly puff adders, rat snakes and boomslangs, a local brand of tree snake. Michael ignored them, even those *inside* the chicken shacks, so I followed his example. Later in life I was to patrol by night in snake-ridden lands for many months at a time and without any worries, but throughout my teenage years spiders scared me witless.

This spider fear is very common, I now know, as is that of snakes. Even among Eskimos (the Inuit) who have never seen a live snake, humans have a genetic ability to spot and identify snakes in movies more quickly than they can spot other animals, including lizards. Four-year-old children can locate snakes faster in pictures than they can other, equally camouflaged, animals. Snakes kill over 100,000 people a year, even nowadays, many of them in East Africa where our ancestors originated, and *their* genetic fears of snakes were deeply embedded prior to their emigrations to snake-less places.

Just as rats born in research laboratories will be automatically terrified of cats, so will a baby human fear snakes, including an Inuit child whose ancestors have for centuries never even heard of snakes.

Over the centuries, all types of creepy-crawlies have infested our minds with fear. Wasps, maggots, spiders, cockroaches and worms, they all arouse a natural human reaction of disgust or distaste. As a result, we often drench our environment with insecticides, even if many of the insect victims have key environmental functions, such as honey-bees, which are our vital global pollinators.

I make an income by lecturing all over the world at business conferences, and as a consequence spend many nights in hotels, often in the capitals of Third World countries. After reading various horror stories about the evil effects of bedbug bites, I have become fastidious about checking the sheets and duvets everywhere I sleep. This bug obsession, I was assured by a psychologist friend, was not related to my spider phobia, and I was relieved to be told that about one person in ten develops a phobia of some sort during their lifetime, the most common concerning animals or heights. Worldwide nearly 50 million people experience anxiety involving animals, and 11 million wrestle with entomophobia (fear of insects).

There are many suggested techniques for ridding yourself of a phobia such as ophidiophobia – a fear of snakes. One that is said to work well is used by the psychiatrist Joseph Wolpe, which involves *gradual exposure therapy*. You make a start by studying photos of snakes in ever more threatening poses, then you graduate to watching them in cages, and finally you interact by stroking harmless varieties.

In the USA, where phobia statistics are helpfully available, it is clear that animal and insect phobias tend to begin at the age of about ten, get worse around twenty and then, if untreated, may stay in place till death. The human condition, which causes virtually no phobias involving fear of fast-moving vehicles or of guns, despite the fact that they kill more every day than American animals and insects kill in a year, shows the power of our inherited instincts. After all, our ancestors lived under threat from lions, spiders and snakes for 4 million years, compared with our experience of being run over or shot in a mere, comparative, blink of an eye.

I had, despite many childhood visits to Cape Town Zoo, always kept well away from lions, but, unlike spiders, they were easily befriended and, after a brief introduction to a friendly lioness at the ALERT lion-cub rescue centre in Zimbabwe, I happily went for a walk with her. And our innate fear of insects is a sensible protective feature, bearing in mind that a common housefly in a modern slum is known to be coated with bacteria, and that stings and bites have led to many millions of people dying from plagues, yellow fever and malaria.

Of all catalogued human phobias, only acrophobia (fear of heights) and claustrophobia (fear of enclosed spaces) are more prevalent than snake and spider phobias. Various specific insect sub-phobias include:

Acarophobia: fear of insects that cause itching
Apiphobia or Melissophobia: fear of bees
Arachnephobia or Arachnophobia: fear of spiders
Entomophobia or Insectophobia: fear of insects
Isopterophobia: fear of termites
Katsaridaphobia: fear of cockroaches
Mottephobia: fear of moths
Myrmecophobia: fear of ants

Pediculophobia or Phthiriophobia: fear of lice
Scabiophobia: fear of scabies mites
Spheksophobia: fear of wasps

An interesting addition to these is the fear of grasshoppers, which was made notorious by the surrealist painter Salvador Dali. As a child he was bullied by other children, who threw large grasshoppers at him. This made him scream, which only encouraged this unique form of torment, to the point where the mere mention of a grasshopper sent Dali into hysterics.

He must have been a touch weird, because his favourite pet was, for years, a bat that he found dead one day being eaten by ants. Because of his resulting lifelong terror of ants and grasshoppers, many of Dali's most famous paintings feature horrific images of both insect types involved in scenes of decay and destruction. When he was middle-aged, he told a journalist, 'If I were on the edge of a precipice and a large grasshopper sprang on to me and fastened on to my face, I should prefer to fling myself over the edge rather than endure this frightful thing.'

Phobia-delving psychologists have long pointed to any fear of insects as being entwined with the allied emotion of disgust caused by images of slime and maggots writhing in rotten flesh. Mark Twain once wrote:

> The fly . . . hunts up patients suffering from loathsome and deadly diseases; wades in their sores, gaums its legs with a million death-dealing germs; then comes to that healthy man's table and wipes these things off on the butter and discharges a bowel-load of typhoid germs and excrement on his batter cakes.

Many insects are cleverly designed for specific tasks that, for their survival and propagation, require them to squirm, ooze, penetrate human organs (such as earwigs into ears in old wives' tales), infest pubic hair, or wriggle into the skin as in the case of bilharzia. There are a million species of insect known to science and there are thought to be another 4 million yet to be classified. It is no wonder that so many people are scared of creepy-crawlies. More than half the earth's organisms are insects.

I would eventually overcome my teenage fear of spiders, but I do have a history of other personal anxieties, some of which have lasted longer than others.

In the 1980s I worked for the Los Angeles-based Dr Hammer of Occidental Oil as his gofer in Europe, and I arranged for him to be the speaker for the host industry at the annual oil-company bosses' black-tie dinner at the Grosvenor House hotel in London.

Only a week before the dinner, Dr Hammer, in his mid-eighties, fell ill and told me to give the speech on his behalf. When I passed this news to the president of the dinner, the most important European oil event of the year, he spluttered, 'Ran, you can't be serious. If your boss can't come, we will invite the chairman of Shell or BP. I don't wish to be rude, but you are a nonentity in the oil world.'

I quickly nodded my agreement, as I was way out of my depth. I phoned Dr Hammer in LA, but he was enraged. 'I can't make it. So my representative *will* make my speech.'

In the event the president did not wish to upset the chairman of Occidental Oil, so he had to accept the lowly me. I asked him who the dinner's guest speaker would be, so that I could do my homework and say polite things about him.

'Ran, I'm afraid that is confidential for security reasons. I cannot tell you until an hour before the dinner.'

My nerves were so tattered with apprehension when the day of the dinner arrived that I contemplated cancelling my speech with some last-minute excuse. But then, I realised, I would lose my well-paid job for sure.

I took four aspirins, donned my dinner jacket and, two hours before the dinner, met the president at the Grosvenor House hotel.

'Our guest speaker,' he told me with great pride, 'is Mrs Thatcher, and here are a few notes about her support for the North Sea oil industry that you can add to your speech.'

This was very bad news. At the time Mrs Thatcher was at the zenith of her popularity, even more so than after the Falklands War. This was due to the sympathy (even from some of her habitual Labour opponents) that she had earned the previous week, when an IRA bomb had exploded in the Brighton hotel where she was staying during the annual Conservative Party conference. She narrowly escaped death, but five people in nearby rooms were killed and thirty-one were injured.

I sat next to her during the dinner and she gave a rousing speech, at the end of which she apologised for having to rush off 'to the House'. Then, as she left the ballroom, the entire room, over a thousand oil bosses, stood up, cheering and stamping their feet, and they continued to do so for several minutes after she had disappeared.

The red-coated toast-master eventually managed to bring the room to order so that the president could introduce the next speaker. When I stood up, I could hear the muttering, which was along the lines of, 'Who the hell is he?' I have never felt more inadequate nor more out of place in my life, even on arrival at Eton, and if I have ever experienced the effects of PTSD, it happened in the aftermath of that dinner.

Even now I feel butterflies before lecturing at black-tie dinners, especially in that Grosvenor House ballroom, despite the fact that I make a living by giving talks at conferences all over the world.

2

Fear of the Bullies

We will catch you in Judy's Passage and break your fingers

Anonymous

After Granny died, my mother managed to sell our Constantia home and one day announced to me and my sisters that we would all be 'going to England'. To her, this must have meant a great relief and a longed-for homecoming. My three older sisters, all over fifteen, still retained memories of an English home, but to me the move meant an exodus to an alien place.

'You will love it there,' my mother assured me. 'There is nothing to fear.'

She managed to buy an old cottage in Lodsworth, a Sussex village beside the woods through which wound the River Lod. Our neighbours, on the other side of the woods, had a nine-year-old daughter with very blue eyes, called Ginny.

I was sent to a boarding prep school in Wiltshire where there were two other boys from South Africa, but I worked hard to lose the last traces of my Cape Town accent. I enjoyed my time there and studied hard enough to be accepted by Eton College, which was where I first learned what it feels like to be a social outcast. Not due to any lingering colonial traces, but because I was a pretty boy.

Not long after my arrival at Eton aged twelve and at the key time for making early friendships, establishing some sort of mini-identity amongst peers, and sensitive to each and every new childish insult, I learned that I had been branded a *tart*. This, I discovered, meant that I sold sexual favours to older boys in return for popularity, or out of fear of threats. The fact that this was untrue did not stop the gossip from spreading and soon being passed to me with wide grins by my leering classmates, who were lucky enough to have less girlish looks. Perhaps because this curse came out of the blue, since my mother had never been advised to warn me of its existence, and possibly because my all-female upbringing (with no brothers) had left me inexperienced in the art of being equally nasty back to verbal bullies, I merely clammed up, deeply hurt, now that I was known as a tart; a word I still hate.

For the next two years I loathed school, lost all my confidence and, at an especially bad period in the summer of 1958, was determined to jump off Windsor Bridge to end it all. However, looking down into the rushing waters of the Thames, I thought of my mother, my sisters and even of the blue-eyed girl back home. With tears in my eyes, I slunk back to my House and knew that I lacked the courage to escape the ongoing taunts by way of taking my own life.

Even the holidays with my loving family were ruined as the start of each new term loomed ever closer, and with it the growing apprehension of the verbal bullying awaiting me. Eventually, even if she wouldn't send me to another school and preferably a day school, I begged my mother to speak to my housemaster and get permission for me to wear a tailcoat and not 'bumfreezers', which were short cut-off jackets that ended at a boy's waistline and left his trousered backside uncovered. This, I well remember, had the effect of making me feel naked as I walked daily from classroom to classroom and then back to my House, hearing the occasional wolf whistles from the windows of other Houses – two dozen of which overlooked the streets of Eton.

The bumfreezer rules were strict. Until a boy reached the height of five feet four inches (or had special dispensation), he would not be allowed to switch to wearing 'tails', which were standard tailcoats as worn by waiters in smart London clubs. These hung down to the backs of your knees. Happily, my mother's heartfelt plea made in person to my housemaster, to whom she poured out my tart story and my resulting character change from a loving, confident child to a morose, nervous mouse, had an immediate effect, and great was my relief when my brand-new tailcoats covered my bum.

But the tails did not alter my looks and older boys still, apparently, 'fancied' me. I therefore developed a permanent scowl, and in the streets looked only at the pavement. Then one day, a boy named Dave Hart, who had joined my House the same term as I had and was also alienated from his peers, told me that he so hated one particular bully that he was going to take up boxing (which was then an alternative to fencing or gymnastics), so that he could beat up his tormentor.

Hart never did take up boxing, but he gave me the idea to do so, and from then on my constant state of fear, shame and derision, began to diminish. Despite my small stature, I learnt to dodge and weave against boys with a longer reach. The instructor, an ex-army man named Reg Hoblyn, was patient and meticulous in his lessons, and as a result I trained extra hard and was soon admitted to the school boxing team at my weight class.

Aged fifteen I began to win matches and, even more important, stopped looking pretty. As new inputs of pretty boys arrived at Eton, the tart taunts were redirected and my self-confidence gradually returned.

At about that time I somehow met a skinny boy called Mike Denny. He was a prefect in his House and had pioneered the art of stegophily at Eton – basically the practice of night climbing the spires, domes or towers of tall school buildings and crowning their topmost feature with a token of the successful ascent, such as a flag or lavatory seat.

I became Denny's number two, and although I suffered from a serious fear of heights, even looking out of third-floor windows, I found that darkness completely removed this phobia and left me with a wonderful sense of excitement and, following a successful climb, of achievement.

Many years later, the adventurer Bear Grylls told me how, during his time at Eton, he had climbed the same school buildings by the same routes.

Denny and I enjoyed many first ascents, including that of Lupton's Tower, but we were eventually spotted on the dome of School Hall at midnight. I managed to escape, but Denny was caught and only avoided immediate sacking because he was due to leave school anyway at the end of that term.

My five years at Eton included two years of dealing with the abject fear of ridicule and humiliation but as I now know, for everything is relative, my experiences of bullying were nothing compared to the living hell of many thousands of children worldwide. Take, for example, the trials of the highly acclaimed concert pianist and TV presenter, James Rhodes, who, back in the 1980s was educated at that 'other Eton', Harrow School, alongside the actor Benedict Cumberbatch. In his autobiography he describes how he was, like me, brought up by a loving mother and sent to an expensive preparatory school. What happened to him there made a nightmare of his next thirty years.

The first official police report on the 'Rhodes case' was filed in 2010, some twenty years after the events took place. Unlike my boxing coach at Eton, whose dedicated hours of instruction over the years hugely boosted my self-confidence, James Rhodes's equivalent instructor ruined his life through fear and shame.

The following statement by one of Rhodes's teachers is unedited and I include it in its entirety since it remains a lesson and a warning to all loving parents:

> In September 1980 I was appointed head teacher of the Junior School at Arnold House, a preparatory school for boys in St John's Wood. It was there that I first met James Rhodes. He was a beautiful little boy, dark-haired and lithe, with a winning smile. He was bright, articulate and confident for a five-year

old. From the earliest of ages it was clear that he had a talent for music. When he was six, in about 1981–2, he was in my form (I was a teaching head in those days). His parents were lovely people, themselves high achievers and they lived just down the road from the school. Although they recognised James's talents for music, I suspect they wanted him to have an all-round experience in education, and sporting activities were to be included. They signed James up for the extra-curricular boxing activity. This was a paid-for activity, and once 'signed up' the parents committed to at least a full year of coaching.

Chere Hunter, the teacher who wrote this report, added:

The boxing coach was a man named Peter Lee, who worked at the school on a part-time basis in the late 1970s. He hailed from the Margate area of Kent. He was a powerfully built man, but not very tall and was probably then in his late forties. In 1981 a new gymnasium was opened and Lee was in his element. He claimed to have been involved all his life with boys' clubs and boasted of his friendship with Jackie Pallo, a famous wrestler.

Quite a few of my boys from the Junior School were sent to boxing to be taught by Peter Lee. Some appeared to really enjoy the activity and I do remember that in the beginning James did too. However, fairly soon after he had started boxing, I noticed a change in James's demeanour. He became rather withdrawn and appeared to be losing his sparkle. The boys who were enrolled for boxing would change into white shorts and coloured house T-shirts in their classroom and then I would escort them over to the gym and collect them forty minutes later.

It became clear to me that James was becoming reluctant to attend this activity. He would take ages to change and often kept the rest of the group waiting. I remember so clearly the time he asked me to stay with him in the gym. I didn't. I thought that he was being a bit of a wimp. However, every boxing day,

> usually twice a week, James would play up and I realised that he really didn't want to be there. On many occasions I did stay with him. I hated the whole thing. These very small children were being positively encouraged to be aggressive. James was a thin little boy and it was clear that he was very uncomfortable.

Chere Hunter thought at the time that when Mr Lee asked James to stay behind to help him clear up the equipment, he was trying to make the child feel special.

> When I took the rest of the group back to change, it was always James who had to go with Mr Lee and help him clear up. I allowed this to happen on many occasions. All this was more than twenty-five years ago, long before child protection became an issue, but there seemed to be an element of trust between colleagues, and children being alone with an adult was never really questioned.
>
> One day James came back to the classroom to change, having been with Peter Lee, and he had a bloody face. When I asked him what had happened he burst into tears, and I went straight back to the gym to question Mr Lee. I was told that James had fallen. I didn't believe him and at that point I suspected that the man was being violent in some way towards James.

Chere Hunter then shared her concerns with her colleague, who was the headmaster looking after the Senior School. She told him about James's personality changes, that he seemed reluctant to go to the boxing activity and that she was worried that Mr Lee was in some way frightening the child. But her colleague told her that she was over-reacting and that little Rhodes needed toughening up. Chere continued:

> I can't remember exactly how long James continued boxing, but I do remember him, on more than one occasion, begging me not to send him to the gym. I also remember explaining to him

that, because his parents had opted for this paid activity, I couldn't take him out of it without their permission. I spoke to James's mum about this and she too had noticed that he wasn't particularly 'himself' and that he appeared withdrawn at home. She was a lovely lady who adored her two sons, but I can't remember the activity being cancelled for him. I sat in that gym week after week. I thought I was protecting him. One day when he returned to the classroom after having helped Mr Lee to tidy up, he had blood on his legs. I questioned him, but he never said a word, just cried quietly. I took him home that day and we played the piano together.

Chere explained that when James left her care to enter the Senior School, he no longer had her to protect him. It was frowned upon for teachers to 'mother' the boys when they became seven-plus.

So I saw this once happy, confident child become paler and paler as time went on. He was a very unhappy boy and didn't stay the course until the usual age of thirteen, but was moved to another school when he was about nine or ten. My colleagues in the Senior School just said that he was very unhappy – and that was the reason for him leaving.

I next saw James when he was seventeen and at Harrow School, where he was competing in a piano competition. My godson was in the same competition. James struck me as a very troubled young man. I later heard that he had had some sort of breakdown. I have recently read an article in the *Sunday Times* about James, who is now an accomplished concert pianist. I was appalled to read his reference to being seriously abused by a teacher at his primary school.

I felt sick with the remembrance of it, and I am wracked with guilt for not realising the hell that James must have been going through. I tried to protect him from what I thought was physical nastiness. It never occurred to me in my naivety that anything of a sexual nature was occurring. I am now in touch with James

> again and he has confirmed the sexual abuse and asked me to name the teacher who hurt him so badly. I got the name right.
>
> Sadly, now I look back and realise that James might not have been the only victim. There were several children who were fearful of Mr Lee, and at the end of the year, because of that, I banned all children from my Junior School from going to his boxing activity. I was regarded as an over-protective female by my male colleagues. Thank God I was.
>
> I am desperately sorry that James has suffered so deeply and for so long. I am also immensely proud that he has come through this and out the other side. He deserves every success and happiness in life. Scars and deep wounds sometimes make us stronger.
>
> I write all this because I know I have to go to the police. Mr Lee might still be alive. He might still be involved with children, even his own grandchildren. It is my view that he is a danger to young people. As a minister in the Church of England and a part-time prison chaplain, I see the effects that serious abuse has on the lives of young people. May God be the judge of these people who ruin the lives of others.

When James Rhodes wrote about his childhood ordeal in 2014, he was already a respected Channel 4 presenter on popular programmes about classical music. He explained his motives for writing of his experience, saying that the first incident in a locked gym closet had changed him irreversibly and permanently. From the moment of his first rape, aged six years old, Rhodes had felt shame that:

> someone could only do those things to me if I were already inherently bad at a cellular level . . . Ask anyone who's been raped. If they say different, they're lying . . . We are ashamed, appalled and to blame . . . Still now, at the age of thirty-eight, I have this empty black hole inside of me that nothing and no one seems capable of filling . . . No relatives or wives or girl-

friends or shrinks or iPads or pills or friends. Child rape is the Everest of trauma.

Rhodes will clearly never forget the physical pain of the oft-repeated rapes. He wrote:

> The damage that the gym teacher's cock had done caused the lower part of my back to explode. Something so big being forced into something so small again and again cannot be sustained without causing catastrophic damage. I woke up at home one day in the holidays vomiting from the pain and was taken to hospital . . . Over the course of five years I had had sex with a man three times my size and thirty to forty years older than me, against my will, painfully, secretively, viciously, dozens and dozens of times. I was turned into a thing to be used.

Unhinged by post-traumatic stresses, Rhodes turned over the following decades to drink, drugs and self-harm by slitting his arms with razor blades. This eventually led to a suicide attempt in a rehab centre.

After Chere Hunter made her 2010 statement, the police traced Rhodes's tormentor, by then in his seventies and living in Margate, *still* working as a part-time boxing coach for boys under ten. He was charged with ten counts of buggery and indecent assault, but was deemed unfit for trial after he had a stroke. He died soon afterwards, leaving Rhodes, and God knows how many other children, with a lasting legacy of fear. In Rhodes's words:

> I am hard-wired to fear the worst, believe every negative voice in my head and expect terrible things to happen . . . War is the best way to describe the daily life of a rape survivor. There are threats everywhere, you cannot relax – ever . . . and you keep going on a mixture of adrenalin and terror.

Torment by a gang whose aim is to terrify their victim is just as soul-destroying as the hell suffered by Rhodes, and it is far more common.

Schoolboy Bradley Parkes from Willenhall, Coventry, attempted suicide early in 2015 after being repeatedly attacked, tormented and threatened by a gang of bullies. The gang was well known to local residents; they vandalised buildings, smashed windows and even assaulted someone with fire, using a lighter and an aerosol spray. But though they had been reported many times, the police did little to intervene.

The gang made Bradley their random target. They mugged him several times at knifepoint. During one mugging, a gang member slashed Bradley's face with a knife. In another incident Bradley had his hand broken.

After taking the brave decision to report the gang to the police – which resulted in the arrest of one of its members – Bradley was labelled a 'grass' by the rest of the gang and the relentless torment and abuse continued. Terrified, Bradley turned to suicide. He hanged himself from a tree in a nearby wood. In his suicide note he wrote that he would rather be dead than suffer more abuse.

Incredibly, Sophia, a friend of Bradley's from school, was walking in the area and she found him and initiated life-saving CPR. An ambulance was called and Bradley made it to the hospital where he was induced into a medical coma. His mother was told that he might not survive, and that even if he did, he might suffer from brain damage. A year later he is slowly recovering.

* * *

One day at Eton I found a note in my study/bedroom written in capital letters:

YOU THINK YOU BOX WELL. WE WILL CATCH YOU IN JUDY'S PASSAGE AND BREAK YOUR FINGERS.

There was no signature and no way of knowing who had left it there or why. My only route to the gym in the evenings for boxing practice was by way of the dark and narrow lane called Judy's Passage, and for the next two years I kept looking behind me on my way to the gym. Thinking back, I realise how slight my fears of that anonymous threat were compared with the contemporary horror that is cyberbullying.

StopCyberbulllying.org defines cyberbullying as 'any situation where a child or teenager is tormented, threatened, harassed, humiliated or otherwise targeted by way of the Internet, interactive and digital technologies or mobile phones.'

Cyberbullying thrives on many social media websites such as Facebook, Myspace and Twitter, and by 2011 cyberbullying statistics (from Internet Safety 101) showed that at least 1 million children had been harassed, threatened or subjected to other forms of cyberbullying on Facebook alone during the previous year; and nearly half of teens aged thirteen to seventeen reported that they had experienced some sort of cyberbullying such as 'sexting' in the past year.

Sexting involves sending sexually explicit videos or photographs of your body, or of a sex act, to another party by way of a digital device, usually as a willing token of love or sexual attraction to that party. Surveys in the USA in 2015 have shown that 20 per cent of teens have sent or posted nude photographs of themselves. The receiver, who may later grow to dislike the sender of the image, may then post the images online or spread them around their school, or simply blackmail the sender by threatening to do so. Closet homosexuals are especially susceptible to such threats through fear of being 'outed' and ostracised by friends and family.

This, according to a US report, seems to have been the case for one Tyler Clementi, who committed suicide very soon after a video of him kissing another man was spread online. Similarly, thirteen-year-old Ryan Halligan committed suicide after a rumour was started at his school that he was a homosexual. Halligan had faced bullying for three years leading up to this point, beginning with 'traditional' bullying and moving on to cyberbullying. At one stage, his fear of physical attack from bullies led him to learn kickboxing for self-defence. Shades of my own reaction to verbal bullying at Eton.

There is often a close link between cyber threats and traditional physical bullying. The British report *I h8u* states that for many boys, 'being a victim of direct-physical bullying was clearly associated with receiving threatening text.' Many victims, as a result, feel unsafe and afraid both at school and at home.

In 2015 the American Academy of Paediatrics reported that:

> Researchers have proposed a new phenomenon called 'Facebook depression', defined as depression that develops when pre-teens and teens spend a great deal of time on social media sites, such as Facebook, and then begin to exhibit classic symptoms of depression. Acceptance by and contact with peers is an important element of adolescent life. The intensity of the online world is thought to be a factor that may trigger depression in some adolescents. As with offline depression, pre-adolescents and adolescents who suffer from Facebook depression are at risk of social isolation and sometimes turn to risky Internet sites and blogs for 'help' that may promote substance abuse, unsafe sexual practices, or aggressive or self-destructive behaviours.
>
> The main risk to pre-adolescents and adolescents online today are risks from each other, risks of improper use of technology, lack of privacy, sharing too much information, or posting false information about themselves or others. These types of behaviour put their privacy at risk.
>
> When Internet users visit various websites, they can leave behind evidence of the sites they have visited. This collective, ongoing record of one's Web activity is called the 'digital footprint'. One of the biggest threats to young people on social media sites is their digital footprint and their future reputation. Pre-adolescents and adolescents who lack an awareness of

privacy issues often post inappropriate messages, pictures and videos without understanding that 'what goes online stays online'. As a result, future job and college acceptance may be put into jeopardy by inexperienced and rash clicks of the mouse. Indiscriminate activity using the Internet can also make children and teenagers easier targets for marketers and fraudsters.

But cyberbullying is, of course, not limited to schools and amongst teens: it happens to adults too, particularly on the social media website Twitter. Here, cyberbullies can create accounts quickly and anonymously, and then harass users without fear of being caught.

A typical example of the many teenage victims of cyberbullying in the USA is the sad case of Rachael Neblett who, in 2006, was a seventeen-year-old student at Bullitt East High School in Mount Washington, Kentucky. It is a small school in a quaint and friendly town. Rachael, a budding gymnast and cheerleader, had a bubbly, open personality and it seemed as though she would tell her parents anything – except that she had become a victim of cyberbullying. Rachael was small of stature, standing at under five foot. While this helped with her gymnastics, it made her an easy target for bullies.

Rachael was able to cope with whatever bullying came her way at school until the summer of 2006, when she began to receive threatening anonymous online messages, primarily through her Myspace account. She didn't confide in her parents – possibly through the fear that she would lose her online privileges and that her parents wouldn't understand. But the threatening online messages continued, and Rachael, terrified, eventually confided in her older sister Peyton, who then told their parents Mark and Donna. They feared for Rachael's safety as these online messages didn't read like 'traditional' bullying. They were of a terroristic nature and contained multiple physical threats and documented Rachael's daily movements. These 'stalking' elements of the messages recorded Rachael's movements at school, and even in her class.

It was obvious that the bully must clearly be a student at the school. Mark and Donna took these emails to the principal of Bullitt East High, and a small-scale investigation ensued. In an effort to ascertain who the bully was and to make Rachael feel safer, a few school officials watched Rachael as she got on and off the school bus and walked to class. This, however, did nothing to allay her fears and the threatening messages continued, making Rachael feel as though she was being watched. She didn't feel safe at school, or even in her own home. The final straw came on 9 October 2006 when Rachael received the following terrifying message: 'I am not going to put you in the hospital, I am going to put you in the morgue.'

After she read this message, Rachael didn't want to go to school, she didn't want to see her friends, she didn't want to leave her own room. Shortly after, Rachael tragically took her own life. While her parents were away at work, Rachael went into their bedroom, walked over to their closet and removed her father's .38-calibre gun from the unlocked case on the top shelf, and she shot herself in the chest.

Even though the police conducted an investigation and even though they found the computer from which the emails were sent, no one was ever arrested for the cyberbullying and online threats.

I was in the British Army for eight years but never experienced any form of bullying at any level, whether among the officers or the men. But as in every walk of life, it does, of course, sadly go on. An example is that of Joseph McCabe, who was stationed in 2007 at a British Army base on the Rhine in northern Germany very close to the one where, in the 1960s, I spent three years.

Joseph attempted suicide several times after repeated and institutionalised bullying and threats. He had a severe stammer that led to his victimisation, but he had learnt to control it. However, when he didn't join his fellow soldiers on drunken nights out the bullying began and his stammer returned, only adding more fuel to the fire.

While serving his 'tour' in Iraq in 2008 the bullying turned into full-on death threats and physical attacks. One soldier put a knife to his throat and said, 'You've got until the end of the tour to kill yourself. If not, accidents happen on tour.' The following year Joseph was stabbed in the leg by a fellow soldier. He went to his superiors, but not only did they ignore the problem, they joined in on the bullying. The more he was targeted for abuse, the worse his stammer became, and the bullies recognised this and kept pushing him.

Joseph's requests for a transfer to a different regiment were denied. He saw a camp psychologist, who ignored the problem and said that all he needed to do was to go to a bar and get drunk. Another psychologist urged that he should be discharged, but this was never acted upon. After these meetings Joseph attempted suicide five times.

Joseph's weakness, for which he was easily picked out as a victim by the local bullies, was his stammer. In Rachael Neblett's case, she was tiny for her age.

Another nest of nastiness where fear is rife is that of domestic abuse, where women are abused by their so-called lovers. I recently watched a BBC television documentary on the topic of bullied partners, which made it clear that many hundreds of thousands of women the world over live in extreme fear of violence within their own homes.

The documentary *Behind Closed Doors* covered the experiences of just three women with live footage of court cases and personal interviews, plus CCTV coverage of police interviews. The overt violence was horrifying to see. One woman named Sabrina suffered a six-hour beating that left her an unrecognisable mass of blood and bruises. She survived only by dialling 999 and throwing her mobile under the bed so that the operator could hear her screams as the blows landed. Her boyfriend tried to claim that Sabrina had been beaten up outside the house by a drug dealer; but the pattern of blood spatters in the house gave the lie to that. Physical violence is hard to cover up, and Sabrina, who thought she was going to die as her boyfriend kicked and battered her, burst into tears outside the courthouse.

'I thought I was gonna hate him and I don't,' she sobbed. 'I still love him, and all I wanted to do was to run to him and wrap my arms around him and tell him that it's OK. I'll be here when he comes out.'

In a way, even more unsettling than Sabrina's case was that of Helen, who had long lived in terror of her boyfriend Laurence, with whom she had been living for many years. The film showed Helen's father, Russell, helping her to move out of her recently imprisoned boyfriend's well-furnished home. Russell, looking bemused, said, 'On the surface everything seemed fine. All these years she's been telling me that everything's wonderful. I mean, you see how nice it is in here. Good life they had. But you never know.'

In fact, as Russell discovered to his horror, the truth was very different, for Helen had, through the years of outward bliss, lived in constant fear of Laurence, who often sent her abusive text messages and regularly beat her up. She had, for instance, been unable to attend her mother's memorial service due to a swollen face and black eye. The point made by this excellent documentary was that Helen, like a great many other abused partners, was desperate to hide the reality of her miserable existence. Laurence seemed to everyone but her to be an amiable and harmless individual.

This brought it home to the viewer that nobody really knows what goes on behind the closed doors of our nearest neighbours, or even our own family members, and the insidious ways in which fear, shame and utterly irrational affection can allow women to forgive the cruel bastards who abuse them.

Looking back, I can now appreciate that my own fears during those years of ridicule in my 'pretty boy' days and the self-induced ruin of my holidays caused by apprehension before going back to hell, as I then saw Eton, were as nothing compared with the fears of thousands of children, teenagers and abused loners back then, now and, inevitably, in the future.

3

Fear of Failure

Bomber Baronet and Screaming Girls in Nightdresses.
Newspaper headline

On my seventeenth birthday, my mother asked if I wanted to stay on at Eton to take my A-level exams. I nodded without hesitation, because I knew that the only career I wanted was to be a carbon copy of my father – to command what to me was the finest regiment in the world, the Royal Scots Greys. When Dad joined them aged eighteen they had six hundred grey horses, but now there were only some four dozen sixty-ton battle tanks.

To become a commissioned officer in the Regular Army I would need a minimum of two A levels. I had managed to pass only four O levels, so when told of my wish to stay on, my housemaster advised my mother that I was unlikely, in his opinion, to obtain any A levels if I did spend another year there. He advised her to send me to a 'crammer' college specialising in 'force-feeding less intelligent pupils'. At least he was honest.

So my future was clear. Get two A levels at a crammer, spend two years of hard military training at Sandhurst Officer Cadet School, join the Scots Greys in Germany as part of the NATO forces facing the armies of the Warsaw Pact countries, and gradually work my way up to commanding the regiment. Dad had dealt with the Nazis; I would face up to Karl Marx.

The crammer college that my mother chose, because my best subjects were French and German, was in Aix-en-Provence, but during the summer months before I was due at the French college, I was caught with a group of local Sussex friends throwing army smoke bombs into the dormitory of a local girls' school. The national newspapers headlined their reports with *Bomber Baronet and Screaming Girls in Nightdresses*, which caused my poor mother a great deal of embarrassment. I was clearly a liability and not to be trusted at home in Sussex. What might I not get up to in France?

So she enrolled me at a language crammer in the seaside town of Hove, near Brighton, and bought me a Vespa scooter on which the journey to the crammer from home was less than an hour.

I was there for a year, and early on I discovered that Ginny, the blue-eyed girl from the other side of the woods at home, by then aged sixteen, was a boarder at a school in Eastbourne, which was near Hove! At the crammer I found concentration in French and German classes extremely difficult, because the contemporary fashion for girls at the time was to wear extremely short miniskirts, known as pussy pelmets.

But I knew that I must pass the two A levels, so I struggled to concentrate on the teacher rather than on the twitching bronze thighs of the female students sitting at nearby desks.

I read textbooks late at night, ate little, was often dangerously sleepy on my scooter between my lodgings and the crammer and, for the first time in my life, began to feel generally depressed due, I assume, to my ongoing nagging sense of failure, inadequacy and inability. In a nutshell, fear that I might not be able to achieve my own long-cherished goal. This fear, nowadays classified as student stress, has increased dangerously in today's climate. Take the case of the Oxbridge equivalent college in the USA, the Ivy League University of Pennsylvania, where in 2014 six students committed suicide in one thirteen-month period. One of them, Madison Holleran, was a top athlete, beautiful, popular and highly intelligent. Yet, despite high achievement, she felt inadequate and was terrified of failure. So she jumped off an upper deck of a multi-storey car park.

Anxiety induced by exam stress can be fatal, even in mid-teens, in atmospheres where goal achievement looms larger than life. In the Palo Alto district of California's Silicon Valley, four teenagers killed themselves in the first few months of 2015.

One student at Palo Alto High School, commenting on the suicides of her fellow students, said, 'We teeter on the verge of mental exhaustion every day. We are not teenagers. We are lifeless bodies in a system that breeds competition and hatred . . . We are sick.'

My own worried state at my Hove crammer was a straightforward fear of failure, but today's twenty-first-century, suicide-inducing factors include increasingly cut-throat competition for places at top universities. This is due to the growing perception that life advancement hinges on admission to *elite* universities, and another modern stress factor is the repayment of tuition fees.

Many psychologists maintain that the reason why exam fears often cause suicides is the age-old fight-or-flight mechanism. In his book *The Fear Project*, Jamail Yogis postulates:

> When I showed up to class, I identified the danger: final exam! That information was quickly routed through my visual thalamus and my visual cortex to my ancient reptile brain, which told my adrenal glands to get ready to survive a sabre-toothed tiger . . . Meanwhile, my modern brain felt all of this adrenal drama and thought, *Oh no, I'm panicking. I'll be more likely to fail*. This 'fear of fear' generated more imagery of how bad it would be if I failed, beginning a downward spiral of adrenaline surges and cortisol pumping. *This is really serious*, my modern brain told my ancient brain, not just one sabre-toothed tiger, but several.

Ginny's father forbade her to see me because of the smoke-bomb incident and other indiscretions, but I managed, when his back was turned, to take her back to school on my scooter. She held my waist and I was in heaven. On one occasion, a mile from her school, a cyclist appeared from nowhere and I swerved to avoid him. I awoke in hospital. Ginny had mere bruises, but her father was furious. I had thereafter to see her secretly by night in a fourth-floor attic at her school, so my climbing experiences at Eton proved useful. One night I was caught on the school's flat roof by a patrolling schoolmistress, and was politely seen off.

With a small group of fellow students, I began to climb and 'decorate' local monuments, including Brighton Pavilion and a number of technically difficult church spires. My proudest conquest was definitely the 'summit' of Hove Town Hall, which towered above the police station.

The following day, the local *Evening Argus* reported: 'An attempt has been made by the Hove Fire Brigade to remove the flag but their equipment could not reach it. No further attempt will be made to remove it. The spire is unclimbable.'

On a student outing to Beachy Head one winter's day, I tentatively tried to walk to the cliff edge, but came to a rapid halt some three paces away as the warning feeling of intense fear grabbed hold of me. Despite the years of night-climbing, often up highly exposed walls with dicey handholds on lightning conductor wires or Victorian drainpipes, I was still as prone as ever to vertigo by day, like some Draculine vampire enfeebled by dawn.

The crammer failed to earn me any A levels, but by passing an O level in German, I had a tally of the minimum five 'O's needed to join Mons Officer Cadet School. If I could pass their five months of basic military training, I would be awarded a short-service commission with the rank of second lieutenant and a total of three years' service with the Scots Greys. Better than nothing.

At Mons I teamed up with Lord Wrottesley, a monocled Irish earl nicknamed Rotters, who knew of a complex climb up the west wing of a nearby girls' boarding school. Unfortunately the police were alerted and we both ended up in prison for the night.

Rotters was sacked and had to join the Parachute Regiment as a trooper. I was awarded fifty-six days of RPs (Restricted Privileges), which was two days longer than my remaining spell at Mons. My platoon sergeant major informed me that I had chalked up the record number of RPs ever awarded since Mons was first formed. Nonetheless I was passed out by the Queen and so became a commissioned officer.

After tank training in Dorset I was sent to join the Army in Germany. At the time the Greys were stationed south of Hamburg and close to the East German border. I commanded twelve men and three sixty-ton Conqueror tanks. We were, in theory, capable of reporting fully armed and alert at specific locations along the border defence-line twenty-four hours a day and with a mere two-hour warning in readiness for any expected Soviet attack.

Our NATO training exercises involved complex journeys through the German countryside, weaving through deep pine forests and along narrow lanes. I found the map reading difficult and my greatest fear was of becoming lost, especially when acting as lead tank for a squadron move on a Brigade exercise, with a great many ears listening in to every critical remark handed out over the Brigade radio network.

With twelve steel monsters lumbering behind you through the narrow streets of a German village, tearing up the cobbles with their steel tracks, a single wrong turn can cause a chaotic scenario, of which other officers will gleefully remind you long after leaving the Army.

There are many dead-end tracks on the vast Lüneburg Heath tank training area, and the experience of having all the other tanks behind you turn around in a forest of narrow lanes just wide enough to take a single tank as a result of your getting lost is the stuff of nightmares. The fault may have resulted from a muddy blotch on your map, as you squinted at it through blinding rain or choking dust, but try explaining that later to an angry troop sergeant.

Or you could end up during a major NATO exercise, as Paddy

Earp, one of my fellow troop leaders, once did with all his tanks enmired in one of Lüneberg's notorious swamp zones, and the whole NATO advance was held up whilst Paddy's tanks were extricated by the Royal Engineers.

At that time, as part of BAOR (the British Army of the Rhine), we faced the Soviet Union's forces at their most aggressive. According to the historian Arthur Schlesinger Jnr, one of President Kennedy's aides at that time, 'This was not only the most dangerous moment of the Cold War. It was the most dangerous moment in human history. Never before had two contending powers possessed between them the technical capacity to blow up the world.'

President Kennedy himself said during the Cuban Missile Crisis in October 1962 that the chance of nuclear war was 'somewhere between one out of three and even'. The superpowers could very easily have stumbled towards Armageddon through mere miscalculation.

During the winter months I took over the regimental cross-country ski team and, in the summer, the canoe team. Ski training was in the Bavarian forests, and I took successive canoe groups up or down the Danube, the Rhine, the Rhone from its source to the sea at Marseille, the Loire and various smaller rivers. There were many scary times, including when, due to a sudden storm, two canoeists went missing off the coast of Denmark for several hours.

Having narrowly missed being made Captain of Boxing at Eton, I took up the sport again with the regiment, but many of the soldiers were extremely large and aggressive street-wise Glaswegians. My own weight was within the Light-Heavy class, where some of the most lethal and agile boxers lurked. I contemplated the normal procedure of losing enough weight to drop into a lighter class, but an elderly major, Tarry Shaw, who had been in the regiment when my father was a boxer, suggested that I take the unusual step of *increasing* my weight into the Heavyweight class, where all the really bulky bruisers awaited their chance to pulverise all opposition in front of the regiment at the annual Boxing Championships.

'They're big,' Tarry explained, 'but they're slow and you can run fast enough backwards to avoid being flattened whilst getting points with quick jabs.'

I ended up in the Finals facing a Glaswegian REME mechanic named Reid and nicknamed The Beast. He weighed over fifteen stone (I was just thirteen stone after two months of food-stuffing) and he stood three inches taller than me. Worse, he was notorious as the most dreaded fighter in the regiment.

Was I frightened? I was petrified. Tarry Shaw had given me extremely bad advice but, once listed as Heavy, I could not withdraw my name without fear of taunts of cowardice. I contemplated getting flu, but there was none about, or falling off my tank turret, but that seemed too obvious. Somehow the time ticked by until the awful moment when I entered the ring to the deafening howl of the assembled Greys, their appetites for violence whetted by the previous bouts of lesser weights. I hardly dared take a look at the grinning bulk of The Beast, fearing that I would disgrace myself there and then.

The first round was awful. Twice a glove like a moon rock contacted my head and my vision exploded in starbursts. Once a sledgehammer swing caught my chest and I hit the floor determined that I was done for. Then, realising that roughhouse tactics could only favour The Beast, I cast my mind back to the long years of Eton training and the feint-and-cut tactics of Reg Hoblyn. This paid off and The Beast began to bleed. His bulk made him tire in the third round, his guard dropped and I was able to damage his face. I won by a narrow margin.

On a canoe training exercise one summer I took the men in our three-ton Bedford lorries to the Kiel Canal north of Hamburg since, although many miles from the actual training area for which I had a permit, it was ideal for training purposes. Unfortunately, one of my corporals fired a flare by mistake at a passing Russian fuel tanker, and this activated the Canal Alarm

System. If a single ship has to stop in the narrow confines of the canal, all ships are immediately halted.

I was in deep trouble and was ordered to report in full uniform to the Divisional Commander, who was then the Duke of Norfolk. For some reason I was heavily fined but not court-martialled, despite the fact that, because of the flare, all canal traffic across Europe had been stopped, which caused an expensive delay.

That winter my short-service commission with the Greys was to end and I was about to apply for a one-year extension, the longest allowed for a short-service officer, when I spotted an advertisement on Regimental Orders for a three-year secondment to the Special Air Service. I applied at once and in February 1966 I said goodbye to my Greys friends and joined 124 soldiers and 12 other officers on the official SAS Selection Course.

By the end of the first week, which consisted of various physical and mental tests, only seventy soldiers and six officers remained. Week Two saw the departure of forty more soldiers and all but four officers.

The course ended with twelve men and three officers being awarded their SAS badge. Because all SAS officers are ranked captain or above, I missed out the rank of full lieutenant and became the youngest captain in the British Army at the time. But not for long because, in the words of my new commanding officer, 'Pride came before a bloody great fall.'

The Selection Course was followed by several months of training in eight personal skills. These were demolition, fast-response shoot-to-kill, parachuting, communications, resistance to interrogation, close-quarter fighting, field medicine and field survival. Failure in the tests for any one of these skills was not permitted.

On leave at home in Sussex I courted Ginny who, at eighteen, was tall, shapely and, as I well knew, much sought after by a number of local suitors. I lived in fear that once away with the SAS I would lose the love of my life.

In June that year I was due for a two-month jungle training course, but an old Etonian friend asked me to join a protest action the day before I was to catch the RAF flight to Malaya.

William explained that Twentieth Century Fox was making a movie, *Doctor Doolittle*, in the Wiltshire village of Castle Combe, recently voted by the British Travel Association as 'The Prettiest Village in Britain'. The Royal Fine Arts Commission had attacked Twentieth Century Fox for altering such 'an exceptional English village' with their film-set activities, including a large dam on the village stream. William's aim was to publicise the depravation of the moguls by disrupting their first day of filming.

He knew that I would be able to create a diversion using 'thunder flashes'. As it turned out, having laid various charges on time fuses, I ended up being apprehended by the police, as were William and the two others in our group. Although nobody was hurt, we were charged with various crimes and, at the subsequent Chippenham Assizes, heavily fined and placed on six-month police probation.

I was thrown out of the SAS, demoted back to second lieutenant and returned to the Scots Greys in Germany. As a convicted arsonist, my chances of ever becoming Colonel of the Scots Greys had definitely diminished. The media highlighted the court case and Ginny's father made sure that she was kept well away from me for a year by sending her to Spain.

Back in Germany, I worked hard at tank training and with the various regimental sports teams, but my brief time with the SAS had fired me with a desire to experience real action. So, when a chance came out of the blue for secondment to the army of the Sultan of Oman, I took it and, aged twenty-three, enrolled for an Army course in Arabic. Before leaving for two years' active posting, I proposed to Ginny, who I had loved since I was twelve. I could not afford a ring, but she said, 'Yes'.

Oman lies along the south-east side of the Arabian Peninsula. The main northern sector of this Sultanate is peopled by Omani Arabs, but a southern province, the size of Wales, contains tribes of African origin known as Dhofaris who were ruled, on a very loose rein until the 1970s, by the Omani Sultan.

So long as the British, with whom the Sultans had a long-standing protection treaty, held sway in neighbouring Aden and South Yemen, the Sultans had no trouble from that quarter. But in 1967, and shortly before I arrived in Muscat, the British withdrew from Aden and the Russians took their place.

For the first time, Marxism had a firm base in Arabia from which to attack Dhofar and thence Northern Oman. The Soviet-trained guerrilla forces would, if successful at removing the Sultan, command the western side of the Straits of Hormuz, the gateway to the Persian Gulf through which two-thirds of the free world's oil needs were tankered daily.

The radio stations *The Voice of Cairo* and *Radio Aden* beamed their Marxist message into many an Omani *barusti* hut, bidding the downtrodden to rise against the oppression of the Sultan, a reactionary dictator who had ensnared them in poverty: 'Join your fraternal brothers in South Yemen and crush the feeble army of the Sultan. Come to us now for training and weapons. Marxism is the only true way to enlightenment.'

The advent of the cheap transistor radio and its availability to people in even the poorest and most remote villages allowed the voice of sedition to spread like a virus. Many young men and women from South Yemen responded to this call to arms, and they were sent to the Soviet Union (or Peking) for military training. Some were specially selected to learn the value and effectiveness of control-by-fear.

I wrote a book in 1975 about my time in Dhofar and I included details of Marxist terror-training as witnessed by two ex-Marxist Dhofaris. One of them, Salim Amr, after training in Odessa, returned early in 1969 to the village of Hauf on the Yemeni/Dhofar border from where the newly formed and Soviet-armed PFLOAG (the People's Front for the Liberation of the Occupied Arab Gulf) would launch its attack on Oman via Dhofar.

Salim was initially posted to PFLOAG's new training camp in

Hauf, which included the Cage and the Lenin School. The Cage was a series of sealed-off caves housing prisoners awaiting torture and execution, and the School was where some 500 Dhofari children, many kidnapped, wore rag-tag uniforms, recited the thoughts of Chairman Mao parrot-fashion and learnt to count in Arabic and English. Later there would also be facilities for reading lessons, but for the moment it was enough to teach the youngsters to hate. To wean them from Islam. To mould them into bitter fighters and fervent Marxists.

One ex-PFLOAG soldier, Ahmad Deblaan, told me that PFLOAG, in both the Yemen and Dhofar, punished people who promoted the 'old' Muslim beliefs in various ways such as flaying the soles of their feet, and the application of red-hot coals to their faces, backs and genitals.

Young Dhofaris, fresh from their Marxist training, returned home crudely shaven and without the long hair and beards that were the age-old symbols of their erstwhile belief. They came back preaching the anti-God and they were strangers to their families and tribes. Many of the older folk tried to stir the communities against these new doctrines, but this largely ceased when two especially vociferous old sheikhs from the Eastern Mahra tribe had their eyes burnt out in public.

The ceremony had been conducted with a fire-heated pocket knife by the nephew of one of the two sheikhs. This nephew had but recently returned from Iraq and was especially talented at converting his kin to Marxism. After the operation on his uncle and the other patriarch, neither of whom died for several days, he had made the words of Karl Marx heard above their screams.

The gathered *jebalis* listened without understanding the new phrases of politics and the ranting of the khaki-clad youngster, whom everyone remembered as an idle child, good only at shirking his duties with the cattle. They failed to see why they should stop praying, why Islam should be discredited, or why such happenings as they had just witnessed should lead the way to a new and glorious way of life. But they understood the meaning of the young men's gleaming weapons and bandoliers.

Salim Amr was later elevated to regional commander where he witnessed an imaginative execution method used by the local *Idaara*, or PFLOAG Execution Squad. Five old folk from a mountain village had been caught praying in the open, contrary to the new, unwritten law that religion was reactionary. The *Idaara* leader had summoned a number of villagers from the locality and held a public trial to give the appearance of justice. All five old men were found guilty and were held down over red-hot coals until their backs were raw with burst blisters. Then they were beaten and taken to a steep cliff where, one by one, and at hourly intervals, they were thrown over the edge.

Slowly but surely, PFLOAG's terror tactics began to achieve results, especially in those regions of the Dhofar mountains close to the Yemen border.

Back in London, the Prime Minister, Harold Wilson, alarmed at the dangerous situation developing in Dhofar as a direct result of his withdrawal of the British Army from Aden, had decided that he would send a token number of officers to help the Sultan's forces against the Soviet-trained insurgents.

The Sultan's navy, commanded by a single pirate-like British mercenary with a bushy red beard, consisted of an old Arab motorised dhow armed with a Browning machine gun. The air force totalled two piston Provosts and a twelve-seater Beaver supply plane, and the army had just three infantry regiments with mostly British officers, some of whom were mercenaries and others, like me, were seconded by Harold Wilson.

On arrival in Muscat I narrowly missed meeting up with the only other Scots Greys officer ever to have served in Oman, Major Richard John. He had just been flown back to Britain with one shoulder and a portion of his chest shot away whilst fighting the Dhofar insurgents.

From Muscat I was driven through mountain passes in a Land Rover by the second in command of the Muscat Regiment. John

Cooper had recently fought for the Yemeni Royalists and during the Second World War had served against Rommel as desert driver to Colonel David Stirling, the founder of the Special Air Service. He had later fought in occupied France, Malaya, and the Radfan Campaign in Aden.

He said I was to take over the regiment's Reconnaissance Platoon with six Land Rovers and some forty soldiers. He described the enemy, or *adoo* as they were known, as the finest guerrilla fighters in the world when operating in their homeland mountains in Dhofar.

'The *adoo*,' he said, 'move like invisible gazelles. They know every *wadi*, every cave, because it is their homeland, and they can smell an army presence a mile away upwind. The moment you arrive in the Jebel, you are under observation. Then, one wrong step, one careless move and they cut you off. Call for reinforcements? You'll be lucky. We have two hundred men to cover an area larger than Wales and, as you will have heard, no means of evacuation except for six mules.'

Later I met the Recce Platoon corporal, Salim Khaleefa, who gave me a wider picture of the Dhofar scenario. 'Many hundreds of *adoo* will come from other lands, from Yemen and Iraq and Egypt, to fight us. It is said that the *Shooyooeen*, the communists, have sent them new *automatiqueeya* guns and many instructors from Russia and China. They will be strong and we of the Sultan are few.'

In Northern Oman, the patrol area of my platoon covered the region south of the Hajar Range, west on to the Empty Quarter and south to the Sharqeeya and the Wahiba Sands. My first patrol was to the Sharqeeya. This entire region was ruled by one sheikh, Ahmed Mohamed Al Harthi, whose ambitions were a growing threat to the Sultan. An armed patrol was sent in by way of the Wadi Tayyin every year to establish, however fleetingly, the Sultan's right of way and to maintain his recruiting rights.

With only three Land Rovers and a dozen soldiers, for the platoon was seriously undermanned, we set out for the Wadi

Tayyin and until we came to the narrow valley of Zayyan there was no trouble, but there, deep into the Sharqeeya, we hit a wall of resentment. The Zayyanis watched us from the *wadi* cliffs in silent groups high on their she-camels. Five-foot muzzle-loaders hung from their shoulders and six-inch soft lead bullets held by criss-cross bandoliers of goat leather festooned their bony chests. Word of our coming had preceded us via the *wadi* gossip system.

We stopped short of the line of Zayyanis and Salim sent the men out on foot across the *wadi* with a machine gun on each flank. Salim and I glanced at each other. 'What do you like us to do?' His English was not as good as usual.

I said, 'Just tell them we are friends and want to ask them some questions on behalf of the Sultan.'

This he apparently did and, by the length of his oration, added some remarks of his own, through which I learned that we of Recce Platoon were but the first unit of an entire regiment coming up to Zayyan.

A thickset Zayyani in a mauve *dishdash* robe shouted back and brandished his gun. Others joined in. Tempers were rising.

Salim turned to me. 'Sahb. These are bad people. They will answer no questions and say they want no Sultan's men on their land. They are for Al Harthi only and he hates the Sultan.' He shrugged. 'I think, Sahb, we would do well to end our patrol here, for these people are not worth our time and trouble.'

So we hightailed it out of a likely calamity and, for the first time, I knew that I had felt the deep stomach fear of imminent armed conflict against a superior force. This was very different from the years of sitting in a sixty-ton tank along the border with East Germany. On return to our base I spent the searing hot summer months recruiting more men, cadging weapons from the companies, overseeing vehicle repairs and training with live ammunition, mostly by night in the mountains. From my own point of view, I quickly learned that, as with climbing buildings, moving in enemy territory by night was a great deal less frightening than in daylight.

Slowly but surely, Recce Platoon became a viable fighting force, which was just as well since alarming reports came daily from Dhofar. As the monsoon clouds began to disperse in September, army units moved into the mountains. Subsequent fighting indicated that huge shipments of arms had come east from the Yemen, and with them new bands of well-trained guerrillas from Russia and China. Their tactics were skilful, their shooting was accurate.

One day I learnt that four Land Rovers of the Northern Frontier Regiment's Recce Platoon had been trapped within a rocky gully when ambushed between three machine-gun groups. The leading two vehicles were shredded, as were the crews, and a massacre was averted only by mists that crept into the gully and gave cover to the survivors.

The colonel called me into his office.

'The NFR's Recce Platoon is written off for a while, so there is no one to cover the desert north of the mountains. *Adoo* camel trains are known to bring in arms that way, so your platoon must take over as soon as you are ready.'

In December 1968 we drove south in five open Land Rovers, one three-ton lorry to carry our rations, including a dozen live goats, and a water tanker. We passed through 500 miles of gravel desert flanked all the way by the sea to our south and the greatest sand desert in the world, the Empty Quarter, to our north. On the third day we reached the sudden barrier of the Dhofar mountains – *adoo* territory.

For months we patrolled the mountains by night, laid ambushes, killed the enemy and, in turn, suffered casualties.

We never maintained a routine for we assumed, unless we had driven far into the desert, that we were at all times watched by unseen eyes. Deep within a sandy valley and many miles from any water source, we camped in order to recover between ambushes and patrols. At one such camp my old fear of spiders came back with a vengeance.

We had posted machine-gun guard positions on the ridge line above the cleft where our vehicles were parked and where we slept on mats with a single blanket, or often with only our daytime clothes. Each vehicle crew and the driver would eat together from a wide tin plate, always goat and rice washed down with strong, hot tea.

One night, under a moonlit, star-studded sky, eight of us were eating and chatting in low voices when a wolf spider hopped onto my bare ankle. Black in colour, with dark eyes, mandibles and five inches across from hairy leg to hairy leg, it was, to me, the sum of all nightmares. I only suffer from two genetic phobias – heights and spiders.

To make matters (in my spider-phobic state) even worse, I had heard of people hitting wolf spiders only to find dozens of little wolf spiders appearing and jumping all over them. The very idea of this made me shiver, despite having been told that such a scenario only occurs if you bash a pregnant mother wolf spider.

My instant reaction was to freeze with fear, to scream and to smash my fist down on this monster. But a simultaneous reaction, as I froze, halted both the scream and the violent crushing of the spider.

I had watched my soldiers' reactions to contact with even bigger wolf and camel spiders, and none of them had exhibited fear. There was no way that I could reveal my utterly irrational terror of spiders in front of the seven men, who day after day and night after night I depended upon, and who, in turn, depended on my judgement in an ever hazardous environment.

So I merely froze, did not scream, forced my jaw into the grinning position and merely brushed the spider off my leg in a 'careless' manner.

My dread of losing respect had managed to trump my lifelong spider phobia and served to break the spell for good, which I discovered soon afterwards when, on donning my desert boots one morning, I disturbed a large camel spider but felt almost no fear.

My godfather Laurence Fiennes, an RAF pilot, who was for a while also my guardian, gave me various tips-for-life that he recommended, and one that I never forgot may have lodged itself so strongly in my subconscious that the word *reputation* won the instantaneous 'brain battle' with that first dreadful wolf spider.

Most of 'Uncle' Laurence's examples of how to (and how not to) conduct myself in life came from his own and others' experiences in the two World Wars.

He told of being a pilot in 76 Squadron flying Lancaster heavy bombers and the terrible strain of each new mission, especially over targets known to produce ultra-high losses of bomber crews, often by burning to death. He recalled the long waiting periods wearing flying suits prior to take-off, and the sheer joy of relief if the 'Mission Postponed' signal was posted.

Those aircrews who found the strain intolerable often feigned bad sickness, dizzy spells or, just before take-off time, would run up one of their plane's engines without switching on the magnetics. This oiled up the plugs and prevented that crew from participating in the raid.

Once a crewman was suspected of having crumpled under the ongoing stress, he was categorized as LMF, meaning that he was of Low Moral Fibre, or, in simplistic terms, a coward. He would then be sent to one of the ARCs (Aircrew Refresher Centres) located in Brighton, Bournemouth and Sheffield. These were, in fact, open-arrest detention barracks where detainees would receive a month or so of lectures before being sent back 'refreshed' to their station, or, if clearly jittery wrecks, posted to a depot labelled as 'unfit for further aircrew duties', where they would be offered the choice of transferring to the Army or to the coal mines. The Refresher Centres were, by 1943, dealing with literally thousands of individuals who had chosen shame rather than an ongoing state of abject fear.

One man who managed to live with his fears was Flight Lieutenant Denis Hornsey of 76 Squadron, who knew my godfather. Hornsey applied several times to fly light Mosquito bombers rather than the cumbersome, easy-target Lancasters, but he was always turned down. Two of his early missions ended with him returning to base without completing a target attack. These were marked on his file as 'Early Returns', which were looked on by Squadron staff as suspicious and made Hornsey doubly stressed, since he was just as afraid of being considered LMF as he was of the actual operations. He wrote:

> Each operation, in my experience, was a worse strain than the last, and I felt sure that I was not far wrong in supposing that every pilot found it the same. It was true that it was possible to get used to the strain, but this did not alter the fact that the tension of each trip was 'banked' and carried forward in part to increase the tension of the next. If this were not so, the authorities would not have thought it necessary to restrict a tour to thirty trips. The line between the living and the dead was very thin. If you live on the brink of death yourself, it is as if those who have gone have merely caught an earlier train to the same destination.

Hornsey was shot down on his eighteenth mission, but he survived. He chose to face his fears rather than give in to the eternal shame of LMF. I chose to grin at a terrifying spider rather than earn the lasting derision of the wonderful men with whom I would endure a great many dangerous missions.

4
The Continent of Fear

Human beings are born free and no one has the right to enslave, humiliate, oppress or exploit them.
Cairo Declaration on Human Rights

In January 1969 I was due six weeks annual leave. The previous year I had planned an expedition using Land Rovers to follow the course of the longest river in the world, the 4,000 miles of the Nile, from its delta north of Cairo to its Lake Victoria source.

Back home, Ginny and I waterproofed the 400 separate map sheets that covered all the Nile-side tracks and, although we had obtained sponsorship for almost everything needed, including an old AA Land Rover and a pair of two-seater prototype hovercraft, we still required a second Land Rover, because one vehicle could only tow one hovercraft trailer.

My South African grandmother had left me £8,000 in her will, and this was my worldly wealth. The court case fines after the Assizes three years before had cut this to £6,000, which was the cost of a new Land Rover.

My mother was adamant that the money would be lost and I would end up with nothing. It was not fair to Ginny whose father, once a millionaire, was now bankrupt and unable to leave her a penny. I argued that, once demobbed, my only career potential lay with expeditions. The £6,000 was, therefore, an investment needed to lay the ground for bigger, more ambitious journeys to come. This appalled my mother, who could see no end to my 'lunatic approach' to life and my failure to settle down to a 'worthwhile profession'. Since there was no alternative, I frittered away my private fortune on the purchase of a brand-new petrol Land Rover, there being no available diesel models.

To tow the two half-ton hovercraft, named Burton and Baker after Nile explorers, behind the Land Rovers, we obtained trailers specially made by a company with a flourishing business in babies' perambulators.

I lay awake at night worried sick that I would never be able to own a home, marry Ginny or raise a family as a result of squandering the money I had been lucky enough to inherit. This worry turned into a never-ending background fear, which I have to this day, that I will never be able to generate enough income to cope with family expenses.

Ginny was to do her best to publicise the Nile expedition whilst doing her day job as secretary to a London vicar. A fellow Scots Greys officer, Peter Loyd, would be our chief hovercraft pilot, selected because he was the regimental helicopter pilot and therefore must be good at hovering.

An old friend from Mons Cadet School days, Nick Holder, was a good Land Rover driver and the original idea to ascend the Nile had been his. Charlie Westmorland was the son of the owner of Hoverair, who manufactured and sponsored us with the two machines. Additionally, following Ginny's urging, we recruited Anthony Brockhouse to make a movie and Mike Broome to take photographs so that we could publicise the trip afterwards.

We drove our convoy across Europe to Genoa and caught the ferry to Alexandria which, at the time, was full of Soviet battleships. Egypt was at war with Israel.

On arrival in Cairo the British military attaché told us that a state of emergency had been declared that very morning. Citizen forces were to be armed and civic buildings were sandbagged and blacked-out by night. Patrol centres had been hurriedly established at each Nile bridge to watch for Israeli commandos in the guise of tourists. No hovercraft had ever before been seen in Egypt, and ours could easily be mistaken by an excitable home guard as Israeli weapons of war. Hovering on any part of the Nile within Egypt was out of the question. However, the attaché agreed to accompany us to the first Nile-side checkpoint in the village of El Wasta. Nothing ventured, nothing gained. In each village crowds of curious *fellahin* closed about our trailers with the cry of *tayyara abyad!* meaning 'white aeroplanes!'

At the El Wasta barrier pole, seething with uniforms and heavy with body odour, we sat for an hour. At length a little policeman came to the cab window. 'You are the helicopter trade party from England going through Africa, yes?' I nodded vigorously. 'You are lucky,' he said. 'All others we turn back but you have the Ministry of Tourism to thank. We give you an escort south.'

Months later we discovered that we had the hovercraft to thank for this piece of luck. One of the Egyptian ministries, perhaps of Agriculture or Defence, was interested in their potential for cotton-crop spraying and for use in swampy zones.

The Russians were building a huge dam at Aswan to control the flow of the Nile, and we were forced to load our convoy onto an ancient ferry to travel the 200 miles of lake that was backing up behind the dam.

We unloaded at the Sudanese border village of Wadi Halfa, where we made ready to split into two groups, three of us to hover and three to take the support vehicles and trailers south through the Nubian desert. The stifling heat was just about bearable, despite the necessity to keep the doors of the hovercraft cockpit closed against the spray.

On reaching Khartoum we gave a demonstration of the hovercraft to the President of Sudan and his generals on an island where the Blue and the White Niles come together. A flood of sales enquiries resulted, for many cotton crops can be sprayed far more cheaply by hovercraft than from the air. The *Daily*

Telegraph later reported that the 'expedition was doing much to improve the friendship and goodwill between Britain and the Sudan.'

The humidity increased as we headed south. The seven-month rainy season was due and the land simmered in sultry expectation. We felt clammy and irritable. Clouds of flying, biting ants attacked us in the grasslands south of Khartoum. Scratches and sores tended to become infected, despite antiseptic cream. Two months earlier, during a training exercise at night, a Baluchi soldier had stomped his rifle butt on my hand and half-severed a finger. This injury now became swollen and reopened where the stitches had been.

We had followed the Nile for 2,000 miles, but the river still ran on upriver for the same distance again. As we continued south, black clouds spat forked lightning across the southern horizon, until finally the storm broke with deafening force. We travelled mile upon mile through drenching rain, and we grew more fearful of being cut off by floods than of being ambushed by rebels. At last we came to the riverside village of Bor, where the Nile was briefly narrow and high-banked.

In return for signed entry permits to the next province, an active war zone, we donated our second hovercraft, Baker, which was now damaged beyond repair, to the district commissioner of Bor. He was a keen gardener and positioned the hovercraft in his Nile-side marrow patch as a hippo-scarer.

Sadly, the peaceful village of Bor, which we found so full of friendly people from the mainly Dinka and Nuer tribes, was later to erupt into a vicious civil war on both sides of the river and deep into the forests south of Bor. This was mostly sparked between these two dominant Nilotic tribes once the South of Sudan achieved its long-fought-for independence from Khartoum.

Prior to independence, these warring southern tribes, mostly Christian or pagan, had joined together as the Anya Nya to fight against the hated Muslim government in the north. They had sunk their traditional tribal enmities in order to fight their common Muslim enemy. We knew that the truckload of soldiers, which Khartoum had detailed to escort us to the Ugandan border, would probably brand us to Anya Nyan guerrillas as a part of the Muslim government with some weird new river-weapon on trial.

Charlie piloted Burton through the endless swamps to the main army camp of Juba, staying at all times close to the river tugboat from Bor, which had sandbagged machine-gun positions on its roof.

Juba was the headquarters of the Khartoum government's army in South Sudan, and throughout the previous seventeen years their soldiers had fought the Anya Nya from there. The Anya Nya, however, simply faded into the jungle on the other side of the Ugandan border whenever the troops issued out of Juba in force.

A ferry took us to Gondokoro on the east bank of the river. Only a hundred years before, this village was a main market way station for hundreds of thousands of slaves seized from their homes all over Central Africa. Gondokoro was truly a place of human suffering, misery and fear on a grand scale, and one of several, including Zanzibar and Bunkeya at the source of the Zambezi River.

Charlie, repairing a rent in Burton's hoverskirt, commented on the lurking atmosphere of unease which he sensed at Gondokoro. 'The slavery captains,' he chuckled, 'came here from Oman. Just as you have.'

In a sense he was correct, for although slavery had existed in one form or another since the days of the caveman, the height of the slave trade in Central Africa, between the headwaters of the Nile, heading north to the Mediterranean, and the Zambezi, east to the Indian Ocean, was organised by the direct Albu Saidi ancestors of my boss in Oman, Sultan Said bin Taimur Albu Saidi.

Slaves were bought and then sold down long chains of brokers, dealers and merchants into the heart of Persia and present-day

Iraq. Baghdad was said to be a significant centre where slaves could always be purchased. Trading dhows went up into the Red Sea to Jidda, from where slaves were taken overland to the holy cities of Mecca and Medina, and even further into northern Arabia. Slavery throughout the nineteenth century continued to be widely practised across the whole land mass covering Arabia, Turkey and Persia – and wherever there were slaves, significant numbers came via Omani-ruled Zanzibar.

Young boys were in particularly high demand because of the constant desire for eunuchs. Castrated males were regarded as unusually trustworthy, and were employed to guard harems and to be administrators. In the holy cities of the Hejaz they formed a special elite to guard mosques. However, even among recognised slave dealers, this traffic in *castrati* was kept furtive, and the operation centres on the Upper Nile and in southern Arabia where boys were 'treated' were not widely known. The mortality rate was terrible – scarcely one in ten survived the terrible maiming surgery – but, as a result, demand for eunuchs was high and prices were at least ten times that of uncastrated boys.

In the 1820s Said's great grandfather, Sultan Seyyid Said, ruled Oman with an iron fist and with the all-powerful British navy at his beck and call. Their main interest was to exclude the French from the region, and therefore from India. In 1841 Seyyid Said had moved his throne from Muscat to Zanzibar, the source of the great wealth to be had from ivory and from human misery in the form of the inexhaustible supply of slaves from the Interior.

Omani slave ships from the Pirate Coast of Trucial Oman, now the Arab Emirates, would sail to Zanzibar at the season of the propitious trade winds. They would arrive with trading goods, take on their human cargo and use the south-westerly monsoon winds to deliver those slaves that survived the voyage to the markets of Arabia and beyond.

In 1866 the Scottish explorer and missionary David Livingstone's reports on slavery, together with the powerful anti-slavery activities of William Wilberforce, had put the British government into a dilemma. They needed to keep the Omanis, whose ongoing wealth was derived from African slavery, on side whilst seeming to halt all slavery. So the Royal Navy patrolled the Indian Ocean to rescue slaves in a highly ineffective manner.

In 1866 John Kirk, the acting British consul in Zanzibar, appealed to London concerning the slavery going on under the very eyes of his consulate. He wrote:

> The death rate, the murder, the rapine inseparable from the slave hunters' pursuit . . . the social chaos, the disorganisation, the absolute destruction of those conditions which help the multiplication of mankind, and ever advancing degradation of the persecuted race; the kidnapping of the thousands for other countries to which our toleration of the slave traffic at Zanzibar opens the way . . .
>
> Surely, no growth in the trade of other commodities could ever justify such a practice.

The British government's response was that slave trading was legal within the Zanzibar state and should not be interfered with. It was none of their business.

By the 1840s the Zanzibar-based Sultans had turned Zanzibar from a mere backwater, a slave entrepôt with a dilapidated fort, into the most prosperous city of the western Indian Ocean. Several thousand Omanis had settled there, as had hundreds of Indian traders and investors in the slavery and ivory markets. They lived in grand villas on the seafront, as did successive British consuls, who were horrified by what they witnessed and did their best, but the authorities in Britain and in India ignored them. Most of the consuls could last only a few months in the disease-ridden city before they died or retreated sick and exhausted.

In 1869 an epidemic of cholera, started years before in Mecca, spread among pilgrims returning across the Red Sea into Sudan and Ethiopia, and thence south along the Nile, where it rapidly infected the slaves in the rest of Africa and, of course, Zanzibar. The consul, John Kirk, estimated 7,000 local deaths in one month, yet slaving ships were still arriving. Local doctor, James Christie, wrote:

> The dhows were literally packed with slaves as close as they could possibly stand, some of them suffering from cholera, many of them in a dying state, and all of them in a condition of extreme emaciation.

This was despite the practice of ships' captains to cull the obviously dying slaves by throwing them overboard before landing at Zanzibar.

Consul John Kirk, his wife and his baby somehow survived the epidemic, but that year of dread and horror altered him. He became utterly determined to put an end to East African slavery whilst he was still in an ideal position to do so.

By the 1870s, on the other (west) side of Africa, the Royal Navy had closed all slave markets and had successfully stopped the export of hundreds of thousands of slaves to the United States. Zanzibar had become the last slavers' citadel of fear and evil.

At a highly publicised meeting of the London Anti-Slavery Society, an abolitionist friend of Wilberforce, who was well into his nineties, spoke out to a rapt audience:

> Thirty-five years ago I went to sleep in the belief the slave trade was finally dead and almost buried . . . that the utter extinction of the traffic was a thing of the past. I now find that a slave trade worse than anything ever known on the west coast of Africa is flourishing and still in vigour under our eyes on the east coast.

This, and other accusations against the government (and the East India Company), were widely reported, and two weeks later the

Queen's Speech included the Government's specific intention to act against the slave trade off the East Coast of Africa.

Back in Zanzibar, Sultan Bargash continued for several years to turn a blind eye to the treaty, but doggedly Consul Kirk browbeat him into eventual submission so that by 1876 few slave-carrying ships were able to evade capture and the arrest of their crews by the Royal Navy.

Nearly a century later I sat in the cab of the old AA Land Rover in Gondokoro, drinking warm Coca-Cola and listening to Charlie Westmorland, as he recounted the little-known story of the Scottish missionary, Fred Arnot, who faced up to two evil despots in the Congo's equivalent of Gondokoro and established Christian missions in the very heartland of Chief Mashidi, a self-styled Lord of Terror.

Arnot had left his job as a Tayside shipbuilder some eight years after Livingstone's death. In 1881 he arrived in the Cape at the time my grandfather was fighting the Boers and working for Cecil Rhodes. Altogether Arnot travelled on foot or by mule over 23,000 miles in south and central Africa.

The land west of the Victoria Falls, then called Barotseland, was Arnot's first missionary target, which he reached after facing death from illness and thirst in the Kalahari desert. The Barotse chief since 1878 was called Lewanika and he ruled entirely through the medium of fear. Arnot, who was often sick with fever, was forced to watch the daily torture and execution sessions in Lewanika's royal court.

An individual accused of witchcraft would have his hands dipped in boiling water and, if the skin dropped away from his flesh, he would be burnt at the stake.

Any judicial decision on tribal matters would be an excuse for an upfront sacrifice, usually of a child whose fingers and toes would be cut off and the blood collected for ritual sprinkling. The child's body would then be cut up and thrown into the river.

Arnot forced himself to accept the innate cruelty of Lewanika and his warriors, and by 1884 he had made friends with the chief and established a missionary school. But when civil war broke out among the Barotse, Arnot moved on northwards to the land now known as Katanga, a province of Zaire. The chief there, an infamous despot named Mushidi, ruled in Garenganze, in the town of Bunkeya, at that time the most active remaining slave market on the continent.

Ever the optimist, Arnot decided to set up a mission in Bunkeya. On his way there in 1886 he discovered the true source of the Zambezi River, some distance from where Livingstone had located *his* 'source'. For this, Arnot was later awarded the Gold Medal of the Royal Geographical Society.

Continuing east towards Lake Mweru, he came to a recent camp of slave-raiders who had been there six days previously and had lashed many weak or lame slaves to trees. Some were still alive, others had been mutilated by wild animals.

On the outskirts of Bunkeya, Arnot was greeted by Mushidi's warriors bearing freshly cut heads of slaves, the blood from which was ceremoniously smeared all over his face and body.

He was then led through the township of Bunkeya, a collection of several thousand huts in the centre of which was the chief's palace. The citizenry consisted of numerous conquered tribes living in sub-villages surrounded by stockades, all decorated with human skulls and macabre displays of freshly hacked limbs and human entrails. In between two stockades they traversed an area of disturbed scrubland where the air was heavy with the sickly sweet smell of decaying flesh. One of the guards explained that the bodies of slaves and executed criminals were left here unburied to feed hyenas and vultures.

The markets thronged with Arab slavers who had been forced inland by the anti-slavery laws of the East Coast, and chained together in hellish clearings were thousands of slaves sweltering and moaning for water. Arnot noted that the pervading stench was of faeces, urine and body odour. He shuddered each time a new slave caravan arrived, and he watched babies torn from their mothers and dashed against trees to save food. Half-castes worked in the slave pens allotted to new arrivals to yoke them together like cattle with wooden hand or ankle cuffs linked with ropes. Children were neck-roped and, like the adults, bled from the wounds opened by the whips of the guards. Next they passed a small stockade which, the guard explained, was Mushidi's dog-house where he kept wild hunting dogs in a state of semi-hunger.

Mushidi had several hundred nubile wives in his harem, but he rarely had sex with any of them. When caught being unfaithful, as many were, they were thrown to the dogs personally by Mushidi who, with his courtiers, enjoyed the spectacle of them being ripped to bits.

As Arnot was about to learn, Mushidi was aware that in order to maintain his reign of terror he needed to keep his reputation for cruelty forever fresh, as do the present-day ISIS (also known as IS, ISIL or Daesh, but referred to in this book as ISIS) and all groups dependent upon the power of fear. One example of this, witnessed by Arnot, was the Chief's personal supervision of the public execution of a senior court official for treason. He cut off the man's ears and made him eat them. Then he did likewise with his fingers, his toes and, finally, his genitals. At last his head was cut off and his corpse was split down the middle.

Soon after his arrival, Arnot was granted an audience with the great Mushidi, who gave permission for Arnot to stay in his kingdom and set up a 'school'.

Arnot thanked the Chief. He knew that, to begin with, he could do nothing but pray and be patient, but God's truths, he determined, must be established here in this hell-hole and Mushidi's barbarism must be ended.

By the end of 1887 Arnot had become a confidant of Mushidi and he had established in Bunkeya a church for his many converts, a clinic for the sick and a school for children. But weakened by ongoing bouts of fever, he was forced early in 1888 to leave Bunkeya and hand over his work to new missionaries sent out from Britain.

Thanks to Arnot and others like him, the curse of slavery in Bunkeya, Zanzibar and the Nile-based markets of Omdurman and Gondokoro was closed down. However, Central Africa remains a region of violent civil war where, in 2014, thousands died all around Gondokoro following South Sudan's post-independence fighting, and in the vastness of Zaire modern-day Mushidis still terrorise the weak. And, despite all the efforts of Arnot, Livingstone and a great many other brave anti-slavery activists down the ages, slavery and all the terror that goes with it, still thrives in our century.

'Slaves,' proclaims *Dabiq*, the journal of ISIS, 'are the spoils of war.' They are referring to the thousands of Yazidi women they forced into sex slavery in 2014. They claim that forced concubinage is a religious practice sanctified by the Koran and, in the same document, they state their hope that President Obama's wife may end up in a slave market. Boko Haram, the Nigerian militant group, clearly share the same views on slavery, having kidnapped all the pupils from a girls' school in 2014 with that same intention.

In Morocco thousands of children work as maids. In Jordan, Syrian refugee camps forcibly recruit girls for brothels in Amman and for Gulf businessmen trawling websites. Following the removal of Gaddafi, Libya's seaports are centres for slave traffic, and Nigerians who can afford them buy 'fifth wives' from neighbouring countries in West Africa.

The wealthy Emirates of the Gulf employ 2.4 million domestic servants, most of whom have no protection under existing labour laws. Many are locked up in their quarters and are easy prey to sexual exploitation.

Because some Asian countries have banned their female citizens from domestic work in the Gulf, recruitment agencies have turned to East African sources, such as Uganda and the lands of the Nile where Kirk worked so hard to abolish slavery.

Under the Earl of Cromer's guidance, Egyptian law forbade slavery at the end of the nineteenth century, and for almost a hundred years – at least on paper – the Middle East was free of slavery.

'Human beings are born free, and no one has the right to enslave, humiliate, oppress or exploit them,' stated the Cairo Declaration on Human Rights in Islam in 1990. The Global Slavery Index (GSI), whose estimates are computed by an Australian NGO working with Hull University, claims that of fourteen states with over 1 per cent of the population enslaved, more than half are Muslim. Prime offenders range from the region's poorest state, Mauritania, to its richest per head, Qatar.

Many Arab states took far longer to criminalise slavery than to ban it. Mauritania, the world's leading enslaver, did not do so until 2007. Where bans exist, they are rarely enforced.

Of course, there are now all over the world, including in the lands of the Nile, brave protesters who do their best to fight the abuses of women, whether as slaves or simply as females. But they often do so in great danger and in fear of their lives.

Mint Moktar in Mauritania, who began to campaign in 2015 for SOS SLAVES on behalf of the rights of the *haratin* caste, the descendants of black slaves, has received a barrage of death threats.

Today there are students in the USA who protest against statues or street names that commemorate wealthy past donors to university funds who once owned slaves. Such protesters do so knowing that they will come to no harm. Their predecessors of the 1950s and 1960s, on the other hand, were involved in the Civil Rights movement only at great personal risk and today they can vividly remember the fear that they often faced back then, because of the violent aggression of racists. There were really two groups of individuals living in fear.

Firstly, there was the fear that enabled the South to maintain a system of ironclad racial segregation, which was crucial in maintaining the humiliation of and violence against blacks. This fear was palpable in the South.

Then there was the fear among black people who grew up in

the South, who understood that they were feared by white people and who knew that this fear led to violence against them. They were at all times fearful of stepping out of line, and mothers cautioned their children not to play with white kids, because they understood what the dire consequences might be.

So eventually the fear of black people that existed in the white population became mirrored in the fear of black people as to what might happen to them. Not all the people in the South had this fear, although they observed the rules and understood the limits of their freedom, but what happened in the South in the 1950s and 1960s was that black people began to overcome that fear of crossing the boundary. The more that black people crossed over this line, the more it encouraged others to do so, and the more courage it gave them to overcome their own fears. So the history of the Civil Rights movement is a history of more and more black people overcoming their fear of breaking the law, of going to jail, or of being beaten. They overcame their fear because they felt the collective protection of their community as more and more people joined the Civil Rights movement.

* * *

After Gondokoro the Nile became impassable to our hovercraft due to the cataracts, so we lashed Burton to our trailer and travelled by red dirt 'murram' roads to Lake Victoria, where we gave a hover demonstration to a large gathering of businessmen and ministers from Kampala and nearby industrial Jinja.

We had followed the course of the world's longest river from sea to source. None of us had succumbed to malaria, despite the weeks of being bitten, although Mike Broome had been badly burnt, Nick had developed bilharzia, and one of my fingers, half-severed back in Oman, had swollen with gangrene.

Some twenty years after our arrival at Lake Victoria, the Hutu Terror of the 1990s dumped many thousands of machete-lacerated Tutsi bodies into the headwaters of the Nile.

In 2011 I was asked to write an anthology of my personal heroes. In each case these heroes proved to be individuals who had faced overwhelming fear without flinching. One was an African named Paul Rusesabagina, who saved a thousand lives in Rwanda by refusing to give in to the genocidal nightmare that raged all about him in April 1994.

After the First World War the United Nations gave Rwanda to the Belgians who already ruled the neighbouring Congo (Zaire). They gave top jobs to the Tutsi and instituted a mandatory identity-card system which soon, by enforcing Tutsi superiority, turned what had merely been a class-based hierarchy into a cauldron of seething 'tribal' hatred.

In the 1930s an influx of Belgian priests worked to make Christianity extremely popular with both Tutsis and Hutus. These priests, who sympathised with the Hutu underdog, persuaded the Belgian authorities to redress the long-standing imbalance of power, and this resulted in a chance for the Hutu majority to revenge themselves on their previous overlords.

In early 1960 Belgium granted Rwanda full independence, and their hasty exit, like that of the British from India, sparked off various massacres of Tutsis. In 1964 ten thousand were killed and survivors were left in terror of their lives.

Paul Rusesabagina was a Hutu married to a Tutsi, and in 1992 he was the manager of a smart hotel, the Milles Collines, in Kigali, the capital of Rwanda.

The Rwandan President Habyarimana, a Hutu, decided to trumpet the external threat of a Tutsi invasion and thereby get rid of all Tutsis in Rwanda by stirring up Hutu fear of a Tutsi fifth column waiting to exterminate them. He also decided that the only answer to maintain ultimate power was to rid Rwanda of every last Tutsi. The name of the game was genocide.

For two years he and his *akazu* power group secretly trained and armed killer groups with help, both practical and financial, from Egypt, South Africa and France. French army and intelligence specialist groups trained the 1,500-strong Presidential

Guard, who in turn trained various Hutu militias. The enemy to be wiped out were quite simply all Tutsis and any Hutus who opposed any aspect of the *akazu* rule.

From 1990 onwards the *akazu* stockpiled arms for the Presidential Guard and the regional militias, mostly from France and Egypt, including Kalashnikov rifles, with 3 million bullets, mortars and shells, rocket-propelled grenades, machine guns, long-range artillery and anti-personnel mines.

Part of the president's policy was to turn all Hutus into murderers so that all would then be complicit and therefore more pliant. By the end of 1992 Paul and many other alert urban Hutus were painfully aware of at least the general gist of the genocide plan, but they did not know when it might take place.

The *akazu* evolved a mass killing system shaped to create maximum psychological terror and planned to the finest detail. The entire Hutu population was to be mobilised to kill their Tutsi friends and neighbours as a civic duty. Anybody who refused to become an executioner would themselves be murdered.

To achieve genocide anywhere, the level of education of the relevant population probably defines the level of sophistication required to mobilise them as killers. Remember that most such killers are average, gentle, decent people like you or me, not brutal psychotics. It is no more natural to murder a neighbour than it is to bungee jump. We have to be mentally trained to kill, to be taught why it is right and then be motivated to act at a certain time. Normally it needs the justification of a war to convince us to join bands of killers (called armies) and accept training in how best to shoot, bomb, bayonet and effectively kill or maim the citizens of those very countries in which we may have been taking our annual holidays for years.

The army and the police, indeed every armed authority in Rwanda, was Hutu controlled. There was no escape for a Tutsi. It was a time of terror, and the end aim of the *akazu* was absolute power through absolute terror.

Just as riots the world over are today organised and advertised on the Internet and often spread like wildfire, so Hutu peasants were incited to kill their Tutsi neighbours by way of their ever-present transistor radios and the few government-controlled newspapers that were passed around the villages and read aloud at gatherings. The borders were officially closed to Tutsi would-be emigrants. They lived like mice among snakes.

With the president's death, an army man, Colonel Bagosora, emerged as the Hitler-figure and Hutu extremist at the nerve centre of the *akazu*, the man who coordinated the 'final solution'.

Roadblocks were set up all over Kigali. Each car was searched and ID cards were scrutinized. All Tutsis were killed with machete blows, and their bodies were used to wall off the checkpoints. The Presidential Guard visited addresses on their lists. Several thousand people were killed on the first day of the genocide.

Over the next week, Paul and Tatiana could see from their window many of their Hutu friends walking the streets holding machetes that dripped with blood.

Thirty-two terrified refugees, knowing Paul's moderate stance, had fled to his hotel before the killer squads had reached their listed addresses. Paul had squeezed them into his living room and kitchen, where they hid.

The Rwandan bishop John Rucyahana was deeply saddened:

> We have often been called Africa's most Christian country, with ninety per cent of the people identifying themselves as Christians. Yet people who had dutifully attended church on Sunday were slaughtering their neighbours by the end of the week. How did those who supposedly followed Jesus pick up machetes and chop children to death?

Here is the testimony of one survivor:

> My husband and my brother were given massive machete blows on the shoulders. I started running with my two-year-old in my arms. She fell and I saw them cutting her up. I ran with all my strength, but everywhere people were screaming as I passed, 'Here she is. Here she is.' These were neighbours I had always considered friends, people I had always been kind to.

For seven days she found shelter with many others in a nearby church:

> On the seventh day the white priest drove away and on the eighth they came for us. With nothing to fight with, our young men broke up the seats and threw them. But they were shot by a soldier. The mob, including many of my neighbours, then closed in. They macheted and macheted and macheted. Never can I forget the screaming.

From the corridor windows of the hotel's west wing you could see through the rickety bamboo fence that surrounded the hotel grounds, and at all hours of the day and night the would-be killers, machetes in hand, patrolled the fence, stopping to peer into the hotel windows on spotting movement.

The rumour had spread among Kigali's hunted and desperate that the Milles Collines hotel was a safe haven, and the guest list soon approached a thousand in a hotel designed for 300 maximum. Paul had Hutu and Tutsi sleeping alongside each other on the floors, close up for comfort, for many had already witnessed unimaginable horror.

Each room held an average of eight frightened people, at night reliving horror in dreams and howling or weeping at the memory of their slaughtered loved ones. And each room was, they all knew, merely a death-row cell. Militia spies with knowing grins and belt-hung machetes came in and out of the hotel when they wished. Cats and mice in the same cage.

A topic of conversation Paul heard discussed more than once, always in hushed tones, was the mobs' killing methods. What was the worst death? The *masu* (wooden clubs spiked with nails), the toilet pits, or the machete? Hundreds of corpses were found with their nails torn from scrabbling at the walls of the Rwandan latrine pits into which they had been thrown. Or one could die of pain and poison from the deep puncture wounds of the *masu*, for the nails are long and go through skin and into bone. Might that be preferable to dying in faecal slime? Or the machete? Survivors of machete attacks had reached the Milles Collines with hideous wounds to their arms and faces.

There were those wounded in the hotel that told of death-squad killers who would select a wealthy-looking target, cut off one hand, then stand over the victim casually sharpening their machete with a whetstone and ask for money 'to avoid further treatment'. Others told Paul that they feared they would develop AIDS because of their wounds, since their attackers' machetes had dripped with the blood of previous kills.

One in every eight of the 8 million citizens of Rwanda was murdered in 100 days, which, by simple mathematics, indicates a degree of commitment and efficiency comparable to that of Nazi Germany.

By the end of May, Paul had 1,268 people crammed into a space intended for only 300. Paul was near to the end of his tether. The endless stress and the daily diet of ever-new tales of terror were wearing him down. He wrote, 'I knew I was going to die. I have done far too much to cross the architects of the genocide. The only question is when and the method of my death and that of Tatiana and our children.'

As the Tutsi-led RPF Army from Uganda closed in on Kigali, the *akazu*'s city killers became obsessive in their drive to locate the nests of those 'cockroaches' clever or lucky enough to still be alive. So they stormed the last remaining redoubts where brave men like Paul had, until then, found a way of saving souls. Churches that had been havens were attacked. In the Catholic church of Ntarama, 5000 people were massacred. In Chahinda parish over 20,000. Hospitals were visited and 'cleansed', as in Butari, where patients were clubbed and slashed in their beds and doctors and nurses were murdered.

Eventually the RPF Tutsis took Kigali from the *akazu*, and the 1,268 people at Paul's hotel were saved. Thanks to his charm and diplomacy, their long period of terror was over.

5

The Lasting Traumas of Fear

The nightmare is still there. I dream of someone coming to abduct me.

Norman Okello, The Lord's Resistance Army

Back in England the doctor warned me not to go back to Dhofar until the poison was out of my system. However, after two months of ineffective treatment, a letter came from a friend in Dhofar. The wording was clear . . . there had been alarming events in the Dhofar fighting. PFLOAG was winning, and some Sultanate soldiers were on the verge of mutiny. All absent officers were urgently needed back.

I decided to return at once, despite my doctor's advice, as my overdue absence must look suspiciously like malingering in view of the critical military situation. No one spares sympathy for a finger. A smashed leg would be acceptable, but a crushed digit is merely an excuse. So, fearful of accusations of cowardice, I bid goodbye to Ginny and my mother and headed back to Dhofar.

When I landed back at Salalah airport, I noticed coils of barbed wire along the perimeter and newly erected searchlight towers. 'The *adoo*,' I was told by a Pakistani porter, 'have new heavy weapons and they mortared the base last month, including a direct hit on the Officers' Mess.'

The colonel soon made it clear to me that it was down to the pitifully few Sultanate units in Dhofar to hold the line against the *adoo* and try to keep them off balance, while they consolidated their manpower and weapons in the mountains prior to attacking Salalah.

Most of the individual Dhofari tribesmen, although indoctrinated and trained in the Soviet Union, had innate skills honed, not in some Russian training ground, but during their years growing up in the very mountains, valleys and forests where they were now actively seeking to exterminate the Sultan's puny force consisting of a few hundred volunteer Omani, Baluchi and Zanzibari men, commanded by a handful of mostly British officers. And by far the most numerically feeble of these units was my own Recce Platoon, which due to my surname, had now been dubbed by the Salalah HQ staff as the Fiend Force.

To survive against such an enemy as the *adoo* in such a place we needed, at all times, to appreciate fully the very real danger of being cut off and wiped out. We, the ambushers, at all times risked being ambushed. We were the hunted as well as being the hunters. Prayers to Allah were at all times silent, not chanted.

The ability to maintain total silence day and night when patrolling or when crouched in an ambush position, sometimes for four days and nights, was key to success, so I never involved soldiers with a cough or cold. One key operation was compromised by my men's extreme fear of *djinn* (evil spirits). Salim Mayoof, one of my machine gunners, a brave Zanzibari, had suddenly halted, shrieked, dropped his gun, and was clawing at the moonlit sky. I ran to him to shut him up. As he looked at me and fell quiet, a yell from behind me came from Fat Hamid, a normally placid man. Later my sergeant explained that *djinns* will fly in an instant from person to person.

Knowing that we were compromised deep inside *adoo* territory and fearing cut-off, I led a nine-hour speedy retreat to the desert hide where our six drivers guarded the vehicles. The *djinn* left Fat Hamid during our retreat, but Mayoof remained in a state of depression, so I sent him back to Salalah HQ.

A week later the adjutant at Salalah sent me a signal that

Mayoof 'wanted his soul back.' My reply confirmed in Morse code that we had searched everywhere but could not find it.

A bedu guide, Nashran bin Sultan, had fascinated me with tales of a fabulous lost city in the desert sands, which he believed had once been fed by a deep aquifer that headed north from the mountains, through the flat gravel *nejd* and, if one could trace this unseen water course further into the sands, it may be possible to locate Ubar, the fabled centre of the incense trade of Arabia.

Whilst searching for a new vehicle route between water holes, we came to the well of Maashadid where the water was some forty-five feet down. I was curious to see how the water was reached. None of the men wished to go down with me, even though I had a torch. It was hot inside and dirty. To help their weary work of filling endless bags, the bedu had fixed bits of metal and lengths of hemp at intervals along the corkscrew descent, and as I clambered lower the heat grew slightly less, but the air was stale and daylight was no longer visible above.

I soon lost count of the twisting turns and came to a narrowing funnel. The beam from my torch picked up a dark hole at its base, but no light was reflected on water. I scrambled down the funnel and thrust my arm into its apex. The cold cling of running water came almost as a shock. I scooped some up and drank: it was only slightly brackish. What a place to work in, filling enough bags for perhaps a dozen or more thirsty camels. Already I streamed with sweat and the air was bad. The impulse to get out grew suddenly strong and I struggled upright in the funnel. The torch struck a rock, and I was in darkness as the bulb had gone.

Straddling the tube of the shaft with my legs, I felt above my head and panic gripped me, for there was space on either side of the rock over my head, meaning that there must be two, or more, shafts leading upwards. I fought back the desire to shout for the men, for they would never hear me and the vibrations might cause a slide.

I decided to take pot luck, for I could feel no rope, nor guiding line. My feet were bare and my toes found crannies in the shaft walls. Suddenly a great flurry set up about me. It was so unexpected that I screamed and beat the air about my head.

Hundreds of tiny squealing creatures flew about like flies rising from garbage. Little leathery bodies brushed against me and, as I clawed the air, so the commotion increased. Shaking my head wildly, I climbed upwards, only to find that the shaft was in reality a mere hollow in the roof above the water funnel, and it was the home of a colony of midget bats. Slithering downwards I lost all sense of direction, knowing only vaguely which way was up and which was down. A foul stench from the streams of bat guano, which my antics had disturbed, added to my desperation.

Then the compact feel of metal touched my hand, and I knew that I was in the main shaft. At once I felt calmer; the nightmare provoked by the bats receded, for that little piece of piping was reality.

I felt my way back up, hold by hold. The blackness softened and grew quickly to an intense brightness as the opening appeared. I breathed in the desert air until my lungs burned, but it was fresh and good. Nashran asked if there were *djinns*, and, thinking of the bats, I nodded with fervour. With hindsight my sudden panic was nothing to do with the fear of bats (*chiroptophobia*), but had everything to do with a form of claustrophobia mixed with my chronic vertigo.

I would certainly never go caving, or try the extreme sport of cave diving, which involves exploring submerged cave systems where divers, like climbers on Everest, are dependent on their oxygen supply. Except that Everest climbers, with luck, can descend to breathable levels should their supply run out higher up. In cave systems, especially swimming against the current, this is usually impossible. Literally hundreds of cave divers have died, their bodies never found for weeks, if ever. And all are aware that, should anything go wrong down in the pitch-dark rushing waterways, fear and panic will only help to kill them, for panicked divers use up their air far more quickly.

It was not much safer above ground. Before a combined operation in Dhofar, where the colonel planned to send my platoon deep into the mountains to ambush a specific feature, I was flown in our twelve-seater Beaver supply plane over the mountains to ensure that I would later identify the exact relevant features. I hated these flights as I knew that the *adoo* had acquired anti-aircraft weapons.

Sitting in the cockpit next to the pilot, I would try to concentrate on the ground below and the map on my knee, but I could not get rid of the thought of bullets ripping up into my scrotum from the *adoo* below, and my buttocks remained taut with apprehension.

This particular fear of being ripped to bits from below also lurked in the back of my mind during all the long hours in Land Rovers. The *adoo* laid mines on all the main tracks in Dhofar, all of which were dirt, not tarmac, and there was never time to send soldiers pushing mine detectors out ahead of our patrols. Very often, following specific Soviet training, the *adoo* would leave their mines just to one side of an especially soft sand stretch, knowing that drivers sometimes skirted such troughs.

There was a remote valley in the *nejd* where, on patrol, we came across the site of a Land Rover blown to pieces by a Mark VII British anti-tank mine. The mine was one of many left behind in Aden when the British Army withdrew from the Yemen two years before.

That mine had been cleverly sited in a dip between two sandy mounds, and I knew that if I had been navigating or driving through the area I would have chosen the same route. After seeing the shredded remains of that Land Rover, we doubled the number of sandbags on the floors of our vehicles.

There was a well at Arzat, famous for its sweet-tasting water, that was used for a while by the Sultan's palace staff to source the Sultan's favourite drinking water. The *adoo* were, therefore, prone to ambush it and I was told to protect the Sultan's men on one water collection day. The Sultan also sent another army unit, who spotted three figures in black running away on a trail above the well. They opened fire and, on retrieving the bodies, found them to be women. Boys of twelve and under were also used by both sides.

On my first action in Dhofar, during the relief of a garrison at Mirbat fort, I had met a young Sultanate askar, not more than twelve years old, who had proudly showed me the bodies of three *adoo* attackers that he claimed to have shot the night before. And one of the dead *adoo* bodies we took away for burial was certainly no more than twelve or thirteen. The intimidation and induction of child soldiers is, these days, more prevalent in Central Africa than elsewhere.

In 2014, Theo Hollander, a Christian Aid researcher, interviewed Norman Okello, a thirty-two-year-old Ugandan who, for two years in the early 1990s, had been a boy soldier of the infamous Lord's Resistance Army (LRA) led by the charismatic Ugandan warlord Joseph Kony.

Norman and his father were at work one day in their family rice field when five soldiers in Ugandan uniforms confronted them. They sported dreadlocks, which identified them as LRA in stolen uniforms.

Norman, aged twelve, was asked if he was with his father. He knew that the LRA murdered parents of abducted children, so he managed to fool the men and convinced them that his father was just a fellow worker. Norman was then brutally beaten by the soldiers and kidnapped. Many other abductees, less tough than Norman, were soon killed off as weaklings, but he made it to the induction stage, where he was told to kill an older LRA teenager who had tried to escape back to his family. After other boys had stabbed this victim with knives, Norman duly bayoneted him to death.

Kony was adept at turning 'normal', nice children into dedicated killers. He favoured catching the ideal raw recruits at between ten and twelve years. Kony's children conducted a reign of terror wherever they travelled from their base in northern

Uganda. Christian Aid believe that there were, during the nineteen-year-long civil conflict in Uganda, a total of 38,000 children forced into the LRA.

After his first killing, Norman found himself identifying with the cult of Kony, who spoke to spirits in mammoth shouting sessions. Kony's child armies were known for their ferocity and their sheer cruelty. After raids, they discouraged village elders from reporting their presence to the Ugandan Army by slitting and padlocking their lips together. They enforced various obscure Kony-concocted rules, such as no riding of bicycles, by hacking off a 'guilty' party's legs and buttocks with a machete. Their routine consisted of: raid a village, disappear into the forest, more raids, torture, rape, kill, steal, then vanish again.

After the first few killings and acts of cruelty, the brutalised children soon began to identify with Kony and to enjoy their feeling of power. Norman told Christian Aid that he had killed many people. After a year, somewhere in South Sudan, his unit was told to attack an army camp and bring back proof of their kills. No one should come away from the operation without the testicles of the dead. His unit, Norman recalled, filled up four big wash bowls with testicles after that raid.

Week after week, Norman participated in the mass slaughter and rape of innocent villagers, but his proximity, by chance, to his own home near the Kitgum region, led him to escape from his LRA Brigade, which was a highly risky process, some two years after his initial kidnapping.

Back home, his mother did not recognise him, and his father soon caught him kicking his sister and beating up other village children. He was unrecognisable as the gentle, studious child that his family remembered.

Years of sponsored group therapy and football sessions with other young surviving LRA escapees eventually helped. Norman later married and had his own children, but ten years after his last contact with the LRA he was still afraid of falling asleep, for he suffered from frequent nightmares which regurgitated the horrors of his past. He would wake up screaming, and at other times he would experience sudden aggressive destructive urges, which he learnt to channel into going for long runs – immediately.

He still lives in dread of Kony's return. 'The nightmare,' he told Hollander, 'is still there. I dream of someone coming to abduct me.'

As I write this in 2016, Kony and his LRA are still at their evil work, spreading fear and destruction in the great forests of Central Africa.

* * *

I began to dread each new operation in Dhofar. I made the mistake of visiting a friend from one of the companies who was in the Salalah Hospital recovering, with other badly wounded soldiers, after bullet and shrapnel removal operations. This experience had a bad effect on my general emotional state.

Even if you are not in any real personal danger, merely observing such unpleasant sights can often sear them into the memory, as journalist and author Mark de Rond found when spending a brief sojourn in a front-line hospital in Afghanistan. He recorded a vignette of a casualty ward that he would never forget:

> One afternoon in early July, for example, a delivery arrived at the hospital: a carton box with a pair of mangled legs inside it. These had been sent to the hospital by well-meaning soldiers thinking that the limbs might arrive in time to be reattached to the torso of their comrade, blown to bits by an improvised explosive device hours earlier. A little later on two badly burnt Afghans arrived. One would be dead within the hour. The other would follow suit . . . A few beds over, a wild-eyed Afghan was blissfully unaware that he had been without a two-square-inch bit of skull for the past twenty-four hours. In the rush of things,

> his skull piece had been left behind in Kandahar. It arrived by plane in the early hours of the morning and was stuffed in our fridge, next to our chocolate snacks and zero-alcohol beer, awaiting reattachment.

At moments of dread before an operation likely to involve enemy contact, I made a habit of praying to God to protect me so that I could 'get back to Ginny, Mum and my sisters'. I also made myself think of my Uncle Johnny and my father in terms of their war service. Having read a great deal about both their wars, I had no difficulty picturing their own pre-battle dread.

My uncle Johnny Fiennes was killed in 1917 leading his unit of Gordon Highlanders 'over the top' and under German machine-gun fire. He was twenty-one years old at the time and had already survived many months of the merciless carnage of one of the greatest killer battles of all time, the Battle of the Somme, with 50,000 dead in a single day.

My father, Ranulph, twenty-six years later, was killed in the next great war not far south of Monte Casino, after being wounded four times previously during tank battles in North Africa.

Both men must have spent months and years living in fear of death in the line of duty. I remember only too well the stomach-churning fear of impending action, when outnumbered in enemy territory and cut off from any support. I have never felt such a deep, primordial fear again.

I keep a Conduct Citation of the Dhofar days that reminds me of those times. It is dated 28 October 1969 and is signed by my colonel. When I find myself frightened by little things, I check the old text just to be reassured that I was not always a coward. The text read:

> Captain Fiennes commanded MR Recce platoon on operations from May 1969 . . . On 30 July his platoon were deployed in an ambush position in thick cover on the escarpment. On leaving

> the position the platoon were engaged by the enemy from five different dominating positions. Captain Fiennes coolly rallied his men and conducted a skilful withdrawal, frequently exposing himself to aimed enemy fire and firing the .50 Browning himself . . . On 3 August the Recce platoon were carrying out a typical patrol in the foothills when they were engaged by an enemy force of between twenty and fifty, armed with automatic weapons. Fiennes so disposed his force as to assault and outflank the enemy groups and force them to withdraw . . . On 9/10 October Captain Fiennes again demonstrated his determination to operate independently with a small force in an enemy area . . . Throughout this and other operations he has set the highest example of dogged determination, tactical skill and physical courage. His independent operations, relying very largely on his own judgement, endurance and initiative, have proved the ascendency of a small SAF force over larger enemy groups on many occasions.

My Uncle Johnny shared with every soldier involved in that deadly trench warfare the knowledge of the *likelihood* of death or horrific maiming. It was a world of rats and lice. If the water table was high, or there had been heavy rain, then the trenches became a sea of mud and water. In some cases the mud was so deep that men had to stand on barrels.

It was not unknown for men to literally disappear in the mud. There were thousands of unburied bodies along the front lines. In the Somme area alone some 200,000 were killed, and most of these were only buried in shallow graves. The constant churning of the earth by artillery fire would exhume the remains, leaving them scattered and in plain view. This also encouraged black and brown rats. The brown ones could grow to the size of a domestic cat and were partial to human flesh.

As a constant state of misery is to a slum-dweller, so was fear to the front-line inhabitants of the trenches in the 1914–18 First World War. Shooting deserters was necessary to help discourage the practice among the terrified men awaiting the next order to 'go over the top' in the knowledge that entire waves of attackers would be slaughtered in a matter of minutes by concentrated machine-gun fire. And even in the comparative safety of a trench, unseen and unheard, lethal mustard gas could arrive at any time to blister the skin, the eyes and cause the lungs to foam.

The personal diaries and photographs of survivors were collated in a 2016 book to mark the centenary of the start of the Battle of the Somme.

On 1 July 1916, 150,000 British troops attacked the German lines. In addition to the 20,000 killed, another 40,000 were wounded. One of those involved was Private Frank Lindley, who remembered:

> You could hear the bullets whistling past and our lads were going down, flop, flop, flop in their waves, just as though they'd all gone to sleep. Second Lieutenant Hirst was near to me, almost touching. He had just got wed before we came away, and was a grand chap, but it wasn't long before he got his head knocked off.
>
> I was in the first wave. There was no cheering, we just ambled across, you hadn't a thought; you were so addled with the noise. Out of the corner of your eye you could see the boys going down, but there was no going back. They had what we called 'whippers-in' with revolvers, and they could shoot you if anybody came back, so we moved forward as best we could. As I laid flat out there in no-man's-land, up on top jumped one of our whippers-in with revolver ready, and we were all laid out in shell holes, and he said, 'Come on, come on.' He hadn't gone two yards before he went up in the air, riddled . . .

Another survivor wrote: 'Arms and legs were flying all over. I didn't know anybody in the shell holes I got in. We were all mixed up.'

Fighting in the air at that time was equally dangerous. At the battle of Arras there were 385 British fighters against 114 enemy aircraft, but even then the average life expectancy of a British pilot was seventeen and a half hours of combat. Their greatest fear in their wooden machines and without parachutes was being burnt to death.

This book does not cover fear in animals, whether hunted foxes or Chinese dogs battered to death in mass abattoirs. But I can imagine the fear felt by the 8 million horses known to have been killed during the First World War, and Private David Polley, 189th Machine Gun Company, Machine Gun Corps, recalled his distress at the slaughter:

> To me one of the beastliest things of the whole war was the way animals had to suffer. It mattered not to them if the Kaiser ruled the whole world; and yet the poor beasts were dragged into hell to haul rations and gear over shell-swept roads and field paths full of holes to satisfy the needs of their lords and masters. Bah! Many a gallant horse or mule who had his entrails torn out by a lump of shell was finer in every way than some of the human creatures he was serving . . . The sight of a team of horses hitched to a limber on a road in the forward areas and screaming with fright at a shell-burst in the ditch beside them, turned my mind . . .

In Dhofar my dread quotient also rose or fell dependent on whether, on any given operation, I had a full thirty-strong turnout with Fiend Force or whether, due usually to the number of soldiers with bad coughs, I would have a lesser strength. Likewise, if we were a part of an operation liaising with one or more of the companies, I always felt much less apprehensive. The simmering fear that lurked like some invisible black raven in my mind during combat conditions was far more nerve-racking than any fear I remember during dangerous expeditions or climbs.

In any combat situation I knew that the human enemy was out to hurt or kill me by any means, whereas crevasses, avalanches or roaring chunks of sea ice, however terrifying, are not. Also, there is the knowledge that my dicing with death by challenging natural hazards is entirely my own choice, which I could cancel at will, unlike army operations in the line of duty.

'Line-of-duty' instances of fearful confrontations for those involved are many and varied. There are two that I rate as particularly impressive. One is Harold Lowe, the Welsh junior officer hailed as a hero of the *Titanic* disaster. Lowe was the only ship's officer who returned to the scene of the sinking in his lifeboat to search for survivors.

Another is Captain Chesley B. 'Sully' Sullenberger, the pilot of US Airlines Flight 1549, who in January 2009 managed to ditch his Airbus A320 passenger aeroplane in New York's Hudson River, after both the engines had been disabled by a bird-strike soon after take-off from La Guardia Airport. In doing so, he saved 155 lives and described the moments before the crash landing as 'the worst, sickening pit-of-your-stomach, falling-through-the-floor feeling' he had ever experienced.

For myself, I well remember when lying in ambushes the bowel-loosening thoughts of specific bullet-damage to my eyes and stomach as a result of seeing others suffering and screaming from such wounds. The worst times for such negative worries were when cut off for hours, days and nights and knowing that one wrong move, one soldier coughing as a local goatherd drove his flock nearby, and we would be surrounded within hours.

On one occasion, our patrol along the Yemeni border in late October was interrupted by a Morse message to go at once back to Thamarit Base. We were met there by our intelligence officer, Tim Landon, who was with a shifty-looking Dhofar tribesman called Sahayl carrying an automatic 7.62 rifle.

Tim explained that Sahayl had taken a violent dislike to two *adoo* commissars who had raped his daughter and wanted to help us capture them.

'This operation is vital,' Tim stressed. 'Sahayl will guide you tonight from the northern cliffs above O'bet to his village of

Qum, where you will ambush and capture, alive if possible, the two *adoo* commissars. This will throw the *adoo* into a state of uncertainty and the locals into realising that we will stand by them in their hour of need.'

We made it to the village of Qum just before dawn and set up our ambushes on all the approach paths. We were in the heart of the *adoo*'s eastern headquarters zone. When the two commissars arrived a few yards from the thornbush where my four-man section was lying, I hissed, *Yid fawq* (hands up), but the leading man, a red star glinting in his forage cap, swung his automatic rifle at me. As did the man behind him. I had to shoot both men at close range.

One of my men grabbed the document satchel off the commissar's corpse, and I gave whispered orders on the walkie-talkie to the other four sections to retreat at speed. The *adoo* only caught up with our long flight through their backyard, ably led by a happy Sahayl, when we were already halfway down the cliffs at O'bet, and only one of Fiend Force was wounded. The rule here was that of fear as a helpful stimulus. The rabbit usually runs faster than the fox as it is running for its life and not just for its dinner.

Tim learned, from the PFLOAG orders sheets in the captured satchel, that the *adoo* were already far better prepared for their planned attack on Salalah than we had believed. The death of the two commissars in the centre of the PFLOAG stronghold had a far-reaching effect, as Tim had hoped. Other *jebalis* in the east took heart from the rebellious example of Sahayl. They too rose up against the aggressive behaviour and tactics of the *adoo*, took up arms against the communists, and generally worked to reassert themselves as Muslims.

There is a book by ex-US Marine officer Karl Marlantes called *What It Is Like To Go To War*, which recalls his time fighting in Vietnam against the North Vietnamese Army (NVA). He wrote about his feelings of guilt after killing people in Vietnam, and he argued that guilt-originated Post Traumatic Stress Disorder

(PTSD) will probably have a lesser effect if the motives for killing someone are, in some way, justifiable:

> It is likely that the young Canadian, British, American, and other NATO or coalition troops who fought in Afghanistan or Iraq will have less guilt the more they believe that they were fighting to stop a clear terrorist threat or overthrow a brutal dictatorship or a religious reign of terror. They will suffer less than those of us who fought in Vietnam for a less clearly defined cause.

The National Institutes of Health in the USA stated recently that 18 per cent of the US adult population suffers from an anxiety disorder during any given year, whether from PTSD or social anxiety disorder or genetic phobias. The part of the brain that involves all these states of fear is the amygdala, which is about the size of an almond and is our primary fear factory.

Back in the 1930s, researchers found that a monkey lacking an operating amygdala felt no fear at all. And the medical journal *Current Biology* described, in 2010, a patient (code-named 'SM' for privacy purposes) who had a congenital disease, which entailed a complete lack of amygdala. By subjecting her to various frightening scenarios including snakes, proven to activate fear symptoms in all amygdalae, and finding 'SM' scared of *nothing*, they concluded that 'no amygdala equals no fear'. The monkey researchers of eighty years before had been right in their assumptions.

The whole fear process is really fairly simple. You are attacked by a growling dog and, instantly, your amygdala triggers the release of certain hormones, including adrenalin and cortisol. Your heart then races, blood rushes into your legs (flight) and your arms (fight) and your muscles tense. This all helps contend with the immediate danger, but the released hormones also ensure that you don't forget this bad experience by firmly filing away a vivid image of it in your long-term – *very* long-term – memory. Hence PTSD.

Unfortunately 'SM's status removed not just fear itself, but also her stored memory of past dangers, e.g. PTSD. So her researchers were not surprised to learn from her family that she had been threatened one night when walking alone through the local park, and that the *very next night* she had again walked alone through the very same park.

PTSD comes in many shapes and sizes and causes many suicides. Sufferers in rehab often describe their worst nightmares as including the face of some past tormentor, and scientists have measured the brain's electric fear pulses shooting up when actual photos of the feared individual are shown to the owner of the relevant nightmare.

I will never forget the face of the commissar that I killed (a millisecond before he would have killed me). My diary after that event stated,

> 'I had often shot at people hundreds of yards away; vague shapes behind rocks who were busy shooting back. But never before had I seen a man's soul in his eyes, sensed his vitality as a fellow human being, and then watched his body torn apart at the pressure of my finger. I tried to force away the image of his destruction, but his scarred face kept watching me from my subconscious. A part of me that was still young and uncynical died with him and his comrade, spread-eagled on a thornbush with his red badge glinting in the hot Qara sun.'

Time magazine told the story of a veteran whose very character was altered by a few months of frontline experience:

> Tim Smith wasn't wounded in Iraq, at least not physically, but he came back strange. His best friend, Norman 'Doc' Darling, had been killed with seven others by an IED in Sadr City in April 2004, one of the bloodiest months of the war. Their unit moved to Mahmudiyah in the Triangle of Death, just south of Baghdad. The war was very bad there too. FOB

St Michael – their Forward Operating Base – was pummelled by mortars and rocket-propelled grenades every day. Tim was never injured, but he was seriously rattled – and that began to manifest itself physically. He developed an allergy to dust. His eyes swelled with severe conjunctivitis whenever he went outside. Tim figures his body was telling him something important: don't go outside.

Tim began to change dramatically when he and his wife Terri returned to St Louis in February 2007. Loud noises jolted him; there were nightmares and anxiety attacks. He slept with a gun under the bed. He wasn't funny and outgoing the way he'd been before. Much of his personality had been deleted – and he couldn't tell his wife why and wouldn't tell her what had happened over there.

Tim Smith's PTSD was the result of suffering over many days the repetitive experience of witnessing death near at hand.

Involved in warfare and killing, but less likely to suffer recurrent dreams about the death and destruction they have instigated are the operators of remote-control weapons . . . men and women, including long-distance bomber pilots who take leave of their families in California at breakfast, drop bombs in Iraq and are back home the very next day . . . or console operators in Nevada, who commute daily to and from their homes to computers that control drones which kill individuals in Afghanistan at the touch of a button.

On the other hand there are individuals who suffer from extreme PTSD attacks for years due to just a single horrific event. As in the sad case of the policeman Dick Coombes, who in 1994 was a member of the eleven-man unit Serial 502, half of whom were trained in riot control, who were sent to the concrete blocks of the Broadwater Farm Estate in Tottenham, North London, where police were under attack from hundreds of youths throwing stones and petrol bombs. Blazing cars were everywhere. Police, four of whom had been shot and more than 200 badly hurt, were being rushed to ambulances. Crowds in the dark shadows of the estate screamed, 'Kill! Kill! Kill the Pigs!'

As the firemen and the police, the latter armed only with riot shields and batons, reached the rioters, three separate mobs of youths, armed with machetes, axes, petrol bombs and long steel rods with sharpened ends, closed in from all sides. Dick's leader, PC Keith Blakelock, stumbled and some thirty rioters closed in on him with a variety of weapons. His truncheon, his shield and his helmet were torn from him, so he raised his hands to protect his face. The mob slashed at his arms, chopping off fingers and exposing his head. Stakes and knives were plunged into his chest and his neck, but he did not die.

Coombes saw the crowd 'like a flock of murderous birds in a feeding frenzy, hacking and jabbing' at his colleague Blakelock, so he ran back to help him but was blocked by a number of rioters brandishing various weapons. A vicious blow knocked him down. He was then set upon by the pack, his visor torn off and his neck slit open with knives. His jawbone was shattered by a machete blade and he lost consciousness. Masked rioters set about his inert body with knives and clubs.

Other constables managed under attack to pull Coombes, who had blood pumping from his face and neck, to the roadway. He was to suffer from crippling epileptic fits for the rest of his life.

I spoke to Dick sixteen years after his experience on the night of 6 October 1985, and he told me, 'That night not only ruined the lives of Keith's family, but many, many others. All of us have been affected. It will never be over for us.' And I thought of the words of Joseph Stanislaw in 1962, 'Wounds heal and become scars but scars grow with us.'

To this day, more than thirty years after Dick's brave rush into that murderous mob, he still cannot work, drive or read a book. He suffers daily blackouts and several serious epileptic fits each month. He cannot enter crowded rooms and he flinches on seeing a knife. In his dreams he sees again and again the man with the machete raised over Keith Blakelock's bloodied body.

David Pengelly, who was the sergeant in PC Blakelock's unit, and his colleague Miles Barton wrote to me in 2010 and confirmed that, down the long years since Broadwater, they have both suffered badly from post-traumatic stress, but that given the choice of a replay, they would again shake away their fear, as wet dogs shake off mud, and go back into hell to help their fallen comrade, and Dick Coombes has told me that he agrees wholeheartedly with this sentiment.

6

The Fear Zone

Never been into the canyon, too many guys drowned in there. Anybody who tries to boat through it is just plumb crazy.

Andy Moses, Canadian trapper

After the killing of the commissars at Qum, Fiend Force continued to operate in the *jebel* and the desert wherever we were sent. In March 1970 I came to the end of my service contract with the Army and said goodbye to the wonderful men, my friends and brothers, of Fiend Force.

As I climbed into the Beaver supply plane with my gun and my backpack, Corporal Salim Khaleefa shook my hand and said, 'I will look after the men, Sahb. Perhaps one day you will come back to us.'

That July my boss, Sultan Said, was deposed and replaced by his son Qaboos. The old man was taken by an RAF plane to a private suite in the Dorchester Hotel in London, together with his palace retinue. He died there two years later, having by then made his peace with his son and successor, Qaboos.

As I write this, Qaboos is still the popular ruler of all Oman and Dhofar and has so far somehow avoided the troubles following the Arab Spring.

Back in Britain, aged twenty-six, with no job and without the khaki umbrella of the Army, I had, for the first time in my life, to face the reality of choosing a career. Up till then I had *always* seen myself as Colonel of the Royal Scots Greys, so I had never bothered to look beyond that goal and, as long as I was in the Army, I had always believed that, somehow, Fate would ensure that the authorities would waive any and all stupid 'regulations', such as A levels, promotion rules, Sandhurst, clean Service Record, and other superior contenders for the job. Even when I was about to leave Sultanate service, I half-expected a request from the Ministry of Defence stating that my service in Oman had been so exemplary that those charged with the selection of Regimental Commanding Officers, whoever they were, had voted for me.

But, back home in Sussex with my mother, I came down to earth with a bang. She was, as always, practical. My sisters were all married; one to an Army officer, one to an American doctor whom she had met at a mission in Zululand, and one to the son of our South African neighbour (who had once called me a wimp for screaming at a rickshaw Zulu). All three sisters were happy and had lovely children, and my mother asked me what, now that my chosen career had proved unattainable, I intended to do? And when was I going to marry my fiancée Ginny, who had waited so patiently for me during my two years in Oman? I had, Mum pointed out, spent over half the money that was left to me by my grandmother on a Land Rover, and now, with no A levels or other CV Brownie points, I should seriously start searching for a worthwhile profession.

I applied for a wide variety of jobs whilst writing a book about our Nile journey, for which Ginny had cajoled a top literary agent into arranging a contract. The book royalties were totalled at £450, which was a mini-fortune in those days.

I spoke German, French and Arabic quite well, so I applied to MI6 for a job. They turned me down without saying why. In desperation I began to give lectures at local town halls using colour slides of the Nile expedition. Slowly I infiltrated the town hall network and, since Britain then had an inexhaustible supply of town halls that paid lecturers £18 a time, inclusive of travel costs, I was unlikely to end up on the dole. The vast majority of my audiences were ladies over seventy who liked each other's company, but found it difficult to stay awake for more than fifteen minutes once the hall lights were switched off for my lecture.

Eventually, using the Nile journey as our template, Ginny and I decided that, once married, we would make a living by lecturing and writing about the expeditions we undertook. Our rules would include never paying anybody anything for anything at any time, which meant we would have to obtain total sponsorship. We would start with short, easy journeys and, once we could attract enough publicity to ensure major sponsorships, we would move on to higher levels of attempting world geographical and physical records.

Our first such plan was a brief excursion to Central Norway's largest glacier, the Jostedalsbre, where we would traverse the high ice sheet by ski and survey one particular icefall at the specific behest of the Norwegian Hydrological Department, their director having stressed that this survey would be of 'extreme topical interest'. To save hauling heavy survey and survival gear 6,000 feet up steep and hazardous ravines, the team would parachute with all the equipment from a chartered aircraft at 10,000 feet.

After the survey was complete the team would descend one of the many icefalls, at the bottom of which they would use small inflatable boats to navigate the glacial rivers back to the nearest roadhead.

The team of volunteers that we selected were all told to learn how to parachute, mountaineer, survey and white-water raft, and they all had to produce proof of full insurance cover.

In August 1970 our sixteen-strong team with three loaned Land Rovers and trailers arrived at Lake Loen in a valley below the great glacier. Don Hughes, the chief instructor of the Army's Netheravon Parachute School, who had taught SAS specialists the latest freefall techniques, volunteered to 'push us out' at 10,000 feet at the moment he estimated we were most likely to land in a crevasse-free zone, and not too close to the 6,000-foot cliffs that fell away on all sides of the ice fields.

On arrival Don told us, 'If we get high winds or bad visibility conditions, I am definitely not letting anyone jump in adverse conditions. Even if you were SAS freefall experts, I'd say the same thing. But you lot are decidedly inexpert.'

I was equally adamant. 'We can't postpone the survey for more than three days, Don. We only have the full survey team until the end of the month, and they can't work on misty days. With no triangulation point sightings, they can't even start work.'

The argument went back and forth, so we agreed to compromise and hope for the best. My sponsored budget allowed for only a single day's charter, so we must be sure of fine weather before calling the aeroplane up from Bergen.

On 13 August the weather looked good, so I took the plunge. When the Cessna seaplane reached our base beside Lake Loen, I could see that it was not the model that I had asked for, or expected. It was, however, the only plane available that could feasibly do the job. We would take off from the lake in two groups of six, fly to 10,000 feet and then jump on Don's prompting.

Since all the previous training back in Netheravon had involved jumping from a spacious Rapide with wheels, whereas this cramped Cessna had metal floats with large rudders, we all needed to retrain at the last minute. Don handled this on the wooden jetty to which the Cessna was lashed. One by one he had us reach out of the little cabin door to grasp a narrow wing strut. Then followed a clumsy lurch from the doorway to reach the float below with both feet. Even with no 120-mph slipstream, this was far from easy.

Simply to let go of the wing strut in this position would be very dangerous as our bodies would almost certainly blow back into the steel float rudders. So Don explained that to avoid decapitation we must jump sideways and outwards just before relaxing our grip on the strut.

I would be the first to jump and did not relish the idea. I glanced at the others. They all looked unconcerned, but I knew this must be an act; they were just as petrified as I was. The *Sunday Times* photographer had hired a helicopter to record the jump. Next day the paper would show a photo of Roger Chapman, my co-leader, dropping towards a dizzy void edged by sharp, black crags and serried ranks of crevasses far below. The banner headline blazed: THE WORLD'S TOUGHEST JUMP.

I did not fancy landing in a crevasse or being battered by thermals against the 6,000-foot cliffs that dropped down from two sides of our tiny target snowfield. I tried to remember how to fall for fifteen seconds in a perfect star shape, how to pull the chute-release handle while remaining stable, and how to steer the chute to a safe landing.

I had learned, at least in theory, the secret of dealing with fear in Dhofar: keep a ruthlessly tight clamp on your imagination. With fear, you must prevent, not cure. Fear must not be let in in the first place. Think of anything but the subject of your fear. Never look at the void you are about to jump into. If you are in a canoe, never listen to the roar of the rapids before you let go of the riverbank. Just do it! Keep your eyes closed and let go. If the fear then rushes at you, it will not be able to get a grip because your mind will be focusing by then on the technical matter of survival.

That jump was memorable. I hit one hand hard against the float and then cartwheeled out of control into space. I narrowly avoided missing the drop zone altogether, but luck was with me and, like most of the others, I made a safe landing. The last man to drop was dragged by surface winds to within twenty-five yards of the cliff edge and bruised his ribs. Most of the equipment chutes were retrieved and we camped as night fell.

In near-lethal ice conditions our survey teams reached their various trig points and completed the survey on time. All but six of the team then trekked down a rocky defile to the rivers and roads far below. This left six of us to tow the valuable sponsored survey equipment and other heavy gear down on sledges. To do this we clearly needed snow and ice, not rocks, down which to slide the heavy sleds. We chose the Briksdalslbre, the steepest of the Jostedal's twenty-eight icefalls, since less steep glacier descents would be split by more crevasses to be bridged, which would possibly prove insuperable. Such was my theory anyway.

To find the upper icefalls of the Briksdal local glacier, guides were essential, so I was relieved when they turned up. Tough and weather-beaten, they knew more about the ice fields than anyone alive. David, the older man, had lived up there at the start of the war when the only parachutists likely to drop in were Nazis. Neither man spoke English, but Henrik, the only Scandinavian in our team, translated. His words were a shock. 'They advise us *not* to proceed with the Briksdal descent, because of the weather and dangerous crevasses.'

I argued with them, but to no avail. Henrik was a man of huge experience. He was also our only ice climber of any note. He said, 'I agree with the Norwegians. I have climbed ice and rock in the Alps, Lapland, Africa and the Himalayas. There are four reasons we should not attempt this. We are now in the period of maximum melt, so there will be avalanches. We have no suitable ice-climbing gear. None of you has previous ice-climbing experience. Lastly, the guides know best.'

The guides then added a new horror story, which Henrik translated. 'Jan says that on the Briksdal this mist and rain will dislodge tons of falling ice all day. He says you must now abandon your heavy-duty gear here and go down by the easier Faberg Glacier. David says that there are icefalls on the Briksdal that even he has never climbed – in fact, he doesn't know anybody who has.'

Realising that I was beaten and sensing that Henrik's words would soon infect the morale of the others, I moved from the attack to the compromise. I was lucky, for the guides wanted to be as helpful as they felt the circumstances allowed. They finally agreed to guide us two-thirds of the way to the Briksdal and then leave by way of another glacier with any of us who wished to follow their advice. In the event, only Henrik left the team, probably because only he truly appreciated the nature of the dangers ahead.

We spent three days and nights descending the icefalls of the Briksdalsbre, an unforgettable and nightmarish experience during which we lost much of our sponsored equipment down crevasses. Halfway down, I made radio contact with Henrik and our Land Rovers. They and some sixty members of the Scandinavian and UK press were scanning the icefalls with binoculars from the valley below.

'You must go back, Ran,' Henrik advised. 'Five days ago a team of Norway's top glacier climbers tried to complete the first ascent of the Briksdal with the best equipment. They failed when their leader was hurt. They say descending is even more dangerous than going up, as you can't see or plan a safe route. Avalanches fall everywhere.'

I would have followed Henrik's advice but, since we were already about halfway down, it seemed less dangerous to try to continue. We already knew about the avalanches with huge masses of ice chunks cascading down the face of the icefalls. So we continued with the descent, and by great good luck we finally escaped with bloody hands, bruised ribs and our lives. Arriving at the glacier's snout, we inflated our remaining rubber boats and careered down the Briksdal River to the roadhead below. The Scandinavian media, who had been predicting our demise for several months, were suitably impressed by our survival, as were our sponsors, and I was ready to move on to a more ambitious expedition – marrying Ginny just two weeks after our return to Britain.

Our next expedition, sponsored by my old regiment the Royal Scots Greys, involved a descent of nine interlinked rivers that traversed the entire province of British Columbia (BC) from north to south for some 2,000 miles from the border with the Yukon Territory to the US border near Vancouver. I selected three soldiers whom I knew from our time together back in Germany during the Cold War days. None of us had experience of rapid rivers or small inflatables, and the nine BC rivers were in parts 'Grade Nine White-Water', which in lay terms meant extremely turbulent. A BBC crew of three and a photographer, Bryn Campbell, from the *Observer* joined the team. Ginny was to drive a sponsored Land Rover towing a trailer full of vehicle fuel and ration packs, and she intended to resupply our three rubber boats wherever a forest track met the river.

On the day we set out from Fort Nelson in the far north of BC, the Liard River was in full flood and semi-blocked by islands of tangled debris under which the river roared. Bryn was struck by a branch and disappeared into the muddy waves. An underwater surge luckily spewed him up further down the log-jam and we hauled him, white, cold and shaken, back into the boat.

Over the weeks and months that followed we all developed a dread of the power of the rivers. At all times we were attended by thousands of singing, biting mosquitoes and tiny *no-see-um* flies.

At a village populated by local Indians we were warned that a grizzly bear had recently killed two young girl campers in their sleeping bags, so we kept our four revolvers loaded in the tents. A French missionary priest knew the Nahanni, the river ahead, and he said, 'At this time the water is high. You have a hundred and forty miles of big fast river. One mistake, and whoosh! The worst place is the Devil's Whirlpool, where the German died eight years ago. After that it is even more difficult. The Nahanni races down like a galloping horse. Incredible.'

A hunter, Brian Doke, told us to go carefully. A moose hunter that he knew had capsized only twelve miles up the Nahanni, lost his kit and twisted an ankle. They found him nine days later; he was half-starved and demented by insects. The previous year another hunter friend had been attacked in thick bush by a black bear, normally non-aggressive to humans. His body, half-eaten, was found alongside his loaded rifle. A helicopter pilot went in to destroy the killer bear, but it attacked him only minutes after he had landed and he stepped back into the revolving heliblade and scalped himself.

At one stretch of the Nahanni the rushing river passed through deep canyons, one of which was named Deadmen Valley. Canadian newspaper articles put the death toll of Deadmen Valley visitors as high as twenty-nine, but after careful research at the Royal Geographical Society and through Royal Canadian Mounted Police records, Ginny had traced only seventeen unexplained deaths or disappearances, plus three straightforward drownings and one plane crash.

In less than 100 miles our boats 'climbed' over 1,000 feet. The final canyon was an impressive display of water force, the river powering past us as though racing to eternity. I felt completely insecure, possibly due to the prolonged effect of the struggle, the noise and the dwindling fuel supply. Each time the boat raced down the back-end of a curling hydraulic, I wondered if the next wave would bury us in its own deep trough.

From the Yukon border and the Liard River, we followed the River Kechika deep into the Rocky Mountain Trench, still heading upriver until the water became too shallow for our boats. Here we split up and Ginny organised for a bush pilot with a floatplane to fly the boats and all but two of us to the south side of the Sifton Pass, the highest in the Canadian Rockies. Jackie McConnell, one of the three Scots Greys soldiers, and I planned to trek on south over the Sifton to the headwaters of the Arctic watershed, but we got lost in deep, tangled forest and waded through swamps with an ever-attendant squadron of mosquitoes and hornets buzzing and biting. At one point the skies to the east darkened with an ominous tinge and there was a vague smell of burning. Fearful of being caught in one of BC's notorious bush fires, we radioed Ginny, but could not make contact.

Earlier we had passed a burnt-out region of utter desolation, with the land rolling black and lifeless to faraway mountains, empty but for ranks of charred and mostly branchless pines. We had been told by Skookum Davis, a local hunter, 'The strength of the grizzly, the speed of the cougar, the camouflage of a million tiny field mice, even the brains of the cunning fur trapper – nothing is proof against a racing forest fire.' Jackie and I felt extremely insecure until a storm arrived, along with spectacular lightning.

As we climbed, the forest became less tangled, and on a high mountain slope we shivered all night between rocks in a howling snow storm. We were running out of food and increasingly fearful of our predicament.

A labyrinth of entwined valleys made a mockery of direction finding, but we were forced to follow their meanderings rather than a compass bearing in order to avoid mountains and ravines.

Jackie McConnell slipped and badly hurt his ankle, so we turned back. By following the watershed we eventually reached our stashed canoe and I said goodbye to Jackie, who would get back to Ginny's current base and fly south to join the main group. Alone now, I headed south. This time I followed close to streams. The going was in every way as bad as before, but it was warmer beside the river than on the slopes of the mountain forests, and for three days there was no rain. By night the temperature dropped below freezing, but I kept a fire going until I slept.

There was a moment of panic when I saw the dark cloud of a forest fire to the east, and again when I lost the river and ran out of drinking water. Twice I became jammed on my back, having fallen off giant tree trunks spanning thick undergrowth. On the fifth day my sores wept poison and I ran out of penicillin. Dizzy bouts affected my judgement and, after two days wading up the river itself, I found myself hemmed in by rapids ahead and sheer rock walls on either side. So I waded back downstream to a place with access to the western bank.

Six hours later I picked up a clearly marked triple tree-slash, which in the territory of those parts indicated a nearby trapline or fur trapper's route. In a while there were further signs and I knew for sure that I had found an Indian trail, which now became easier to see and was no longer a will-o'-the-wisp passage through undergrowth, but a trodden path with blaze marks every so often.

In due course I made it to the southerly watershed on the far side of Sifton Pass. All streams and rivers from then onwards would flow into the Pacific and not the Arctic. At Fox Lake the team were all there but for Ginny, who was organising things further south.

Jackie took me to one side and warned me that the BBC team were planning to popularise their documentary by adding the theme of officer-to-soldier bullying by me, to add to the excitement of the journey itself.

I had counted on a fair BBC film of our journey, an honest reproduction of our struggles, not an artificial *Mutiny on the Bounty* stirred up, then recorded by the film team. If the BBC TV series *The World About Us*, with its audience of 8 million, gave me a bad name for brutality, inefficiency and glory-seeking, the damage would be irreparable, because Ginny and I were painfully aware that the sponsor companies on whom our future totally depended would blacklist us. Sponsors were as crucial to our expeditions as creditors are to a small business. There was nothing unusual in our sensitivity to the feelings of sponsors; it is the ingrained and ever-present worry of all expeditioners without funds of their own. It can affect the judgement and the ability to make correct decisions and was, in the years ahead, to come within an ace of destroying my career.

Ginny arrived in the tiny floatplane. She was worried about the tensions in the team.

'Don't let things get worse,' she counselled.

I shrugged. 'There's little that I can do. The film crew seem determined to make trouble. Let's not talk about them.'

We spent an hour together in an empty mosquito-free warehouse. It was the first anniversary of our wedding. Ginny gave me the maps that she had waterproofed and marked with warning comments learned from the Mounties and game wardens with whom she had been in contact. Not all the news was rosy. The

Fraser River was, by all accounts, infinitely rougher than the Nahanni and was riven with whirlpools, sinkholes and twister waves. Before we could reach the Fraser, we must cross wide lakes jammed with logs and navigate rivers too shallow for outboards.

Over the long days and weeks ahead my fears were a mixture of dread about the state of the rapids in the canyons ahead and the ongoing machinations and intentions of the film team.

At the end of the Finlay River, where once the unnavigable rapids of Deserters Canyon blasted south, we came up short against a jostling carpet of logs that blocked our way for three miles or more, caused by the world's largest earth-filled dam, 600 feet high and a mile-and-a-half wide. The dam itself was hundreds of miles away, but the waters of the Finlay were still backing up into its boundary forests and whole trees daily detached themselves from the lake floor, spearing to the surface like corks and adding to wind-driven log-jams. Another hazard, Ginny warned me, was the risk of mountain mudslides, which caused tidal waves that swept across the lake without warning. We moved through loosely packed logs, but after an hour a wind caused the jam behind us to shift and the pack to contract. Remembering cinema films of loggers riding tree trunks through rapids, we set about dragging our stricken boat over the spinning, grinding jam, wishing that we had spikes on our boots as the wood was wet and well-polished by ice action from previous winters. At length we found an open channel and, thankfully, slid the boat back into the lake.

Hidden at the south end of McLeod Lake we found the mouth of the Crooked, our eighth river since leaving the Yukon border and the last before the mighty Fraser. This was a fast, shallow and confusing waterway, which twisted and turned through myriad oxbow lakes and split side-channels. For many days we bumped and pulled our way along, and tempers frayed. One night Ginny waited in a thickly forested muskeg swamp beside the river. I had asked her on the radio to be there at dusk with spare propellers. Our schedule proved impossible to maintain due to delays on the river, and Ginny waited for four hours in the dark. The batteries of her torch died and strange noises sounded all about her as the night hours advanced. Muskrats and beavers, racoons and deer all came to the water and, finally, so did a black bear. The bear did not see Ginny until they were near to each other. Ginny lost her nerve and screamed. The bear came closer and she pulled her .38 Smith and Wesson revolver out of her anorak pocket. Somehow she pressed the trigger before the gun was clear and a bullet passed through the outside welt of her rubber boot – within a couple of millimetres of her foot.

The bear departed, and so did a terrified Ginny. Next time I met her she was furious. Why had I not made the rendezvous? Why did she have to wander through stinking woods and portage heavy gear? Nobody ever thanked or acknowledged her.

I did, I pointed out.

'No, you don't. You just use me. You couldn't care less what happens to me so long as I'm in the right place at the right time.'

The Crooked River took us at length into Summit Lake, from where we portaged the boats for eleven miles across country to the town of Prince George on the great Fraser River, which would take us for 850 tempestuous miles all the way to Vancouver and the US border.

Seventy miles south of Prince George the river penetrates a deep trough valley, which is many hundreds of feet below the surface of the surrounding land mass. The river responds to the new resistance of the enclosing walls by seeking a sinuous route through a succession of nightmare canyons, livid with foam and mad with the roar of boiling water to the exclusion of all other sound.

The uncertainty of not knowing the state of the river ahead wore at our nerves, especially Jack's. Each day the cataracts grew more powerful and more frequent. In a small rubber boat even a twelve-foot wave can seem awesome. When they are legion and explode from every side, some boiling up from beneath the hull, they can make any passenger edgy. In the back of my mind lay the fear that around the next corner, or the one after, we would come without warning and without any chance of extrication to an impossible maelstrom or bottomless whirlpool.

With great difficulty we managed to descend the notorious Iron Rapids, but at camp that night the film team were as sullen as monsoon storm clouds. Around the campfire my attempts at a cheerful analysis of our progress were met with silence. Part of the trouble was the team's awareness that the worst lay ahead. The constant cliffhanging apprehension of the past weeks rendered nerves raw and tempers inflammable. The power of the Fraser had impressed us all. There was no doubt that it had controlled us, rather than us controlling the river. Our survival was largely a matter of luck and every new canyon had surpassed its predecessor in successive displays of unpredictable violence. Ahead lay the Moran Canyon, followed by a series of awkward major rapids.

To glean knowledge of the Moran, we visited the shack of Andy Moses in Kelly Creek, where he had spent fifty years beside the river. 'Never been into the canyon,' he said. 'Too many guys drowned in there. Anybody who tries to boat through it is just plumb crazy.'

After three days in Clinton I feared that the men's morale was beginning to plunge so, although I hated to enter the canyon unprepared and ignorant, I knew that we must go before any further delay sapped our will.

We entered the canyon, a rushing, rolling alleyway squeezed between black walls a thousand feet high, wherein the current gained momentum mile by mile down to a curving gut no more than fifteen yards wide between rocks. The underplay of currents was impressive. Stanley would shake his head in disbelief as the boat shot sideways in total variance to the commands of tiller and propeller. Huge surface boils, bubbling like hot water in a saucepan, twice turned us completely about and thrust us chaff-like against the granite walls.

We stopped, fearfully, above the great killer rapid of the Bridge

River confluence. The Press were waiting in Lillooet town below the Bridge River Falls; they sensed drama. Ginny's morale was low, not helped by hearing tales of others who had attempted the rapids. Four months earlier a muscular Frenchman had arrived in town. He had canoed every major rapid in North America, including the Lava sinkholes of the Colorado. Now he had come to tame the Bridge River Rapids. The Mounties retrieved his battered body from the whirlpools below the falls.

All of us rose early to preview the rapid and, in descending the rocky slope from the road to the river, I slipped and one foot landed on a jagged rock. The rubber sole of my gym shoe was slit and the heel of my foot was gashed open. I limped down to the river, leaving a bloody trail, and I squeezed the cut foot into a black rubber frog-shoe. Our first look at the cataract was off-putting, and the boom of the water was hypnotic.

Nerves on edge, I pushed our boat off. The rapid was explosive, but we survived and in an eddy below it we beached and shook hands. We clambered up to the film team's vantage point. Jack was silent. The culmination of weeks of fear had come to a head. He knew that our boat had remained upright through sheer good luck, both in and under the falls. In the temporary grip of hydrophobia, he decided not to risk this rapid.

That evening the Lillooet doctor stitched up my injured heel and said that we had been luckier than we deserved. He had seen the bodies of three young men, who had attempted to shoot the Bridge River cataract, off to the Lillooet mortuary.

Later, after the Black Canyon, we fought through nameless rapids hidden from the world by the gorges they had forged. We plunged down the rearing hummocks of eighteen-foot waves at China Bar – a rapid that caught us by surprise with its giant breakers, but which gave Jack back his nerve. He was committed by the time he saw what he was in for, and he clung to the C-Craft as it tossed and dived like a junk in a hurricane. The experience gave him confidence to face the Fraser's final monster rapid, Hell's Gate. This rapid was caused by rock-falls from a rail line that had been dynamited through the cliff-face and, in 1913, by landslides from both sides of the canyon. The river descends through the resulting bottleneck at up to fifty miles per hour. Water drained from an area of 84,000 square miles tears through a sheer-sided alley less than forty yards wide. Thirty-four million gallons pass the point every sixty seconds and the undercurrents are vicious, sucking flotsam down towards the river floor 175 feet below the surface.

We navigated the Gate with ease, a simple affair compared to the Bridge River rapids, but a mile downstream we came to near-disaster in a vicious rapid about which no one had warned us. Further on at the narrows called Sailor's Bar, we slithered through saw-toothed rocks where, a year before, a thirty-foot rubber raft had capsized and the helmsman had drowned.

Four days later the river split into three wide channels below New Westminster, once the capital, but now a sprawling suburb of Vancouver. We passed through the beautiful city with its backdrop of snow-clad peaks and into the river delta. A sea mist covered the marshes so we navigated with care into the Pacific until a police launch met us with a bullhorn. 'This is it, folks. You're in Yank territory now.'

The two BBC films led their 8-million-strong British audience to believe that I was a cruel and incompetent publicity seeker. The innuendoes that helped to paint this picture certainly added spice and colour to the films, and they did surprisingly little to discourage my sponsors in the future. They also helped me, in a small way, to develop a tougher skin in readiness for future events which would lay me open to public scrutiny and criticism.

7

Fear of Disease

I didn't want to stagger around naked, moaning and glassy-eyed, as the infected often did before they died.

Will Pooley, health worker

Some three months after returning to Britain after the Canadian expedition, Ginny was stirring the stew when she came up with a weird suggestion. 'Why don't we go around the world?' She had mooted the idea once before, during a brief Highland holiday, and I had ignored it as impractical. She envisaged a perpendicular route – through the Poles – which was, I knew, neither physically nor administratively possible. Even the world's polar experts had never managed it. We must, she added, *never* fly at any point of her 52,000-mile planned route.

I could see that Ginny was determined, and so, having selected a suitable team of volunteers and found sponsors for an ice-strengthened, forty-year-old ship and a small aeroplane that could fly with both wheels and skis for purely polar resupply purposes, we spent the next seven years unpaid and full-time obtaining everything needed from some 1,900 sponsors.

The SAS Group became the overall hosts of the project and provided us with ample space in their barracks close to Sloane Square in London's West End.

Although most of our team, under the leadership of our friend Anton Bowring, were on the ship's crew, we chose two men, out of 800 applicants, for the Ice Group with whom I hoped to cross both of the world's icecaps. One of the men, Oliver Shepard, had for nine years been a beer salesman, and the other, Charlie Burton, had left South Africa when his meat business there had gone bust. Neither had ever been anywhere cold, but then neither had Ginny or I.

At the time I was receiving a pay packet as a Territorial Army SAS captain and first I had to complete a two-month SAS jungle course in Brunei with a squad of four Regular SAS men. The patrol leader, Simon Garthwaite (who was killed by *adoo* in Dhofar a year later), slipped on a wet rock and cracked open the back of his skull. Our medic sewed him up, and a day later stitched back my ear lobe when it was partially ripped off by an *atap* thorn. Then our radio operator needed evacuation with dengue fever, so we demolished a clearing in the jungle for a helicopter to land and remove him. The explosion sent thousands of insects sky-high, and a big spider, landing on our medic's neck, bit him and caused a great black swelling. Apart from leech sores, I escaped further serious damage.

We all needed to learn how to travel in Antarctica, so we applied to the RAF to fly us, our sponsored two-seater tracked snow machines, and 30,000 lb of sponsored equipment to North Greenland. As we were all Territorial SAS soldiers, this was arranged using a routine RAF flight. The Greenland Ice Cap trials taught us a great deal about the do's and don'ts of polar travel on land-based ice with crevasse dangers. But Arctic sea-ice travel would involve a completely different set of problems and the temperatures would (unlike Greenland, where the coldest we experienced was –15°C) drop down into the minus forties. So we completed a second trial, which involved a journey from Ellesmere Island, at the most northerly tip of Canada, towards the North Pole.

The Canadian Army let us camp in two abandoned shacks on the northern coastline of the island and close to their Soviet-submarine-monitoring outpost of Alert. Of our first night there, Oliver wrote, 'The huts are deplorable. Minus 48°C. No heater and so, so cold. I slept wearing ten layers of clothing. Day and night were both as dark as pitch when the moon was hidden, and flesh glued itself to metal. We could manage about half an hour outside in a stiff breeze before retreating into the hut to thaw out.'

On our snowmobiles, which were like motorbikes with skis, we set out on 1 March and managed to progress five miles along the coastline while travelling at –51°C. The torture of the cold at night was such that we could not sleep without taking Valium tablets.

Ginny sat at her radios for ten hours a day, often longer, knowing that we were passing through areas of unstable, breaking ice. She never missed a schedule and hearing her faint Morse signal or, in good conditions, her voice in the tent was the happiest moment of any day.

One morning the wind blew at a steady forty-five knots, with gusts above fifty knots. The wind chill factor was –120°C and the natural liquid in our eyes kept congealing, making it difficult to navigate through the broken ice-blocks. Vision was all important. To progress at all meant choosing the least nightmarish route through the rubblefields and ice walls. We dreaded axe work because of the body sweat it caused and, later, the shivering when sweat particles inside our clothes turned to ice, which cascaded down our underwear when we moved. A typical stint of axe work would last nine to eleven hours in order to clear a skidoo lane of between 500 and 3,000 yards.

At first, aware of the danger from polar bears, we each carried a rifle, but we soon dropped the practice through sheer exhaustion. Slipping, sliding and falling into drifts made it difficult enough to manage a shovel and axe.

Our daily en-route ration of two frozen chocolate bars each wreaked havoc with our teeth, and by the time we returned to London we had, between us, lost nineteen fillings.

The fear came when my skidoo rolled over, down thirty-foot ramps of hard, sharp-edged ice slabs, and I flew off to land yards away with the wind knocked out of my lungs, my head buried and my goggles stuffed with snow. The ridge and ice rubble zones were the most exhausting.

By the end of April we had exceeded the northerly records of the Swede Björn Staib, the Italian Cagni, and the Norwegian Nansen. By the end of the month we had surpassed all but the journeys of the three Pole conquerors, Plaisted, Herbert and Monzino.

Early in May we were a mere 180 miles from the Pole when we were stopped by too much open water. With difficulty we found a flat floe just long enough for a ski-plane landing. Ginny then hired a search flight, but it failed to locate us. This was unnerving, but a second attempt on a rare day of clear skies enabled the pilot to pick out our yellow tent and he just managed to land on our narrow floe.

Back in London we packed and labelled over 3,000 heavy-duty boxes bound for eighteen different remote bases around the world. A year before, I had finally opened an expedition bank account, and the day we left England with a mind-boggling array of equipment for the ship's 110,000 sea-mile journey, a team of thirty, a ship and an aircraft, we were in credit to the tune of £81.76.

We left Greenwich in our old ship, the *Benjamin Bowring*, nicknamed the *Benji B*, on 2 September 1979, knowing that the journey, if successful, would take a minimum of three years. On the day we set out, the *New York Times* editorial column, under the heading 'Glory', stated: 'The British aren't so weary as they're sometimes said to be. The Transglobe Expedition, seven years in the planning, leaves England on a journey of such daring that it makes one wonder how the sun ever set on the Empire.'

More or less following the Zero Meridian, we drove from Algeria to the sand dunes of El Golea, a sticky-hot hell-hole dubbed 'El Gonorrhoea' by Oliver. We were pleased to leave the sweltering sands and head south to the 8,000-feet-high Hoggar Mountains and from there we travelled over trackless miles of sand and scrub to Timbuktu and then on to the port of Abidjan in the Ivory Coast, where we would meet up again with our ship *Benji B*.

The expedition's self-taught 'cook', Simon Grimes, was in charge of local purchases and he worked out various ways of cooking yams. Water collection was not easy, but he did his best from village wells, ponds or, when the track was near the Niger, directly from the river.

I recalled a letter I had once received from Nick Holder, who had contracted bilharzia during our Nile journey down the other side of Africa. He wrote about this waterborne sickness:

> Bilharzia, otherwise known as Schistosomiasis, is a disease occurring in most tropical countries, and it currently afflicts over 200 million people worldwide. It is caused by any of three species of fluke called schistosomes and is acquired by bathing or wading in infested lakes, rivers and irrigation systems. Schistosome eggs are passed from an infected population into water, and they are particularly prevalent in the waters of the Nile valley in Egypt. The eggs develop into tadpole-like creatures known as Cercariae which enter the human body, usually under finger and toe nails. Once in the bloodstream they mature into adult worms.
>
> Complications of long-term infestation can cause cirrhosis of the liver, bladder tumours and kidney failure. Since the 1980s, treatment of the disease has been revolutionised by a single dose of a drug known as Praziquantel, which kills the flukes and prevents damage to internal organs.

However, back in 1967 when I'd organised the British White Nile Hovercraft Expedition such remedies were unknown, and Nick was cured in a more basic fashion, as he went on to describe:

> We had been provided by our Nile sponsors with both water-purifying kits and tablets. The tablets were easier to use because they dissolved in a glass of water, the only problem being that

the taste of the resulting liquid was quite awful and it tainted everything we drank. 'Nice' cups of tea were no longer 'nice'.

The alternative was the water-purifying kit, which involved pouring the water into an open receptacle and then waiting up to a quarter of an hour as the liquid passed through gauze layers which filtered out the various contaminants.

I'm afraid that patience was a virtue I wasn't born with, and I noticed that the purified water didn't look or taste very different from the unpurified water which, after all, fifteen million Egyptians drank every day and they seemed to be OK.

However, after the end of the expedition when we returned to the UK we were all checked out for the early signs of such diseases as malaria, sleeping sickness, etc. and to my utter amazement I was diagnosed with bilharzia.

At one local Niger well Simon drew up a gallon or so of water in his roped bucket, and then poured this into a jerry can through a filter. 'Little bastards,' he muttered, blowing at the filter's gauze. I peered over his shoulder and a dozen miniature, hook-tailed tadpoles writhed in alarm as the warm air struck their horrid little forms.

'Hook worms, liver worms, toe worms, every sort and kind of disease carrier, and those are just the visible ones.' Simon seemed delighted. 'Imagine what a drop of that water would look like under the microscope. The locals here must be eaten alive from within.'

In fact, the only fever one can contract from water is Lassa Fever, and for this to happen you need to have exposed skin in water contaminated with rat urine, or inhale droplets of such contaminated water. There are, of course, waterborne diseases that do result in fever, but such fever is a manifestation of the immune system fighting infection, and not a direct effect of the bad water.

I watched Simon apply sterilisation and purification tablets to our bottles once he had pumped the water into them through lime candles; even then I doubt I would have drunk any of it but for my thirst.

As with our fight-or-flight inbuilt instinct, so with contamination, since every time our nomadic ancestors needed water they had to decide if it was safe to drink. Every time one of their family was struck by a fever, they knew that they were all at risk even though, unaware of air-borne viruses, they had to learn about quarantine the hard way. Those people who handled and buried diseased corpses were the ones most likely to succumb to the same illnesses. Faeces, especially human waste, was long known to host fatal bacteria such as cholera, and the link between someone drinking contaminated water and then spewing watery vomit and diarrhoea to spread further disease was easily apparent.

Simon, bitten by a great many insects and mosquitoes during our Niger-side travels, developed malaria, as did two members of our ship's crew then waiting for us off the Ivory Coast.

Because Oliver Shepard had various tasks to complete for the Natural History Department of the British Museum, including finding out about skink lizards in the Sahara, bats in the sub-Sahara, and water snails in the Ivorian jungles, we camped in lush forests along the Bandama Rouge River.

Charlie Burton found an eight-inch black scorpion in his sleeping bag one morning, and en route through thick jungle I filmed an army of thumb-sized black ants on the move in a metre-wide restless carpet over a hundred metres long.

By the light of his Land Rover, Oliver put two dead bats, which he had netted in a deep well into which we had lowered him, into a jar of formaldehyde. The bats were rare and were exactly what the museum had requested. Oliver had heard that a dreadful disease called Ebola had caused a pandemic in the Congo jungles and that a bat bite had transferred the disease to a pygmy. Charlie disagreed and said that a jungle monkey was the guilty party. Either way, the blood-curdling description that Oliver gave us of the deadly sufferings experienced by Ebola victims, about which he had been taught during his army-sponsored medical training, made me wish to keep well away from Oliver's pickled bats.

In January 2016 I interviewed Will Pooley, a health worker who had suffered from Ebola and was one of the lucky few to survive the killer disease. Will had flown from his home in Suffolk to Sierra Leone as a volunteer field nurse for a small Sierra Leonean charity just prior to the Ebola outbreak. He talked to me about his memories of that time:

> I was working as a nurse in a small clinic in Freetown, Sierra Leone when the World Health Organization (WHO) announced the detection of the virus in neighbouring Guinea. In the following weeks, increasingly alarming reports reached us on the radio and through Sierra Leonean colleagues that the virus was spreading into the east of the country by the Guinea border. An NGO worker stopped by our clinic on his way back from the east and told us that healthcare posts and hospitals were shutting down in fear of the disease. A BBC World Service report that I heard one evening told of staff fleeing from the Kenema Government Hospital, our main treatment centre in the east of Sierra Leone, as it was overwhelmed by victims infected with Ebola.
>
> Kenema Government Hospital was the site of one of the only two Ebola Treatment Units in the country at the time. It developed additional, very basic treatment facilities on one side of the hospital grounds in an improvised fashion, which grew haphazardly in response to increasing numbers of patients. Immediately staff began to fall sick and most of those died. The mortality rate for healthcare workers infected with Ebola, above seventy-five per cent, was higher than the average, but it was not clear why this was so. Few healthcare workers were willing to continue working with these risks.
>
> Back in Freetown these reports left me feeling uncomfortable in the knowledge that they were desperate for nursing staff and here was I, a nurse, doing little to help. It soon became morally

clear that I must go to Kenema. At this point I had no fear of what I might find there. Rather I was quite excited about seeing for myself a situation that was being described in apocalyptic terms by people on the streets in the capital.

When I reached Kenema and went to the hospital I met the deputy matron, who put me on the next morning's training workshop for hospital staff being engaged to work in the Ebola Unit. About forty local staff and myself were given an introduction to Ebola, Ebola patient care and infection prevention and control by three WHO doctors (British, American and Japanese) who had been drafted in to help the unit. I remember fear being discussed. 'I know you are all afraid,' we were told, 'but if we are careful and observe precautions, we can do this safely.'

I thought, 'I'm not afraid.' It wasn't that I saw a terrifying opponent and stood fearlessly to challenge it. I simply didn't care that much. Things would change however, and despite not having a strong concern for my personal safety, I would, before long, be gripped by fear.

The day after the training workshop I turned up to work and the small, tired team I met there didn't seem surprised that I was the only one of the trainees to do so. One of the WHO doctors showed me how to don the full body suit, gloves, apron, boots and headgear that constituted the personal protective equipment (PPE) designed to protect healthcare workers from the virus.

We then went inside the Red Zone where the infected patients were isolated. Patients lay moaning on beds, buckets by their sides were brimming with faeces, vomit and blood. One of the patients was staring at the ceiling with his mouth wide open. He had clearly died some time ago. Inside were children, mums with babies, young men, a couple of older people – a real cross-section of the population. My heart rate started to rise; I could hear it in my ears.

From then on I turned up every day at eight and went home sometime in the evening. The local nursing team consisted of a handful of those who hadn't fled or been infected. Six nurses survived Ebola, more had died. Sister Ubalu was the nurse in charge, though when I arrived she was at work but obviously unwell. She died a few days later and Nurse Nancy Yoko stepped in to lead the team. For the next couple of weeks a member of staff died every other day or so. It was only a matter of time for Nancy, but she came in every day and said that she had no fear because everything was in God's hands . . .

Eventually I got sick. One morning I woke dizzy and aching after a feverish night's sleep. Once in work I could barely walk for fatigue and I went to have my blood tested for Ebola. The prospect of entering the suspect ward as a potential Ebola case was a terrifying one. Indeed the suspect ward was now nicknamed the 'terrordome' by the WHO team, as it was the site of the worst horrors that the unit produced. I chose to isolate myself at home, and through the fugue of my illness pondered my potential outcomes and options.

I received news of my positive result that evening. I wasn't afraid of dying, my odds were fifty-fifty, I thought; the potential for not existing anymore did not bother me. What put a sick dread into me was the mental picture I had of the unit and what I had witnessed of the symptoms. God, I didn't want to be squatting on a bucket shitting blood, or lying incapable on a maggot-infested mattress.

I didn't want to stagger around naked, moaning and glassy-eyed, as the infected often did before they died. I was afraid of pain, and I would do anything not to suffer. When the WHO team said that evacuation by the British Government was an option, I jumped at it. At least in England they could knock me out with sedatives . . .

On the flight home, inside a bubble isolator on a trolley lashed down in the middle of an otherwise empty RAF cargo plane, I spiked a temperature peaking above 40°C. I started to see and feel how bad things might get.

Before long I was in the Royal Free Hospital in London receiving experimental drugs that seemed to improve my condition dramatically. These included Z Mapp, created in the USA from tobacco plants.

Within a week I was out of isolation and in the clear. Nancy wasn't though, and I received the news that she had been infected. She died a grim death a week later. I don't know if she kept her fearlessness until the end, but I imagine that she put herself in her God's hands and accepted her fate.

Soon afterwards a Scottish nurse, Pauline Cafferkey, who was working for the global charity Save the Children, went to Freetown in November 2015 in response to the worsening pandemic. She wrote of her experiences there, 'I feel sorry for our poor patients, especially the little children, who are so very sick and are handled by strange foreigners in masks who are making them drink bitter medications.' She was deeply moved by the plight of one boy whose family had all died, but she knew that this was a regular occurrence with whole families and villages being wiped out in a week.

Five weeks after her arrival in Sierra Leone, Pauline began to feel feverish and, having by then watched the symptoms of many Ebola victims, she knew that she was in danger. Nonetheless, health officials let her fly back to Britain without any quarantine arrangements.

After her initial recovery, she had a relapse, which was a truly frightening experience following the great relief of thinking that she had escaped a horrible death. But nobody knew how long the virus can hang around in various nooks and crannies after it has disappeared from the actual bloodstream of a survivor. Some suspect sites include testicles, spinal cords and eyes.

Pauline wrote in the *Scotsman* that she had begun to dream about Ebola, and this had become an all-consuming obsession. She described her protective suit as horrendous to wear in the heat. She also noted that Sierra Leoneans are, by nature, friendly and love to hug and kiss friends – clearly a dangerous trait in an Ebola-infested zone.

In neighbouring Liberia, 4,800 people died of the outbreak. The main hospital in the capital of Monrovia had become overrun with desperate Ebola suspects within days of the initial outbreak there, and chlorine supplies ran out, as did even the most basic protective clothing, and diseased refuse piled up in corridors. Of the sixty doctors working in Liberia at the time, six died in the first three weeks. The chief doctor, who was working in Monrovia for the International Rescue Committee, summed up the whole experience, 'If we learnt anything, it was fear.'

Doctors later treated Pauline Cafferkey with Will's plasma in the hope that she would develop her own immunity to the virus, as he had. Both of these brave individuals did, luckily, prove resistant to Ebola, but hundreds of other volunteer nurses did not.

Early in 2016 a panel of twenty experts from around the world published a scathing report in the *Lancet* saying that the World Health Organization reacted too slowly and that the epidemic 'exposed deep inadequacies in the national and international institutions responsible for protecting the public. Without addressing key issues, we will remain wholly unprepared for the next epidemic, which might very well be more devastating, virulent and transmissible than Ebola or previous disease outbreaks.'

The epidemic was summarised by a panel convened by the London School of Hygiene and Tropical Medicine and by the Harvard Global Health Institute, which stated that the outbreak had caused 'immense human suffering, fear and chaos.'

Pandemics caused by newly emerged bugs make for good horror films because, as film producers know, few things are scarier than incurable new diseases that spread rapidly. And globalisation allows plagues to travel far and fast. Diseases such as HIV/AIDS, SARS, West Nile virus and Ebola appear demon-like from remote jungles or from Chinese poultry farms to spread panic worldwide. Today, as I write this, a new mosquito-carried bug has downgraded even the latest ISIS horror stories.

The Zika virus, originally spotted in Uganda way back in 1947, is now infesting Latin America and the Caribbean and is liable to spread all over the Americas, except to Canada and Chile where the transmitting agent, the *Aedes aegypti* mosquito, cannot survive. Although not lethal to most humans, the Zika virus is associated with microcephaly, whereby infected pregnant women produce babies with abnormally small heads and underdeveloped, damaged brains, who are likely to suffer seizures and premature death. More than 4,000 Zika-infected babies were born in Brazil alone in the last three months of 2015.

Some medics in South America are suggesting that Zika is also being transmitted sexually, and the very uncertainty of many of the bugs' characteristics adds to the dread of people living in the known danger zones. Health advisers are in a quandary. Are the risks so high that countries lucky enough to be Zika-free should advise their citizens to stay away from those countries known to have it? Will Zika sweep through entire populations like cholera or the plague, perhaps creating group immunity, and, if so, should all vulnerable women avoid getting pregnant until that time? Some Latin American governments have already advised such a precaution. So now their women live in fear of the results of having sex.

At the same time as Zika spreads panic in Brazil, an outbreak of H1N1 swine flu is spreading across Eastern Europe from St Petersburg to Armenia and Georgia. Despite efforts by the authorities in eastern Ukraine to hush up the scale of the spread of this disease, some three hundred deaths have been reported in Donetsk town alone, and in Kiev, where up to 40,000 are expected to contract the bug in one week, schools have closed and government departments have issued face masks to all employees.

Various bird- and cattle-originated 'killer influenzas' have

Salvador Dali had a lifelong terror of grasshoppers and ants. These insects appear often in his paintings, as shown above.

Of all catalogued human phobias only fear of heights and enclosed spaces are more prevalent than fear of spiders and snakes.

Wolf spider.

Carpet viper.

By the 1870s, Zanzibar had become the last slavers' citadel of fear and evil.

1968, Memphis, USA. Involvement in the Civil Rights movement
in the 1950s and '60s came at great personal risk.

Rwanda, 1990s. It was a time of terror. There was no escape for a Tutsi. All were killed with machete blows; several thousand people were murdered on the first day of the genocide.

Auschwitz prisoners lived in a state of acute fear, for they knew a dreadful death awaited them at a moment's notice.

I had learned, at least in theory, the secret of dealing with fear in Dhofar: keep a ruthlessly tight clamp on your imagination. We the ambushers, at all times risked being ambushed.

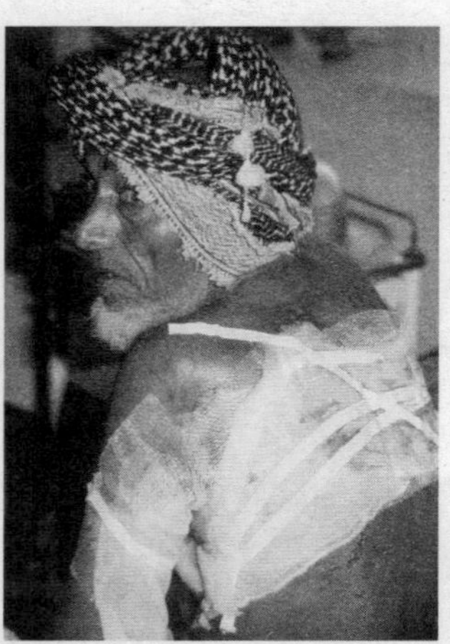

Marxist Dhofaris punished people who promoted the 'old' Muslim beliefs in various ways such as the application of red-hot coals to their faces, backs and genitals.

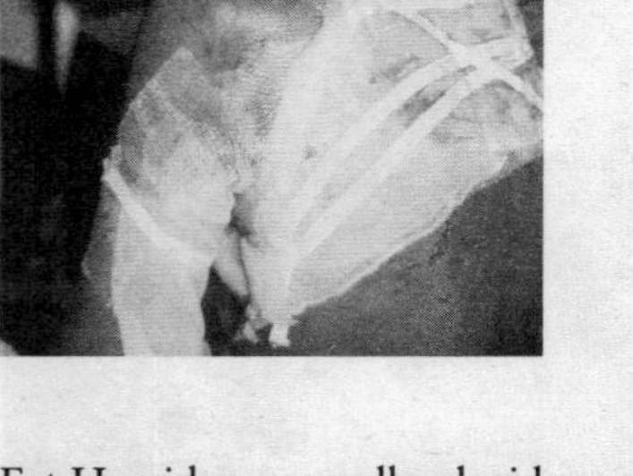

Fat Hamid, a normally placid man, was overcome by extreme fear of *djinn* (evil spirits), and his behaviour became a danger to us all.

Never look at the void you are about to jump into. If you are in a canoe, never listen to the roar of the rapids before you let go of the riverbank. Just do it!

Parachute training for the Norwegian Expedition in 1970.

The Bridge River rapids, Headless Valley Expedition in 1971.

Warning sign for bilharzia, Zimbabwe.

Fetching water in a snake and parasite infested lake, Homa Bay, Lake Victoria, Kenya.

'Hook worms, liver worms, toe worms, every sort and kind of disease carrier, and those are just the visible ones' found in a gallon of Niger well water. Simon Grimes, my wife Ginny and locals.

With Will Pooley in 2016, a health worker who had suffered from Ebola and was one of the lucky few to survive the killer disease.

Sarah Outen in her tiny rowing boat 'Gulliver'.

Tony Bullimore (centre) pops up to the surface as rescuers were about to cut a hole in his capsized yacht.

Both kept their heads, despite their fearful predicaments, and fortunately both were rescued.

over the years created panic in threatened populations, including the great 1918 worldwide influenza that killed millions just after the carnage of the First World War had ended. The rat-infested trenches and the wastelands of rotting bodies were ideal breeding grounds for this new virus, soon to be christened Spanish Flu, which caused five times as many deaths as had the Great War itself. Originating in chickens and thence passing to pigs and humans, the virus struck in the spring of 1918 and killed an estimated 50 million people, and maybe more.

A loving embrace exchanged at the end of the war between two people who may not have seen each other for several years risked the immediate transfer of the disease. The huge crowds of people who attended the Armistice celebrations in Trafalgar Square in London and in hundreds of communal spaces up and down the country intensified the chances of the disease spreading. In Arizona handshaking was outlawed, and in France spitting became a legal offence. Railway workshops turned to coffin manufacture, and Red Cross ambulances became hearses.

Whole classes of children were kept away from school by their wary parents, and instead they filled the city's playgrounds, singing:

I had a little bird
Its name was Enza
I opened the window
And in flew Enza.

Spanish Flu emerged in two phases. In the late spring of 1918, the first phase, known as the 'three-day fever', appeared without warning. Few deaths were reported, and victims generally recovered after a few days. When the disease surfaced again that autumn it was far more severe, and some victims died within hours of their first symptoms. Those afflicted were first aware of a shivery twinge at breakfast. By lunchtime their skin had turned a vivid purple, the colour of amethyst or the sinisterly beautiful shade of the heliotrope flower, and by the evening, before there was time to lay the table for supper, death would have occurred, often caused by choking on the thick scarlet jelly that suddenly clogged the lungs. One eye-witness account recorded that patients 'died struggling to clear their airways of a blood-tinged froth that sometimes gushed from their nose, ears and mouth.' Up to 20 per cent of those infected died.

Just as horrific, although no longer taught as a topic in most modern history lessons, was the Great Plague of the seventeenth century. In carrying out research for a book about the village folk of Eyam, a remote spot in the Derbyshire Peak District in the year 1665, I relived a faint echo of the fear that they experienced.

The 350 Eyam villagers, on the advice of their vicar, chose to stay in their isolated hamlet after the plague had arrived in their midst, rather than flee to escape infection and spread the disease to other villages.

Some years ago I had a massive heart attack and I have also had a common form of cancer, but neither of these ailments caused me lasting pain. Some illnesses kill without causing any suffering, and others are horrible to suffer or even to observe, despite the modern availability of morphine and pain relief.

To know that a horrific form of death lurks all around you, but to stay where you are in order to help others, as in the case of Will Pooley and also the people of Eyam, is to be truly brave.

The first known outbreak of the Black Death in Britain in 1351 killed off half the entire population. Between then and 1665 the plague resurfaced many times to kill millions all over the world, and it last struck Europe as a major epidemic in 1720. Today the plague bacterium is still alive and kicking, but it is kept at bay by antibiotics to which, as yet, it has not become drug-resistant.

* * *

Because there was no warning of any sort when I suffered a massive heart attack in 2003, and when I 'awoke' in hospital three days later, I had no memory of the event, there was no worry of any sort associated with it. However, ever since I have felt considerable concern and apprehension at the slightest twinge anywhere in the general area of my chest.

Likewise, when at my annual medical check-up with my GP I was diagnosed with possible prostate cancer, I had a six-hour operation to remove the tumour within a couple of weeks, so the period of anxiety and worry over whether it would prove to be terminal was very limited. However, the experience of knowing that cancer *had* infected my body, planted the awareness, previously absent, that I had already hosted the unwelcome killer, which probably still lurked within me, waiting for another, probably far nastier, return attack. This ongoing, often thankfully latent, anxiety raises its alarm status with each new ache or pain that I feel from time to time, especially, for some reason, in the region of my stomach.

Any contact I have ever had with a contagious bug has given me subsequent periods of worry. In 1981, when the HIV/AIDS virus first hit the news with announcements of immediate contamination should any body fluid from an infected person even touch you, I spent an unnecessary two weeks not daring to touch or breathe close to anyone, even my wife, due to my potential contamination after tending two injured parties at the scene of a road accident.

Not long ago my wife and I visited the Fiennes Institute, a care home in Antigua, which was founded originally in the 1920s by my grandfather in the Seychelles when he was the Governor-General there. Then and now the 100 inmates of the Institute are mostly destitute and sick and have no family to look after them. I am currently the Patron of the Institute and was pleased to be invited to visit. Only later did I learn that a small number of the dear old folk I had met and greeted were, in fact, lepers. This piece of news immediately set alarm bells ringing loudly, as I had suffered an aversion to leprosy ever since a midnight rendezvous with an informer on the Yemeni border, to whom Tim Landon, my intelligence officer at the time, had sent me to gather information.

The informer, a gnarled old tribesman had, on receipt of some money, grasped me closely and whispered in my ear. This involved a liberal amount of dribble and spittle, so when my colleague, Corporal Salim Khaleefa, informed me that the old man was a noseless leper, I spent several weeks carefully scrutinising the state of my fingers and toes.

More recently I was flown by helicopter to an island distillery north of Glasgow to celebrate a new blend of malt whisky, which was being announced by a well-known whisky producer. I lectured to a group of journalists from European luxury magazines over dinner in a large marquee the company had erected beside a loch, which was half a mile's gentle walk from their distillery. The water from the little loch sourced their whisky. All went well at the delicious dinner, but ten days later an email was sent to all the attendees with apologies and advice that all should get their blood tested for Lyme Disease. Apparently two of the guests had contracted this potentially lethal sickness, having been bitten by ticks on the way through the heather from the distillery to the loch-side marquee. On our Exmoor farm we are surrounded by heather, and I know of several trekkers on the nearby moors who have suffered badly from tick bites. I was greatly relieved when my post-whisky-event blood tests came back Lyme-free.

I still have a worm-laden tale in a letter from Nick Holder following his own bilharzia infestation on our Nile journey. He wrote:

> I was admitted to the Royal Hospital for Tropical Diseases in St Pancras, London. At that time the cure for bilharzia was the injection of 10cc of some drug directly into the stomach through the muscles of the abdomen. For someone of my age and fitness,

such an exercise was difficult to perform if I was conscious as I would automatically tense and tighten up. So it was decided that I would be admitted to a hospital ward and given a general anaesthetic.

In the next door bed was a poor fellow who had also just returned from Africa, but with an infection from a tapeworm. These parasitic worms, called cestodes, live in human and animal intestines, are ribbon shaped and can grow up to thirty feet in length. They are usually contracted by eating under-cooked meat or fish. The head of the worm has suckers or hooks which are attached to the wall of the human intestine.

My poor friend was naturally permanently hungry, and the highlight of every day was the arrival of breakfast, lunch and dinner, served by two nurses. The routine was the same: the meal would arrive, my friend would attack his with gusto, and then, having finished in record time, his hand would shoot up, with a request to the nurses for some more. But this request was not granted.

As the days went by, my poor friend got thinner and thinner and the tapeworm got longer and longer until, one morning, we were all surprised to see him emerge from his bedclothes and slowly shuffle out of the ward. A couple of minutes later we were amazed to see our skeletal friend arriving back in the ward, dancing with glee and informing us that he had got rid of the worm.

We all trooped out of the ward and headed for the lavatories, where we stared in amazement at the worm. It resembled tagliatelle and completely filled the lavatory bowl, and even spilled out onto the floor. An incredible sight which I will never forget.

My fear of bedbugs, which I have mentioned earlier, although not exactly an obsessive–compulsive disorder such as David Beckham is said to suffer from, was unreasonable to some extent, since in many years of hotel-bed searching, I have yet to find a single one. However, I continue the search purely out of fear of my body being bitten by a bug that has the night before bitten a victim of HIV/AIDS, or some such blood-carried disease.

With insects on my mind whenever a planned expedition involves a hot country, I always take a tube of Anthisan cream to apply to any bite or sting from any itch-causing insects for, as in Dante's *Inferno*, a serious itch can be hell. But itching is, of course, a potentially lifesaving problem, which is why our immediate primate ancestors spend up to 20 per cent of their time grooming themselves and each other. Scratch an itch as an insect lands and you may save your life, and squash the culprit quickly before it bites, for mites cause typhus, fleas the plague, tsetse flies sleeping sickness, and mosquitoes malaria.

Back on our Transglobe Expedition, once Oliver had successfully completed his water-snail collection in the Ivorian jungles for the British Museum, we followed tracks of deep mud south out of the jungle-kingdom of the insects and met up with our old ship *Benji B* in Abidjan's teeming port, where the crew hoisted our Land Rovers on board. More or less to the schedule Ginny had planned some seven years before on her six-inch school globe, we headed south of the Equator and into the fierce Benguela Current.

After a fortnight loading a thousand drums of fuel and sponsored food in Cape Town, we headed further south, heavily overloaded, into the Roaring Forties and bound for Antarctica.

8

Oceans of Fear

I can't see a thing, it's so dark; this must be what it is like to be buried alive.

Tony Bullimore

We celebrated Christmas well into the Roaring Forties with the overladen ship rolling and diving in grey-black seas. A Christmas tree, lashed by the crew to the mast, was torn away by storm winds, and walls of green water curled over the down-plunged prow, then buried the bow and fo'c'sle with shuddering blows that were felt by everyone on board. Our skipper, a retired admiral, nearly swallowed his pipe.

Because I had always suffered from seasickness, Ginny and I had been put in the tiny quarantine cabin amidships, where the ship's giddy movements were least acute. Nonetheless we awoke one midnight to find that the motion of a wave from an unusual direction had literally picked up the extremely heavy ship's iron safe and flung it onto its back beside our bunk. The next day it took three of us to get it back to its proper position. In another cabin Charlie was woken when his ashtray, heaped with cigarette butts, was thrown from his bedside table and the contents emptied all over his pillow and his head.

If there had been *any* other way of reaching Antarctica rather than by ship, I would have given my eye teeth, as the saying goes, to have used it.

Recently I have lectured on a series of fear-filled ocean

experiences under the boring heading of *lilapsophobia* (which means an obsessive fear of hurricanes, tornadoes, and the like). Certain experiences of individuals at sea and in trouble struck me as distinctly fear-inducing. The following are a few examples.

In 2013 a charity, of which I am a trustee, sponsored an adventurous girl, Sarah Outen, to row, kayak and cycle all the way round the world from London to London, mostly on her own. After thousands of miles and many excitements she began her solo rowing voyage across the North Pacific Ocean from Japan. Three weeks into her row and, although it was not the normal hurricane season in the seas off Japan, the lone Sarah, who is quite small in stature, in her tiny rowboat *Gulliver*, was told to expect Tropical Storm Mawar. She wrote:

> Waiting for Mawar was a weird mix of adrenaline, calm and anticipated fear . . . As it got closer, I prepared *Gulliver* as best I could and took to the cabin with my helmet to hand. I strapped in and awaited the worsening conditions. By the evening of 6 June the wind and sea were a roaring mess with winds in excess of seventy miles per hour. Knockdowns and capsizes became the norm as waves throttled us from all angles. Water had started to leak into my cabin via the hatches, and before long a ribbon of water was streaming in through my main hatch, like a tap left open. Given the extraordinary force of the waves I wasn't surprised, and I gritted my teeth each time a wave smashed directly into the bulkhead as I waited to see what would happen.
>
> The conditions worsened through the night. Wave heights were up at ten metres and still growing. The sea anchor was now taking huge strain – I could hear it and feel the g-force as I was thrown back in the harness when *Gulliver* was swung round into different wave sets. Over and over. A few times *Gulliver* was upended off the back of a wave, then slammed down again with an ear-splitting thud, followed by another roll.

By daylight we had rolled eight times and been knocked right over onto the side many more. The waves were now at fifteen metres. Worst of all, the damage to *Gulliver* had clearly reached a critical state. Everything inside the cabin was wet, including the electrics box and water-maker. The sea anchor had gone from the bow of the boat and was attached only by its retrieval line on the side of the boat. This was holding us broadside to the waves, meaning increased risk of capsizing. The retrieval line was getting caught around different parts of the boat, breaking off critical equipment, and all of the communications aerials were damaged or ripped away.

I could hear that the rudder was damaged, and it sounded as though it was damaging the hull. One of the safety rails had been ripped out, damaging the side of the companionway and potentially opening up the forward cabin to flooding. The satellite dome on the front cabin had also gone, as had the GPS antenna – all serious leak paths into the front cabin, and *Gulliver* was taking longer to right himself after each capsize, given the water that had been taken on.

With all this damage, and knowing that I already had water coming into the back cabin, I had no option but to call in for help. My feeling was that with the further inevitable capsizes, there was a very real likelihood that the forward cabin would flood and I would be trapped in my cabin under water.

The most frustrating thing of all was that I was powerless to do anything else to prevent or repair the damage, given the sea conditions. To open that hatch would have meant a wave coming into the cabin, followed by an irrecoverable capsize, and even if I had made it out, I risked being swept overboard and seriously injured, if not drowned.

Sarah was lucky: Japanese Coastguard located and rescued her from the badly damaged *Gulliver*, and she was rushed, severely bruised and dehydrated, to a hospital in Japan after her terrifying ordeal.

Tony Bullimore, another sea-going Briton, also a loner, who had been voted Yachtsman of the Year in 1985, was sailing in the Southern Ocean in January 1997, some 800 miles north of Antarctica in increasingly evil sea conditions. He was aware of the potentially lethal consequences that can quickly appear as though from nowhere, should any one of a hundred circumstances occur in such a remote region. He explained:

> I never curse the sea, no matter what she throws at me. I've always shown utter respect, because I know the power she has to swallow ships the size of the *Titanic* and break a person's heart. Over the years she's taken a lot of good friends of mine and never given them back.

His recorded memories of his next few days show him to be a master of understatement. In his shoes I would have been scared out of my mind. Here are some excerpts:

> Visibility is down to a hundred metres. Every so often I see another rogue wave, and I begin imagining that if they're in front of me then they must also be behind me. Clipping on a safety harness, I surf down the swells, steering sharply before I reach the bottom of each trough so that the bow doesn't dig into the water. I look round and see a wave on my port side. It's bloody huge, with a face that looks almost vertical. I look at it in awe, and realise that one of those only has to catch me at the right moment and I'm in serious trouble.
>
> Late afternoon and I've been at the helm for nearly five hours. The rogue waves must be mighty because the average waves around me are all about sixty feet high. I can hear them coming, rumbling like thunder. They build and build, pushing forward until they peak, and then split at the top, sending water rolling down each side. The previous storm, ten days ago, lasted eighteen hours. Maybe I can steer through this one if I manage to stay awake and fight off exhaustion.

The wind speed indicator is nudging seventy knots – surely it can't go any higher? Every so often I look back and see a huge wave building behind me. I come up with the wave and see the whole world before me surfing down into a trough at twenty-six knots. The entire boat is vibrating with the speed. It's not built to go this fast in these conditions.

Suddenly, the boat heels sideways – hit by a wave. I feel the pressure in my shoulders as they brace against the bulkhead. The masts must almost be touching the water. Slowly she rights herself, pulled upright by the weight of the keel. The boat heels to leeward again; I brace myself.

Crack! What was that?

All of a sudden the world turns and I turn with it. It isn't slow motion; it's very, very fast. I keep thinking about the 'crack'.

I'm sitting on the ceiling of the doghouse, with the floor above me. Looking down through the windows I can see foam and water surging beneath me. It's like being in a glass-bottomed boat.

Shit! The bloody keel has gone. I can't believe it. No keel, no chance. I could have lost the masts or the rudders and still been okay, but the keel is almighty.

The boat's not going to sink. It's a foam sandwich design with watertight compartments. With any luck, I can probably stay reasonably dry in the doghouse.

In the pit of my stomach, deep down where even the butterflies are afraid to go, I know that I'm knocking on death's door, and I'm over a thousand miles from the nearest shipping lanes, and the nearest race competitor, as far as I know, is 800 miles ahead. Oh, Tony, what a mess!

You're going to die, Mr Bullimore, sometime in the next few days.

Okay, Tony, be realistic, what are your options? If a rescue operation is launched, what form will it take? I'm too far from land to be reached by helicopter, so that's out. So where does that leave me? I might be lucky and get picked up by a research ship heading for Antarctica, but there's probably only half a dozen all year, so that would be like winning the lottery. I probably have more chance of drifting to Antarctica.

I think the wing masts were probably heeling the boat over, bringing the keel near the surface just as a wave crashed down. A funnel of water explodes into the hull with such force that it hits the roof above my head. It's like an upside-down waterfall, and for three or four seconds I stare at it blankly, frozen in shock. I hear a faint groan of exclamation, and know it must be mine.

Already seawater swirls around my knees, then my thighs, rising at a tremendous speed. Bloody hell, it's cold! I know it has to stop at the waterline – that's the law of physics – but there doesn't seem to be much logic about anything that's happening to me. The boom has smashed the window – punching a neat hole about eighteen inches high and three feet long in the deck beneath my feet.

Water surges upwards, now at my chest. It sloshes from side to side in the cabin; I'm in the washing machine from hell. I keep telling myself, it's a foam sandwich boat with watertight cells. It's not going to sink. Tell that to the waves! The lights have gone; the hull is dark. Someone who is six-feet, six-inches tall can stand in the centre of the cabin. I'm only five feet four, and water is nearly up to my chin. I try to keep to the sides, where it isn't so deep.

Now the window has smashed and it's a whole new ball game: a desperate situation has become critical. The boat rolls and I tumble off the shelf, landing with a splash instead of a thump. Water? Somehow the cuddy is beginning to fill. Does it mean that I am sinking? I can't see a thing, it's so dark; this must be what it is like to be buried alive. Wiping my eyes, I stagger into the engine room, and using my knife I open an emergency sachet of water. I only have two left now. And the realisation hits me that I really am going to die. No one's coming. Even if they did send a plane, they'll take one look at the hull and fly home. They'll think there's no one alive inside here. Face it, Tony, you're history. And morbid thoughts turn madly in on themselves. But I make a silent agreement with myself that I'm not to think about dying at least for another day.

The water is up to my chin, and occasionally I have to hold my breath as a mini-wave rolls inside the hull and covers my face. My tongue is swollen, making it difficult to swallow. Don't worry, Tony, you've got nothing left to eat now. One less problem to worry about. In a peculiar way it's refreshing to be faced with no choices. I can't free the life raft, I'm out of food, the boat is lower in the water, my fingers and toes are starting to blacken with frostbite . . . all unavoidable facts.

Cold is such a creeping, insidious enemy. It's going to take me piece by piece. That's what happens with hypothermia. And it's started already. My hands and feet feel like lumps of petrified wood and are about as useless. I have never felt so wretchedly alone. What on earth was I thinking when I took on this challenge? It seems almost stupid now to pit oneself against something as ageless and unforgiving as the great oceans of the world.

That's the problem, whenever we start thinking of ourselves as anything loftier than or the equal of Mother Nature, she reminds us that she can wear away at continents and create storms that flatten cities. Better and braver sailors than I are now dead and part of a marine food chain.

The truth is, I've run out of ideas. In total darkness, crammed in a corner full of diesel fumes and rolling grey water, there is no hope. The only warmth I can feel in my body is deep in my chest, but I keep thumping my feet and tapping my fingers.

What if the Argos distress signal has stopped transmitting? How long do the batteries last? If the signal stops for any length of time, I'll have drifted miles away. In the rough seas and mist, they might not find me.

Find me! What am I saying? They're not even bloody looking!

> They're not going to come all the way down here for me. You've bought it this time, Tony. How much longer will you wait before you swim outside? It takes more courage to commit suicide than it does to stay alive.
>
> Exhausted, I lie shivering and watch the white dots dance in front of my closed lids. A voice inside my head keeps saying, *You're going to die. You're going to die.*

But, like Sarah Outen, Tony had luck on his side. The Australian Air Force and Navy eventually located his distress signal and coordinated a skilful rescue some 2,500 kilometres from the south-west coast of Australia. Hearing his rescuers tapping on the upturned hull, Bullimore surprised them by swimming up and out of his tiny air pocket in the hull some five days after his terrifying ordeal began.

Both Sarah Outen and Tony Bullimore kept their heads, despite their fearful predicaments and both were rescued without lasting trauma to their physical or mental health.

In 1819 the men of the American whaling ship *Essex* were not so lucky. Two thousand three hundred miles west of the South American coast, they were rammed by a great sperm whale and their ship sank. The twenty-one crew members took to the three lifeboats and landed on a remote island. After a week they began to starve, and so all but three of them resumed their boat journey.

Starved and dehydrated, they were ravaged by diarrhoea, their skins erupted in weeping boils, and oedema affected their limbs. They suffered blackouts and their behaviour became bizarre and, when they had the energy, violent, and they stole food from each other.

On 10 January 1821 crewman Matthew Joy was the first man to die. Others soon followed. The first six to perish were sewn into their clothes and slipped over the side.

On the night of 28 January the three boats separated. One, with three crewmen aboard, was never seen again. Those who still lived knew that they might be many days, if not weeks, from land. The little food that they had would soon run out. When the next man died, Captain Pollard ordered that his body should remain in the boat and their shipmate's corpse would be the men's next meal.

Three more men would die and be eaten before 1 February, at which date the survivors ran out of food again. They now faced an unthinkable crisis. In Pollard's boat, four men lived – Brazillai Ray, Charles Ramsdell, the captain, and Pollard's young cousin Owen Coffin. In the depths of their desperation the men decided that unless one of them was sacrificed, they would all die long, lingering deaths. The chance to live became a lottery, and every man had a one-in-four chance of drawing the black spot. The man who pulled it from the bag was the unfortunately named Owen Coffin.

Horrifically for Coffin, the three remaining men then drew lots once more to see who would execute him. This hideous duty fell to Coffin's friend, Charles Ramsdell, and he shot Coffin. The boy's remains were consumed by Pollard, Ray and Ramsdell.

Shortly after, Ray also died and for the rest of their torturous days in the boat Pollard and Ramsdell survived by gnawing on the bones of Coffin and Ray.

It was ninety-five days since the *Essex* had been sunk by the whale. The other lifeboat, with three survivors who had also resorted to cannibalism, was located by a British merchant ship. Altogether, eight men lived to tell their tale. Of the original crew, six were lost at sea and seven were eaten.

Whether the fear of being eaten by human colleagues is less than that of being torn to bits by sharks is debatable, but the latter fate befell dozens of US Navy sailors during the war against the Japanese in 1945.

That July the cruiser *USS Indianapolis* delivered its cargo of enriched uranium to a US air base on the Pacific island from which the atomic bomb attacks on Hiroshima and Nagasaki would be launched. On her way back to Guam, the *Indianapolis* was hit by torpedoes from a Japanese submarine and she sank in less than twelve minutes. Three hundred men were drowned, leaving 880 survivors adrift in the middle of the night amongst the flaming wreckage. The surprise and speed of the sinking meant that only a handful of lifeboats had been launched, and many men were without lifejackets. They could no nothing but cling to anything that floated and then wait to be rescued. What they couldn't have imagined was that help was five days away.

It was brutally cold in the water at night. With dawn came a little welcome warmth, but it also brought something dreadful: sharks. The oceanic whitetip shark is a notorious hazard for survivors in warm water and the attacks continued until the men were rescued five days later. One survivor, Woody James, wrote:

> The day wore on and the sharks were around, hundreds of them. You'd hear guys scream, especially late in the afternoon. Seemed like the sharks were worse late in the afternoon than they were during the day. Then they fed at night too. Everything would be quiet and then you'd hear somebody scream, and you knew a shark had got him.

During the day the temperature reached 27°C and the men were exposed to the full strength of the tropical sun, but at night they faced the prospect of hypothermia as the temperature plummeted. Some men suffered from severe peeling of the skin, and there were many sailors who had been badly injured in the torpedo attack. Their wounds made them weak and the blood in the water attracted the sharks. They developed sores in their mouths and throats, which were exacerbated by the salt water, and as they became dehydrated and took in seawater, the levels of sodium in their bodies increased, which led to weakness, oedema, seizures, dementia and death. Some of the men killed themselves or one another as the hallucinations and madness took control.

Although the ship had sunk so quickly, the radio operator had managed to send out distress calls, and three separate stations picked them up. However, tragically for the men in the water, no one acted on these calls. One station commander was drunk and another had ordered his men not to disturb him, and a third thought the call was a Japanese prank. So the men spent nearly five days in the ocean before any rescuers arrived.

Of the 880 men who had survived the sinking, only 321 were rescued. The sharks had fed well as the human contents of their floating larder spent those five dreadful days and nights awaiting amputations by their unseen predators.

The ship's captain survived and was court-martialled later in 1945 for 'hazarding his ship by failing to zigzag'. He committed suicide in 1968, and was exonerated by Congress in 2000.

There are, of course, many thousands of stories of shipwreck survival following great storms at sea, but I rate just as fearful the tales of those who fled before tsunami waves heading inland, most of them being Japanese.

On the day of the earthquake that caused the 2011 tsunami, David Chumreonlert, a teacher, was on Japan's north-east coast lecturing in a school in the small seaside town of Higashimatsushima when someone yelled, 'Tsunami is coming.' The class fled into the school gymnasium, which was on slightly higher ground. They just managed to survive by grasping high bars in the gym as the flood water tore through the town and submerged most of the school.

Setsuko Uwabe was a cook at a nursery school a mile inland from the coastline of north-east Japan, and she found herself gazing at a strange dusty-white cloud in the distance and over the sea. It was long and flat across the horizon. Panic ensued. Sirens began to shriek and Setsuko fled with hundreds of the children to nearby high ground, barely escaping the dark, boiling waves as they engulfed the nursery buildings below.

Toru Saito in the coastal town of Oginohama was parked up watching live news on his car's small TV screen when he spotted movement further down the main street. To his horror he saw houses rushing by propelled by a wall of water. Down by the harbour his father, Masafumi, had bravely saved many lives, in the nick of time, by locking the sea wall floodgates just before they were hit by a thirty-two-foot-high wave.

* * *

After arriving at the South Pole on 17 December 1980, Ollie Shepard, Charlie Burton and I made it safely to the Pacific coast where we were picked up by our ship *Benji B*, which then took us up the other side of the world to Alaska. We had completed the first major obstacle of the Transglobe Expedition, but we knew the Arctic Ocean would be a far greater challenge. Sadly, Ollie had to leave us at this point in order to save his marriage, so our Ice Team would from now on be only the two of us.

The ship dropped us off in two twelve-foot rubber boats at the mouth of the Yukon River, and over the next fourteen months we fought our way up the Yukon and Mackenzie rivers, and then made the first open-boat navigation of the Northwest Passage from West to East. We finally reached the North Pole on 11 April 1982.

Almost four months later, after ninety-nine days adrift on a melting ice floe in the Arctic Ocean, I saw two matchsticks upon the broken horizon. I blinked and they were gone. Then I saw them again; the distant masts of the *Benji B*.

I cannot describe the joy of that second. I found tears smarting in my eyes and I yelled to Charlie. I think that was the single most wonderful and satisfying moment of my life. Until then I could never bring myself to accept that success was within our grasp. But now I knew and I felt the strength of ten men in my veins. I knelt down and thanked God. For three hours we heaved and paddled our two aluminium canoes across the floating pack ice. Sometimes we lost sight of the ship briefly but always, when again we saw her, she was a little bit bigger.

Shortly before midnight on 3 August, Jimmy Young, the New Zealander engineer who was up in the crow's nest with binoculars, shouted down to the bridge, 'I see them! I see them!'

On the bridge, gazing into the low wan sun, one by one the crew identified amongst the heaving mass of whiteness the two dark figures that they had dropped off so long ago at the mouth of the Yukon River on the far side of the Arctic Ocean.

At 0014 hours on 4 August 1982 at 80°31'N 00°59'W, we climbed on board. The circle was complete.

Each one of us retained the image of that moment when, amongst the floes, we came aboard the ship. We would never forget it, and we shared something that no one could take from us: a warm sense of comradeship between us all – Swiss and American; Indian and South African; British, Irish and New Zealander.

Ginny was standing by a cargo hatch. Between us we had spent twenty years of our lives to reach this point. I watched her small, tired face begin to relax. She smiled and I knew what she was thinking. Our impossible dream was over. So, too, were the weeks, months and years of stress and fear of failure.

After the Transglobe Expedition, Ginny and I settled down to the less ambitious business of trying to make an income. I wrote a book and gave lectures; she worked to pay off the expedition's debts partly by selling leftover sponsored kit at a street market in Camden Lock.

In 1984, an American octogenarian millionaire, Dr Armand Hammer, who had sponsored parts of the expedition, offered me a job in the London-based PR department of his company, Occidental Oil, and this kept me employed until he died a decade later. He was prepared to give me time off work to do expeditions, and Ollie Shepard suggested that we use our hard-gotten ice-travel experience to man-haul to the North Pole without air resupply, a world record that we knew was being planned by the Norwegian polar fraternity.

At that time the TV drama, *The Day After*, was very popular.

It was a nightmarish look at life in small-town America before and after a nuclear attack. In 1984 many novels featuring nuclear war were published. The fear was real and intense. It filled the streets of Europe and America with millions of protesters, and countless heads with nightmares.

The Cold War had been getting hotter since the 1979 Soviet invasion of Afghanistan and the 1980 election of Ronald Reagan as US President. Mikhail Gorbachev became leader of the Soviet Union in 1985, and we know now that Gorbachev and Reagan later met and steadily reduced tensions so that the Cold War ended peacefully and the Soviet Union was dissolved within a few years. But in 1985 what actually happened would have seemed wildly improbable – which is why almost no one predicted anything like it. But nuclear war? That looked terrifyingly likely.

The London unit of the Territorial SAS, of which Ollie, Charlie and I were all members, had long trained us to live in specific foxholes with periscopes and NBC (Nuclear, Biological and Chemical) protection in North Germany along the likely routes that an invading Soviet army would take.

Ginny joked that, when the trouble started, the Arctic polar ice would be as safe as anywhere. So, in the winter of 1985, Ollie and I began a series of attempts to reach the North Pole unsupported.

Meanwhile, earning a predictable income, thanks to the Occidental work, was a novel and very welcome experience, which enabled Ginny and me to buy a near-derelict farm in the middle of the Exmoor National Park, where she started a herd of Aberdeen Angus cattle and a flock of Black Welsh Mountain sheep as a commercial business.

After Ollie and I had completed some successful sledge trials up North, his employers, unfortunately, threatened him with the sack for spending too much time away from work. So Ginny recruited an experienced Antarctic sledger, Dr Mike Stroud, who, at thirty years old, was eleven years younger than me and extremely strong.

The only drawback for me of having Mike as my polar co-traveller over the years to follow was his enthusiastic scientific research into 'bodily reactions to stress'. This entailed him taking our blood on numerous occasions in the tent. I have always hated injections, especially the slow withdrawal of blood, so I would screw up my eyes as soon as Mike produced his hypodermic kit. Fear of needles, apparently, has its own name . . . *aichmophobia*.

In 1986 Mike and I broke the existing world record for unsupported travel towards the North Pole, which had stood at ninety-eight miles from land for the last eighteen years, and in 1990, from the Siberian coast, we reached to within eighty-nine miles of the Pole before we ran out of food and had to radio for a Russian helicopter from a floating scientific Ice Station to take us back to Siberia.

At one point on that memorably uncomfortable polar journey, we passed the fresh footprints of a bear only a few days after we had abandoned our radio and our only weapon, a .44 magnum revolver, as being too heavy for us to continue to carry. By then we were seriously weakened by hunger and by the after-effects of several immersions in the sea after breaking through thin ice. Our only way of continuing had been to lighten our sledge loads.

Neither of us had felt any undue fear of polar bears until that moment of seeing the footprints when, for the first time ever in the Arctic, we had no means of self-defence. At that point I was distinctly scared. I acted as navigator, and led the way with my hand compass and watch for direction finding. This meant that Mike was always behind me which, since polar bears if hungry will always go for the rear person, naturally gave him a far greater reason to be frightened.

A friend of mine, Spike Reid, was in his late twenties when he led a team of a dozen students on a British Schools Exploration Society expedition to Spitsbergen. The group camped on the edge of a glacier and were subjected to a raid by an old and hungry polar bear. Spike told me his story:

It was early in the morning and we were collectively asleep. Our team was camped on the edge of the Von Post glacier. It was the beginning of a great adventure, and we planned to hike unsupported high up across glaciers to a mountain for the rest of the expedition. We hadn't set a night watch as we thought it to be a low-risk location. As part of our evening preparations and in order to stave off the risk of a polar bear attack, we had erected a perimeter defence around us with flares on the posts. Somehow a polar bear got through without triggering the flares.

Then it attacked. The first thing we knew was when my co-leader Andy and I heard shouting. We leapt from our sleeping bags and found that a starving bear had torn into the tent where Horatio Chapple and two other team members, Scott and Patrick, were sleeping. We left our tent through opposite flaps and I took the rifle. The first thing I saw was a huge polar bear, metres away, attacking Horatio, a superb man and team member, and towering above him. He had been dragged out of his tent and had bravely tried to fight the bear.

I quickly cocked the rifle, aimed carefully at the bear and squeezed the trigger. Nothing happened. The rifle didn't fire. I cocked it again and it spat the unfired round out. I repeated the attempt to shoot the bear, then tried repeatedly until the magazine was empty, but with no luck. Four bullets lay on the dusty ground by my feet, the bear was still attacking and I had not yet succeeded in shooting it. It turned then from Horatio towards me and charged. It threw me to the ground and I could not fight it off. It swiped me several times with its mighty paws and then bit hard into my head. I distinctly remember hearing loud cracking noises.

Luckily, Andy, the other team leader, was there, and he saved my life. As the rifle lay close to both the bear and to me, and as we had no other gun, he resorted to throwing rocks at the beast until it stopped attacking me. For all his labours, the bear then turned on him, viciously attacking his head and jaw.

Without mercy, the bear returned to Horatio's body. Quickly, it spotted Matt, another member of the team, who had grabbed the rifle and tried to get some more rounds into it in a valiant attempt to end this nightmare. The bear chased Matt around the tent, but he skilfully outwitted the animal. Four of the team slipped out of the back of their tents and started to escape from the camp and the attack. Others hid in their tents, for there was nothing they could do without a loaded rifle.

Patrick and Scott were keeping a low profile in the remains of their destroyed tent, but the bear found them there. It attacked Patrick in his sleeping bag, breaking his arm and hitting his face. With the huge animal less than a metre from him, Scott tried to escape. He ran with the bear close on his heels, and it attacked him, badly wounding his head and jaw.

Eventually I was able to get up after the attack. I reloaded the rifle swiftly with a round I recovered from the ground. Seeing me standing, the bear came towards me again. It charged and, just in time, I fired the rifle. I shot it in the head and it fell to the ground in the middle of the camp, a metre or two from me. The attack had ended at last, but with the terrible loss of a good young man.

The bear was dead and the team rallied to keep the injured members alive. The four of us had all suffered facial trauma, and I found out later that Andy and I were in a critical state. This meant that the team had no designated leaders. Rosie, one of the youngest in the team, took it upon herself, with Matt's help, to raise the alarm and get things in order.

Even though most members of the team were no older than seventeen, they were exceptional that morning. Andy and I would certainly have died without their care, and we are both forever indebted. Furthermore, I would not be alive without Andy's brave attempt to get the bear off me and away from the camp. None of this will ever be forgotten.

The loss of such a good team member in the attack will always be with me. Horatio aspired to be a doctor, and he would have made a great expedition medic. I don't think I will ever get over the loss of that wonderful young man.

We were evacuated very swiftly to Longyearbyen and then to Tromsø on mainland Norway where the closest hospital was – 1,000 km from the scene of the attack. The nightmare was finally over, but this was just the start of my story and in that hospital began a very long road to recovery.

One way or another over the many journeys I have made, both alone and as part of a team, in the Arctic pack ice kingdom of the great white carnivores, I have been extremely lucky never to have been mauled by a bear, nor have I ever had to kill one.

9

The Power of Fear

My journey is at an end. My summit was just out of reach.
Henry Worsley

I returned to London from the Arctic whilst still working as vice-president of public relations for Occidental Oil North Sea, and one night I was called with news of a tragedy on one of our oil platforms. Piper Alpha was Britain's biggest oil- and gas-producing platform, bringing more than 300,000 barrels of crude a day (10 per cent of the UK total) from below the seabed north-east of Aberdeen. The unit had suffered from a sudden explosion and over 160 of those on the platform at the time had been killed. The CEO of Occidental, Dr Hammer, flew over at once from the USA in his private jet, and after collecting him from Heathrow, I drove with him to Aberdeen where many of the badly burnt survivors were being treated.

Over the past few years I had done my job, as advised by my PR predecessor, in terms of wining and dining in posh restaurants with top journalists in the national and international oil and gas sector and all related media. The purpose of this was to 'keep them on side for when you need them'.

Very fearful of bad publicity, I found that in our Occidental hour of need, all the years of wining and dining had no beneficial effect whatsoever, and the press coverage was about as critical of Occidental and our Health and Safety behaviour as it could be. This was not surprising, for the disaster proved to be the world's deadliest ever oil-rig accident and cost the Lloyd's insurance market more than £1 billion.

Dr Hammer died in his nineties, and I was sacked by his successor. So it was then back to a life with no reliable income, and I lived off Ginny's income from her thriving cattle and sheep farming whilst continuing with Mike Stroud in our ongoing fight to keep one jump ahead, polar record-breaking wise, of the Norwegians. Their top explorers at the time were Erling Kagge, Børge Ousland and Rune Gjeldnes.

In 1990 a three-man team, including Kagge and Ousland, set out to break the same North Pole Unsupported record that Ollie, Mike and I had by then attempted four times and for which we held the 'furthest north' record. Despite the fact that the third Norwegian in their group, smitten by frostbite, was removed by ski plane en route, Kagge claimed that he and Ousland had 'reached the Pole unsupported'.

Mike and I repudiated this claim, which was made in the media, since the unwritten definition of 'unsupported', agreed by the Russians and the Canadians, was that *no* aircraft contact was to be made between land and Pole.

From that time on, our great fear was of being beaten at the remaining world polar records by the Norwegians. So when in May 1991 I heard that Erling Kagge, our earlier rival in the Arctic, was planning an Antarctic record-breaking journey, I quickly contacted Mike Stroud. After obtaining the relevant sponsorship support, we set out in November 1992 to attempt the first ever unsupported crossing of the Antarctic Continent, beginning our journey at the same time as Kagge, solo, began his.

Of our many polar journeys north and south, the most perilous incident occurred only a week after we had set out over the ice shelf and in a zone of great instability. Thunderous roars warned us that the whole ice shelf had entered a hyperactive phase, causing hitherto safe snow-bridges to collapse all around us into their crevasses. No amount of ice lore could keep us out of trouble here. A gaping hole opened up with an explosion of snow spray as we watched. Some 10 paces ahead of Mike, and 45 feet wide by 120 feet in length, it lay directly across his intended path. Had it occurred but a few seconds later, he and his sledge would have disappeared, along with several tons of plunging snow-bridge. All around us renewed implosions announced further cratering.

The sensation was memorably frightening. We must escape at once to a safer area. But where was safer? Only the looming bulk of Berkner Island offered certain stability. We roped up with nervous fingers, fearing that at any moment the snow beneath us would open up and dump us hundreds of feet below. The surface of the ice shelf all about us rumbled and reverberated again and again. Geysers of snow dust rose into the air. The feeling was similar to closing on enemy troops when under mortar fire. As each new crump exploded at random, the fear increased that the next catastrophe would have our name on it.

The nylon rope between us was sixty feet in length. We moved as fast as the sledges and the wings of fear allowed. Time stood still. I came to an abrupt halt as a wave of cold air rushed past, accompanied by the loudest and closest of the explosions. I ducked, for the all-engulfing sound seemed to pass both overhead and underfoot.

Immediately between Mike and me an immense crater appeared. One moment the ice shelf ahead was solid and white. The next a maw like the mouth of the Underworld, steaming with snow vapour, lay across our intended route, wide enough to swallow a double-decker bus. The roaring echoes of imploding snow cascading into the bowels of the ice shelf returned in successive waves, like shore ripples from an undersea volcano. Although a cold wind scoured the ice sheet, I sweated with fear. The next hour was a nightmare of apprehension; nowhere was safe. Only pure luck enabled us to escape from this volatile zone.

On that 1992 Antarctic expedition, Kagge beat us to the South Pole, but we achieved the longer record, which was later confirmed by Guinness Records as, 'The longest totally self-supporting polar sledge journey ever made and the first totally unsupported crossing of the Antarctic landmass was achieved by R. Fiennes and M. Stroud. They covered a distance of 2,170 kilometres (1,350 miles).'

A few years later Ollie phoned to say that he had heard that Ousland was about to attempt to cross Antarctica solo and unsupported.

With little time to prepare for such a trip, I was landed by ski plane on the very edge of the Atlantic side of Antarctica in a high, cold wind. I felt unusually lonely as the little plane disappeared back north. Ahead, the frozen white wastes stretched over an area bigger than China.

From the edge of Antarctica's ice, and with a sledge-load of almost 500 lb, I set out south over a long island called Berkner, where Frost Spur, a steep ice rampart of several hundred feet, blocked the way forward. To my vertigo-haunted brain this obstacle looked insuperable, but the fear of failure so early in the journey made me realise that the only way was to attempt to scale it.

In the end I made the climb five times before all my gear and the sledge itself was on the top of the spur. Luckily I was still able to use my frost-nipped fingers to erect the tent and start the cooker. But it had been a near squeak.

The next day I began the long trek to the Pole over the ever-rising plateau. Unlike my previous travels in Antarctica, this time I was now totally alone and in an area known to be crevassed. Normally in such a zone I would be tied by a safety rope to somebody else. I spent many hours, as I hauled through successive whiteouts, rehearsing in my mind exactly what I would do following a sudden plunge into a hidden crevasse.

I knew only too well the details of the events in 1912, the year of Scott's death, that occurred on the survey expedition of the Australian geologist, Douglas Mawson, a fearful episode caused by a single crevasse fall.

Mawson and the experienced Swiss doctor Mertz had placed

their companion, Belgrave Ninnis, a twenty-two-year-old Briton, and his dog-drawn sledge at their rear with all the rations, the tent and the most valuable gear, having assumed that to be at the back would be the safest place. This proved false, and Ninnis plus his sledge and all his dog team fell some 200 feet into a crevasse over which the other two men had already sledged.

Without rations or a tent and over 300 miles from their coastal base, the two survivors' outlook was grim. To replace their rations they killed and ate their dogs one by one. Unaware that the dogs' livers were poisonous due to their Vitamin A content, the two men continued to devour them even as their nails and hair fell out.

Mertz was the worst affected. He became violent and tried to tear to bits the makeshift canvas that Mawson had fashioned as a shelter. One morning the doctor, in front of Mawson, chewed off one of his own fingers. Then he died.

By the time Mawson had buried Mertz, he was himself in an emaciated state, but somehow, in an amazing feat of determination and endurance, he made it back to his base.

Some three weeks inland from the coast, I began to feel ill. That night I was violently sick and my stomach was seized with painful cramps. To my horror I recognised the symptoms of a kidney-stone attack, two of which I had experienced before. I took morphine tablets, Voltarol and Buscopan, as advised in my notes from Mike Stroud. The relief did not last long, and a couple of tent-bound days later, I ran out of painkillers and writhed about in agony.

With a good deal of luck, my emergency radio call ended up with the Patriot Hills Camp sending out a Twin Otter rescue flight with a doctor and medicines. My relief on being fed a heavy dose of morphine was great. So ended my very real fear that I would die alone and in pain and beaten by my rivals.

I was flown to a hospital in Punta Arenas, and thence to London for laser treatment. I was lucky for, years later, I read of an ex-SAS officer, Henry Worsley, who, also man-hauling solo across Antarctica, suffered from a peritonitis condition some 900 miles from his start point and not far from his finish line on the other side of the Antarctic continent. This must have been extremely frightening. He sent a message to his wife before he died, which said, 'My journey is at an end. My summit was just out of reach.'

I am generally against solo expeditions in areas of natural hazards, such as cycling in the UK on busy country lanes, or travel on Arctic sea ice, or crevasse zones in Antarctica and Greenland. Such activities make me feel permanently uneasy (which could be translated as scared).

This fear of imminent trouble when travelling alone was proved justifiable one dark night on the Arctic Ocean when attempting to be the first person to reach the North Pole solo and unsupported from the North American side of the world. I had worked out that previous individuals had all failed in their various attempts at this record because they had waited until early March, when the sun first rose above the polar horizon before they set out. This made for a safer start, but by the time they reached the Pole, the summer break-up had begun and there were barriers of large areas of open water. Too late! So I had decided to set out in the dark in mid-February at the time of the full moon.

Bad luck meant that the benefit of the full moon was cancelled out by a period of dense cloud cover, and the effect of the full moon on the sea was that of a full tide, which cracked up whole areas of the sea's ice cover that I was trying to negotiate by the feeble light of my head torch.

Whilst crossing from one floe to another over a moving bridge of ice blocks, my sledge slipped sideways off the side of the fractured causeway and into the sea. I hit the quick-release catch on my harness in order to save myself from immersion. One leg was wet to the knee, and one hand, the one with which I then pulled the sledge rope back out of the sea, was also wet and quickly lost all feeling.

I realised that I was about thirty minutes at best from death by hypothermia, and the aggressive fear of that fate lent me the strength to haul the sledge out of the sea, back up the side of the rapidly disintegrating ice ramp and on to the adjacent ice floe.

By the time I was safely on to a flat patch of the floe and well away from the nearest edge, my hand that had fished under water for the rope had lost all feeling, and the other one would soon be equally useless. I managed to insert one long metal pole into one of the sleeves of the tent, enough for a crude, but droopy, wind shelter into which I brought my sleeping bag, the petrol cooker and my lighter.

Using my mouth, since I had only one usable hand, I held the cooker steady whilst I pumped petrol onto the burner. I stopped once I could smell petrol fumes. Taking the cooker out of my mouth removed the parts of my lower lip and tongue which had stuck to the metal, but the blood flow quickly froze. Shivering violently, I lit the burner and found that I had indeed pumped enough fuel, since a three-foot-high flame ignited and started a fire on the droopy tent roof-lining. This I extinguished with my sleeping bag, and then I began the process of defrosting. It was a close call and one which enforced my fear of solo travel thereafter.

Once I had warmed up my body core and rubbed life back into my sodden foot and better hand, I forced myself out of the shelter, reloaded the sledge as best I could, and headed back south towards the vague outline of the coastal mountains. I realised that I had been extremely lucky. A fortnight later in a Montreal hospital I was told that the top half of five of my fingers must be amputated.

Back in Britain, Ginny reacted with humour to my news when I telephoned her. 'Typical,' she sighed, 'we are already short-handed on the farm.'

A UK doctor advised against amputation until five months after the date of the accident, on the grounds that the middle of each affected finger must recover fully because its skin would be used to form a flap to cover the new 'end' of each shortened finger.

Unfortunately, I found it very painful whenever I touched anything with the mummified black ends, which stuck out like large grapes. After two months I could stand this no longer and I bought a Black & Decker vice and a micro-saw, with which I cut off the dead portions. This seemed to work well.

I have over the years had many close calls and I recognise the 'superman' factor that our Creator has buried deep in our make-up . . . deep, but *instantly* available on call. On that nightmare polar night when my sledge crashed into the sea and, suddenly, I became aware that death was mere minutes away, my mind and my body went into overdrive at full throttle and gave me what Charlie Burton used to call 'super strength'. It comes from nowhere and just in time, having spotted that you are about to be terminally trapped. Trapped by some, usually unforeseen, disaster.

As an avalanche explodes from above, you scuttle with a speed and dexterity that is normally beyond your physical ability to the safety of a nearby overhang. That is super strength triggered by terror.

On that dark night in the Arctic, I hauled a heavy waterlogged sledge up a ten-foot-high ramp of slithering ice blocks with one semi-useless hand – a physical feat that I know, in normal circumstances, I would not have managed. That too was super strength, for the wonderfully capable wiring of my amygdala had recognised the imminent hypothermic trap that I faced but for the intervention of an instant superhuman effort. Sometimes this super strength involves not muscle, but willpower.

An example of the latter is the case of a twenty-seven-year-old climber and mountain-rescue volunteer, Aaron Ralston, who worked in an outdoor-gear shop and lived in Aspen, Colorado. He favoured hiking and climbing by himself and one morning set off for a day's hiking and canyon-climbing in Canyonlands National Park.

Towards the end of the day, working his way up a narrow crack towards the top of a ravine, he was trapped by a sudden slippage of an 800 lb rock, which came to rest on one of his hands. He tried, without success, to pull his hand free, and he made his penknife blunt after many hours digging at the rock.

Aaron had stupidly told nobody where he was going, so he knew it was unlikely that he would be found. This was a truly frightening situation. Wearing only shorts and a T-shirt, he shivered in the gloomy confines of the narrow rock chimney. When his water bottle ran dry, he drank his own urine.

He tried using his climbing rope to lever the rock to one side. This did not work. On the fourth day of his entrapment, ready for death, he etched his name and the letters RIP on the rock wall and used his camera to record a goodbye message to his parents.

On the fifth morning, Aaron had a clear dream of a little boy being picked up by a man with one arm, and he awoke with the conviction that this was a divine message indicating that he was destined to have a son and *must* save himself.

Super strength took over at that point, for he knew that every moment counted if he was to survive.

His problem was mechanical. How to cut off his trapped hand with a blunt penknife blade. He knew he could not slice through his two forearm bones, so he broke them one by one by throwing his whole weight against that wrist until, with loud cracking sounds, the bones broke and he was able to dig away at the nerves and muscles. Once the hand was completely severed, he applied antiseptic to the bleeding stump of his forearm and, with the remnants of his fear-induced super strength, abseiled back down to the canyon floor and staggered back, semi-conscious, to a used tourist trail.

Three years later he married and had a son.

Hiking alone in a canyon or on polar ice in the dark are activities where lethal hazards may be anticipated. Offices in central New York are usually safe by comparison except, of course, offices in the twin towers of the World Trade Center on 11 September 2001, when they were hit by jihadi-hijacked airliners.

The North Tower was hit first and set on fire. Then came the turn of the South Tower, which collapsed from the top down after burning for nearly an hour.

Down on the twenty-seventh floor of the North Tower (out of over a hundred floors) Captain Jay Jonas and his firefighter five-man crew suddenly heard a sickening roar from above. Jonas knew that, since their tower had been hit first, they were likely to suffer a collapse, but his mission was to fight the fire which was still above them. Nonetheless his intuition clicked in with the conviction that he must *instantly* head downwards. He did not explain this decision to his startled crew: he just ordered them to head down immediately.

Carrying 100 lb of firefighting gear each, they descended, rescuing a limping woman en route. After a sixteen-floor descent, Jonas and his crew had to stop where they were, as the entire building collapsed around them. A million tons of falling steel and concrete rushed by them in a thick cloud of choking dust; the roar of Armageddon.

Unbelievably to onlookers, including TV audiences of millions around the world, five flights of the North Tower's stairwell remained poking out of the sea of rubble as the dust cloud slowly settled. Jonas and fifteen others survived; 2,752 people did not.

The fear suffered by those entrapped on the upper floors of both towers involved, for many of them, the agonising choice of burning to death or jumping to death by pulverisation on the concrete road far below.

Nine years later, thirty-three miners in Chile experienced excruciating fear in a dark, claustrophobic mine following a massive rock-fall. At the time they were working half a mile underground and, for the next seventeen days, had no hope of rescue. They had to resign themselves to the likelihood of a slow and lingering death. The *New York Times*, following the miners' eventual rescue after nine weeks underground, quoted one miner as saying, 'The silence just destroyed us . . . Without a positive sign, your faith collapses. Because faith isn't totally blind.'

The same human terror as experienced in a burning tower block and a deep, dark mine was clearly the lot of the 1970 Apollo 13 astronauts when, 199,995 miles from Earth, they were shaken by the sound of an explosion that sounded like a meteorite strike and the simultaneous malfunction of vital electrical circuits.

They found, after a desperate search, that a short circuit had ignited an insulating cover in the module that provided their life-support systems. The fire also ruptured a key oxygen tank, and the whole mission was immediately aborted by the NASA Flight Director, Gene Kranz, whose efforts back on earth to save the crew were made doubly difficult, as the spacecraft was by then within the moon's gravitational sphere of influence.

As Apollo 13 headed round the dark side of the moon, the crew would have realised that they were more than likely to die in space. It was also increasingly probable that they would suffocate slowly due to too much carbon dioxide in their stricken craft. Only a clever 'Heath-Robinson' modification removed the poisonous air just in time.

When Apollo 13 eventually re-entered Earth's atmosphere, the world held its breath in fear of the heat shield having been damaged. The crew's families lived through seat-edge apprehension at that time.

Two years after the Apollo 13 crew's misadventure, a chartered aeroplane took off from Uruguay with forty passengers, including a rugby team who were due to play a match in Chile. The plane was scheduled to fly over the Andes, but due to bad weather and a navigational error, it crashed into remote mountains on the border between Chile and Argentina. With both wings and the tail ripped off, the fuselage came to rest on a snow-covered slope at nearly 4,000 metres. There were twenty-seven survivors, including many injured, and because they had expected to land in sunny Santiago, none of them had warm clothes with them.

Eight days after the crash, the survivors, already desperate with the cold and ravenous with hunger, heard on a transistor radio that all searches for their plane had been abandoned. This news made them decide to eat the flesh of the dead, many of whom were their friends or relations.

One night an avalanche crashed down onto the fuselage and eleven more deaths occurred. A plan was then hatched to send three of the least weak men out west to seek rescue. After a desperate nine-day trek over high mountains, two of the survivors, both students, finally reached a village, and helicopters soon located the crash site.

Years later I met Nando Parrado, who was one of the two students, at a conference and I listened spellbound to his vivid memories of his terrifying experience.

At least Nando and his rugby-team colleagues had each other's company when they faced their predicament. In 1984 I was given an exploration award by the *Guinness Book of Records* and, at the ceremony, I met a Serbian lady, Vesna Vulović, whose award was for holding the record for surviving the highest fall without a parachute. She was a flight attendant on a plane that was torn to pieces in mid-air as a result of a bomb detonated at 33,330 feet, and she was the only survivor. It is thought that she probably survived the impact on a frozen mountainside due to her low blood pressure, which caused her to pass out quickly and prevented her heart from bursting. Today, over forty years later, Vesna is still alive and she flies quite regularly, for she never suffered any psychological trauma as a result of the incident.

She told me of a seventeen-year-old German girl, Juliane Koepcke, who experienced a similar mid-air explosion on a flight with her mother from Lima in Peru to visit her father at a wild-life research station that he managed in the Amazonian rain-forest. The plane was hit by lightning, and she survived a two-mile fall and found herself alone in the jungle. She had been flung clear of the aircraft at 10,000 feet, but was still attached to the row of seats where she had been sitting, and these spun like a helicopter rotor, slowing her descent and hitting the jungle where the forest canopy was thick.

It is not difficult to imagine the fear of the young girl in a miniskirt on waking from a concussed state with dead bodies lying around her in upturned seats in an unknown jungle. Her collarbone was broken and her skin was gashed in many places. The other ninety-one passengers, including her mother, were all dead. She waded down waterways for ten days with crocodiles on the banks, piranhas swimming around her legs, and maggots feeding off her wounds. On eventually reaching a riverside loggers' camp, she was taken to hospital and eventually on to her father's jungle camp.

One way of training for polar expeditions that I practised, in order to overcome my tendency to avoid exercise through sheer laziness, was to enter team adventure-racing sports and mountain marathons. On winning the Veterans Elite Team prize one year, my team leader and I were each given a smart running vest emblazoned with the slogan: *Simon Yates Climbing Gear*. On two subsequent marathons when wearing this Yates shirt, I heard other racers shout at me, 'Simon Yates Cutting Gear!' followed by sarcastic-sounding laughs.

Curious as to this substitution of 'cutting' in place of 'climbing', I questioned my team leader who, although not a climber himself, knew all about Simon Yates, who was apparently famous amongst mountain fraternities everywhere for having once cut the rope that held his climbing partner dangling above an abyss. To my mind this was another example of fear-induced super strength willpower.

In 1985 I learnt that Simon and his friend Joe Simpson, a Sheffield climber, had achieved the first ascent of a remote Peruvian peak in the Andes, but they ran into trouble on the descent when Joe fell and badly injured one knee. Unable to climb on his own, Joe was lowered gingerly by Simon down some 3,000 feet of the mountain's steep west face. With only 300 feet to go, Simon lowered Joe, unknowingly, over an overhang where he dangled. He was unable to climb out of this predicament and Simon, who was slowly being pulled downwards, realised that *both* of them would soon die. So he cut the rope, and Joe plummeted down onto a snow bridge in a deep crevasse, in agony but alive. Simon searched for him, but finding no trace at all, had to assume that he was dead.

After a miraculous escape from the crevasse, Joe dragged himself over snow and rock for three pain-filled, dehydrated days and six long miles to reach the Base Camp and an extremely relieved Simon. Joe subsequently said that the most frightening time for him was when, on landing on the crevasse's snow bridge, he had realised that it was only loosely attached to one wall of the crevasse and, with one wrong move, he would send it crashing down into depths from which even his survival knack would not save him.

To be trapped against your will anywhere is liable to be a fearful experience, but far more individuals are trapped by other people than by natural hazards.

For example, in August 2015 the Peruvian Army was led to a well-hidden jungle camp of the Maoist rebel group known as Shining Path, whose insurgency over a forty-year period had caused 70,000 deaths. The former captive who guided the Army to the camp was one of many hundreds of slaves of Shining Path who was kidnapped from his village as a child; his father had been killed in front of him and his mother and sister were raped. Like others of his age, he had been forced to work in the coca fields harvesting cocaine until he was twelve, when he was conscripted as a rebel soldier. He told his liberators, 'I was there for twenty years against my will. I lived in fear.'

Such kidnappings and enslavement by terrorists or criminal gangs are rife in many parts of the world. A Scottish woman, Naheeda Bi, who was born in Glasgow, was drugged and then kidnapped from Islamabad International Airport after a visit to relatives in Pakistan. She was held captive in a slave camp in northern Pakistan for over ten years and forced to make munitions for Taliban-bound arms smugglers, along with many other kidnapped slaves. Naheeda survived year after year with minimal food, frequent beatings, torture, ongoing bouts of disease and diarrhoea and the constant fear of execution. A foray by the Pakistan Army into the criminal-held areas of the kidnappers caused them to release many of their captives, including Naheeda, who eventually made it back to Scotland after her ten nightmare years. On her release she was thirty-eight years old.

Natascha Kampusch lived with her divorced mother in the Vienna suburbs and, aged ten, was walking from home to school when she was kidnapped by a man in a minivan. A massive police hunt failed to find her, and her captor, a retired engineer who lived by himself in a house not far from Natascha's home, kept her locked in a soundproofed cellar under his garage. He beat and starved her regularly, tortured her by holding her head under water, and kept her entirely alone as his slave until, aged eighteen, she managed to escape. When her kidnapper realised that the police were after him, he committed suicide by jumping under a train.

Natascha later said that she had been more afraid of the long periods when she was locked up entirely alone than she was of her captor's harsh treatment.

Naheeda and Natascha experienced very real fear throughout their captivity, but they always knew in the back of their minds that they might escape or be released. Long-term prisoners, including those sentenced to life, a few of whom have been wrongly sentenced, know that they have *no* hope of release other than by suicide.

In the 1980s while researching the background to a mass murder in San Ysidro, California, by a serial killer, I interviewed a recently retired prison warder. Having described the fear experienced by a survivor of the dedicated killer as she feigned death among the bodies he had already shot, the ex-warder looked me in the eyes and said, with the force of pent-up years of harsh experience, 'Her fear was nothing and was gone in no time. I have lived in a cauldron of real, living fear from which there is no escape . . . the fear of a state prisoner.'

I asked the ex-warder how I could get a permit to interview a specific prisoner in San Quentin State Prison. He advised me that no prisoner would speak to me for fear of retribution from fellow inmates. He described some of the facts of prison life:

> Once incarcerated and introduced into toxic prison environments, many formerly non-violent offenders become violent. Simply put, prisons and jails are stressful, fearful places, and rather than stem violence they tend to reproduce and even provoke it. The fearful, older and more socially isolated inmates primarily use avoidance behaviours to maintain safety, whereas younger inmates tended to use 'pre-emptive self-defence' tactics to convey a tough exterior and thus avoid victimisation or exploitation.
>
> One of the most troubling aspects of current trends in American mass incarceration is the extent to which criminality is produced within prison walls, primarily in the form of inmate–inmate or inmate–staff assaults. Most methods of prison or jail control have the adverse, and perverse, effect of increasing inmates' levels of fear, terror and, ultimately, violence – with stabbings, beatings and other types of assault being common occurrences. Prison or jail 'violence' can take many forms – from mental abuse and racial slurs to sexual predation and rape, theft and property damage, ubiquitous systems of coercion, constant surveillance, stimuli deprivation, lack of privacy, crowding, excessive noise, the 'violence' of resignation and despair, perceived threats of bodily harm – to actual beatings, stabbings and other types of physical assault.

Groups of prisoners often murdered others and, to protect themselves, gangs were formed, usually in racial groupings such as the Mexican Mafia, the Hispanic Nuestra Familia, the Black Guerrilla Family, and the white Aryan Brotherhood.

Many inmates have their bodies and often their faces covered with gang tattoos. Knowing that guards do frequent spot checks for hidden weapons, drugs and cell phones, which only rarely include rectal and oral checks, prisoners keep razor blades in their mouths in readiness for self-defence against gang attacks in the exercise yard or mess hall.

Prisoners also fashion weapons from bunk-bed spars, which are known as *bone-crushers* and can be aimed through cell doors at a specific prisoner passing along the corridor.

Guards, according to my ex-warder, make a habit of checking jail cells when the occupants are out, and they have learned to check bars of soap for their size and shape. This is how they know what type of cell phone a particular prisoner is apt to hide up his rectum. To keep this hiding place supple when the cell phone is not there, the bar of soap is put in its place. Hence flat, rectangular bars indicate an iPhone, whereas stubby bars are likely to substitute for old Nokias.

New arrivals are quickly quizzed by gangs using 'kites', which are rolled-up paper questionnaires, easily passed by hand or slid under cell doors, and the answers will tell the gang leaders all about the person. Failing to fill one in is not an option. Cell phones are then used to check details on the 'kites' against Facebook entries.

The omnipresent fear of other gangs and even of others in their own gang, which is felt by gang members in prisons, is accentuated by the most murderous outfit, the Aryan Brotherhood, members of which are often kept in single cells as so many have murdered their cell mates.

The Brotherhood was formed in San Quentin in the 1960s as a counter-gang to protect white inmates from attacks by black and Mexican gangs. But a good many of the Brotherhood's murders are of suspected informers or fellow members who disobey the rules of the gang. Outside prison, the Brotherhood keeps discipline by shooting, beating or burning to death their enemies, including individuals trying to quit the gang. The gang motto is *God forgives. The Brothers don't.*

The influence and reach of the most powerful prison gangs who rule by fear is felt on the streets of many American cities, because all criminals know that they may end up in prison, where their personal history will affect how they are viewed, treated and possibly murdered.

A 'grapevine' system, known as the BNL or Bad News List, circulates and is attached to any new inmate who has stolen from somebody 'outside' who has a friend 'inside', or somebody suspected of being a police informer 'rat'. Such individuals who know they are on the BNL will live in permanent fear of attack.

Overall I would grade the slow-burning dread of a prison attack, or of a worsening cancer condition, as infinitely worse than the brief moment of terror when falling from a rock face or into the depths of a crevasse.

10

Cities of Fear

The voice of God in me screams of wealth in abundance. Thanks be to the Father.
The 'Money Prayer', Nigerian Crime Enterprise

After my 1995 kidney-stone attack in Antarctica and the loss of five of my finger ends in the Arctic, I worked for a while with Ginny as her cowman and tractor driver, in between giving lectures to conferences and slowly but surely following up the life story of a man who, the previous year, had asked me to write the account of his ten-year search for the killers of his wife and child.

He had phoned me out of the blue in March 1994. He had a Welsh accent and called himself Alex Goodman. He said he was an accountant by profession and had read my book *The Feather Men*, a UK number-one bestseller that year, and he had decided that I was the right person to write *his* story. A London publisher contracted me to produce a draft by mid-1996, and my subsequent researches in Bristol, Birmingham, Peckham, Los Angeles, Miami and Grand Bahama to corroborate Goodman's data, led me into worlds of fear many miles apart from my own normal stamping grounds. I called the resulting book *The Sett*.

My research was greatly helped by a number of police officers who knew two of the criminals Goodman accused of the murder of his family back in 1984. One of these suspects was a Birmingham drug dealer, and the other a Jamaican who was active in London, Birmingham and Kingston, Jamaica. I published photographs in my book of Goodman, the Yardie, the police officers, and the Birmingham drug dealer, and when the book came out in 1996 I was threatened by the latter's gangland friends, even though by then he had himself been killed (by a man with whom I subsequently became friendly and visited in prison).

By the time I had finished the resulting book, I understood all too well why Goodman had a nervous tic and why he stared into mirrors and shop windows; not to return his own haunted gaze, but to see who was behind him.

When the Goodman book was published, *The Times* compared it to the work of Ernest Hemingway, with the comment, '. . . a *tour de force* in its scope, ambition and eclecticism', and it reached number four in their bestsellers list.

The media in Britain do a great job informing us of daily horrors occurring around the world, whether in the form of bombings, wars, jihadi massacres, drowned refugees or tsunamis, but we seldom hear about the ever-present state of apprehension in which thousands of our fellow citizens, young and old, live their lives in many towns and cities throughout Britain.

When news editors are short of more sensational stories, they do resort to reporting the occasional UK urban murder, rape or suicide, but they fail to spotlight the true nature of the dark underbelly of Britain's many zones of fear, which I would never have known existed but for my need to verify Goodman's story.

Sadly, what I learned about urban terror in UK cities in the mid-1980s and early 1990s is still the ongoing state of affairs in Britain today.

My months of research took me to the urban haunts of drug dealers, pimps and prostitutes and to the concrete labyrinths of council estates in many areas of London, Birmingham and Leeds. By the end of my travels I had met a great many people whose daily lives could accurately be described as a living hell. There were many reasons and many evil people responsible for this sad state of affairs, and I will attempt to highlight a few.

Goodman had, I confirmed, lived for a while in a tiny flat belonging to Sara, an Asian prostitute whom he had befriended at an early stage of his dangerous quest. Her window box, he had noted, of which she was so proud, suffered from used condoms and fag-ends being dropped onto its geraniums every night like darts from the flats above. This, Goodman said, summarised life in Britain's huge urban council estates.

Sara was protected by an old school-friend turned gangster called Columbo and his close-knit clan of West Indian cousins, who were known locally as The Family. His parents had arrived in Stoke Newington, North London from Trinidad in 1967 when he was two. His father had disappeared when he was eight and his mother was dirt poor. He and his sisters learned self-sufficiency in the uncaring, often hostile, world of the Woodberry Down Estate, just off the Seven Sisters Road.

Aged ten he was sucked into the sad and dangerous world of London rent boys, cruising known homosexual pick-up points such as the public toilets at Manor House and Clapton Ponds. For £15 he would accompany one, sometimes two, elderly men down nearby backstreets to dark doorways. He kept his activities away from other West Indians, who called gays 'battyboys' and beat them up.

Columbo hated his gay work, but he needed money to help his mother get food for the family. Back at school he kept his secret to avoid being bullied as a 'queer'. By the age of twelve, and less attractive to pederasts, he started to procure other, younger lads for closet homosexuals, mostly married businessmen from the stockbroker belt. He was paid £15 for a teenager and more for younger boys. He found suitable merchandise at railway stations, where they arrived fresh from areas of high unemployment, many of them giving their earnings to an alcoholic parent. Some, as young as seven, were glue sniffers from the Woodberry Down Estate, and they would do anything for glue-cash. He described the nightmares some of these children went through when needing a fix.

One girl of eight used to kneel with her head under a refuse bag held over a parked car's petrol tank, and then sniff deeply. She would later scream and scratch walls until her fingers were bloody. 'Keep away . . . the snakes!' she would cry. Another boy would steal fire extinguishers from council-estate landings and inhale the bromine fumes as he triggered them. He said his mother made his baby sister sniff felt pens when she cried too much. Other favourite fume-sniffables included Tippex, Evo-Stik, hair sprays, fly sprays, nail-varnish remover, paint stripper and shoe polish.

Columbo pimped for many boys whom he had initially recruited by recognising them as sniffers who were desperate for cash. He could identify them by their red eyes, their smelly breath and the spots around their mouths.

He had finally stopped his pimping activities when Jason Swift, a twelve-year-old friend of his, also from Woodberry Down, was murdered by members of Interchain . . . 'A paedo mob from all over the bloody world who are into sado-stuff like RFI, rectal fist insertion. Six of them took an hour to kill Jason; buggered him every which way, stuck knives up him, then suffocated the poor little lad with a pillow when he screamed.'

For a while Goodman was bidden by the Family's chief honcho, James, to learn the slang they used for drug-related items and activities because the Family were involved in maintaining a mobile amphetamine laboratory, mobile in case of a raid by police or another drug-dealing gang. Whenever they needed a new site, they merely broke into an empty flat or rundown squat which was rarely checked by the council, especially following the chaos that resulted from the abolition of the Greater London Council. They then simply changed the lock and kept the keys.

A member of the Family nicknamed 'Chemist' taught Goodman about the devastating effects of using cocaine and crack. Cocaine, Goodman learned, breaks down the body's ability to reconstruct itself. The veins and arteries of long-term users split and they haemorrhage to death, their bodies rotting through lack of cell regeneration. Those who absorb cocaine through their nostrils can end up with ulcerated, perforated noses.

Each smoker experiences for a minute a taste of ecstasy, a mile-high rush like the best sex they have ever had. Then, for the next ten to twenty minutes they gradually float back to earth. Unless they light up another £60 worth of crystal, a miserable comedown sets in, inducing paranoia and aggression.

A third method, known as freebasing, involves a smokable variation of coca powder with a 95 per cent purity level plus a solvent such as ether, which is heated using a naked flame to hasten the moment of smokability. Since ether is highly flammable, explosions have caused many fatalities.

Smokable forms of coca paste were developed as small pebbles or 'rocks', which addicts lit and dropped into empty Coke cans. They then sucked up the smoke which, in many cases, addled their brains and they ended their days in mental institutions.

The 'rock' form of crack addiction is highly expensive, and in the 1980s the cost for a single night session was £1,000. Break-ins and a spate of street muggings resulted. A single example of this is evident from the court case at Christmas 1993 when, at the Old Bailey, 19-year-old crack addict Duane Daniels admitted 600 burglaries, 130 muggings, and 220 car break-ins, all to feed his habit.

Multiply the example of Daniels a thousand-fold and the equation is clear. Cocaine makes for a great deal of fear, and Yardies are the main merchants of cocaine in a great many UK towns and cities. This is no more a racial slur on Jamaicans than to blame all Italians for Mafia misdoings.

I was very lucky with my research into Goodman's time spent in the Jamaican world of Tottenham thanks to unpaid help from a local Crime Squad policeman named Taff Jones. He was Welsh, an ex-bricklayer, and one-time landlord of The Beehive pub in Tottenham before he joined the local Beat Crime Desk and thence the Crime Squad's surveillance unit. He and his colleagues wore bomber jackets, carried binoculars and used rooftop perches to watch the streets. Taff introduced me to various aspects of the hellish netherworld inhabited by many thousands of my fellow UK citizens.

Taff and his specialist squad often selected their rooftop perches in areas where no CCTV cameras operated, but they also relied on sudden calls from City Council street surveillance centres, who had spotted a dealer in action.

Taff told me how such centres and their operators were so feared and hated by drug rings that they had to operate in secret, and their staff told nobody what their job was. There had been arson attacks on their centres and, in one case, gas had been pumped into a local surveillance HQ via ventilators, thus rendering the staff unconscious.

There are some 5 million active CCTV cameras in Britain, the greatest number per citizen in the world, and they are increasingly being updated by their council owners with the installation of high-powered, super-magnifying cameras situated, like Taff's men, on suitable rooftops. They can be zoomed in by their surveillance centre operators to observe an entire street scene and to read the details on a number plate.

The operators at these centres have had to watch horrific scenes of stabbings, old folk being kicked to death, and suicides where they can do nothing to help, other than phone the nearest available police contact. Nonetheless they know that their film footage can be used to identify dealers and murderers.

James, the head of Columbo's clan and an ardent Rastafarian, had come from JA (Jamaica) in the mid-1970s, escaping from the hellhole of West Kingston, then a contender for the title of murder capital of the world, for the promised land of the mother country. At first, life had been an improvement, but that had all changed, according to James, with the advent of crack cocaine replacing the traditional drug of Jamaicans, cannabis, known as ganja or weed, which he described as 'harmless like Players No. 6 cigarettes or Tennents Bitter'.

Since the arrival of crack, hundreds of UK-based Yardies (to a Jamaican, 'Yard' means home) had become rich beyond their wildest dreams. Single-minded, ruthless violence was their code of conduct. London was no longer a haven of peace and the traditional ganja trade for the likes of James and Columbo. Killings and torture, rape and armed theft were on the increase and creeping out from such Yardie enclaves as Tottenham, Brixton, Peckham, Stoke Newington and Lewisham as crack cocaine addiction spread plague-like and without distinction as to class, sex, age or race. Only 40 per cent of black killings in South London were reported, and since most of the dead were illegals, few ripples were caused.

The vast majority of the victims were black. Shootings, often with sub-machine guns, death by machete slashing, kidnap, rape and torture were all rife. Yardies blew one another away for the sake of it, and often merely to enhance their own 'respect'. In parts of Yardie-infested cities, the normal dress code for their wheelers and dealers included a semi-automatic pistol, in the same natural way that I wear my watch.

The result in a great many black communities was vicious intimidation, bereaved families, and ongoing apprehension as to what new horrors tomorrow might bring.

Unlike Chinese Triads, the Italian Mafia, or even Colombian crime networks, Jamaican posses, as their gangs were known, were divided and unstable, doubly dangerous because of their spontaneous, almost natural, violence towards one another as much as to outsiders. They controlled their street dealing in cocaine and crack through the exercise of extreme brutality and cruelty, even when they could easily have got their way using mere threats. They killed without compunction, often without forethought, and fatal knife fights were common, even over mere arguments about a game of dominoes. They were arrogant and racist, feeling innately superior, even to fellow Caribbean islanders.

With no code of ethics and virtually no ties of internal allegiance, the posses fought within themselves and then split to form further factions, abruptly turning on their original organisations. This, of course, created a nightmare for pursuing lawmen.

British police and customs authorities had been warned in the mid- to late-1980s that crack had wreaked havoc and death all over the USA. Los Angeles, which only a few decades before had been a paradise of verdant parks and sandy beaches, had now become a concrete hell locked into a spiral of crime and armed response. Media accounts of killer youth gangs maddened by crack and senseless car-borne shootings had led to a fear-ridden fortress mentality among many honest LA citizens.

The authorities in LA tried to contain the lawless in certain zones like Skid Row, east of Broadway. The weak and helpless poor were forced to live jowl-to-jowl with the evil in such places. By 1985 Skid Row contained arguably the most lethal ten square blocks on earth, ruled by gang warlords, slashers and night stalkers. Seven per cent of the 150,000 gang members in metropolitan LA were, at that time, female. Many carried guns and had blown opponents' brains out as handily as had any macho male.

LA's *Clockwork Orange* world of murderous street gangs was a multi-ethnic one. More than 400 street gangs included 236 black and Latino gangs and 84 Asian 'sets', controlling great chunks of the inner city and seemingly impervious to the temporary inconvenience of police raids. Salvadorians killed Chicanos for narco-turf, *Lord of the Flies* Cambodian boat-children murdered their elders and chance passers-by for a dollar. But the highest-profile groupings were the two hostile mega-gangs, the Bloods and the Crips, often distinguished by the colour – red or blue – of their clothing. Both gangs had originated in 1972 in ghetto high schools.

Californian schools were first integrated in the 1940s and white groups like the Spookhunters terrorised blacks, who reacted by forming black gangs. The arrival of crack from Colombian cocaine in the early 1980s escalated all forms of inter-gang violence. The three most violent black gangs in LA were working on a truce in 1992 to end twenty years of bloodshed, but they were finding it hard to attend meetings for fear of being shot en route. The Renkers, being Jamaican not American, ignored the truce and continued to kill with abandon. They were headquartered deep in the gangland jungles of the Crenshaw district and were made up of vicious men and women with sleek German cars, Motorola mobile phones and fast reactions.

Over in New York in the mid-1980s Yardie gangs quickly found roots, especially the powerful Renkers Gang (the word 'renkers' in JA patois means the smell of human urine), whose brand of terror was stamped on their new territory by their well-publicised treatment of a teenage street dealer suspected of stealing Renkers cocaine. They beat him all over with a baseball bat, scalded him with boiling water and left him to die slowly in chains hung from a basement ceiling.

As would later occur in Britain, crack arrived with the Yardies, and as New Yorkers took avidly to the new drug, so occurred an unprecedented rise in child abuse, split families, murdered policemen, and intimidation of whole communities.

The Head of New York's Drug Enforcement Administration, Robert Stutman, warned his UK counterpart in 1989 that, 'of all the kids who died by battering in New York City, forty-six per cent were the children of cocaine/crack using parents.'

Subsequent alarming drug statistics included the facts that by 2008 drug overdoses in the USA, mostly from heroin and its pharmacological substitutes, overtook car crashes as the leading cause of accidental death. And that the annual number of known heroin users in 2007, then 370,000, had nearly doubled by 2013.

In 1985 Colombia produced 10 per cent of the world's cocaine, and the other 90 per cent passed through Colombia from its Peruvian and Bolivian sources en route to the USA. Eighty-two per cent of the street value of all Peruvian and Bolivian cocaine was paid to Colombia.

The total of Colombia's non-narcotics export earnings was only $5,750 million, a tiny fraction of the $375,000 million from cocaine. Small wonder that all aspects of Colombian life were influenced by the drug. Even the Church had been corrupted. Avianca, the national airline, was heavily involved in drug transport. The government, the military and the local police, with a few valiant exceptions, were rotten to the core.

Medellín was the mile-high Andean metropolis famous for gold, coffee, orchids and cocaine. It is Colombia's second biggest city after Bogota, but the first in worldwide notoriety. Narco-crime supplied the oil on which Medellín ran. Churches, the centre of life in the 1970s, provided a rendezvous for drug dealers by the mid-80s in their echoing emptiness.

Two great suburban shanty towns, Comuna Noroccidental and Comuna Nororiental, were bordered by open sewage canals and were rife with violence, prostitution and poverty. Both communes had been established to soak up the mass of terrified refugees from rural areas during the 1950s when La Violencia, a genocidal civil war, killed off 300,000 Colombians.

The majority of contract killers used by the Medellín drug cartels came from the slum of Barrio Antioqua. From this hell on earth the Cartel derived its most accomplished assassins. Barrio Antioqua had schools that taught how to pick pockets, how to kill and how to be a child prostitute of either sex.

In Europe most people would find considerable difficulty in locating a paid killer. Not so in Barrio Antioqua, where contract assassins advertised openly. *Trabajito* – 'little job' – experts were two-a-penny and could be picked up at a dozen or more street corners. Any taxi driver would tell you where to find one. To have a family member, a noisy neighbour, or somebody pressing you for payment terminated would cost $100, or thereabouts, but a judge with a bodyguard might cost $10,000. You had only to furnish your street assassin with a photo of the victim, an address and some basic information on day-to-day movements. If you were suspicious that your *asesino* was a fake, you could demand a *muerto de prueba*, a test kill, which could involve any chance passer-by.

Some killers specialised in *asesinato de la moto* just within the El Poblado district north of the Medellín River. Riding pillion on motorbikes, they would fire split-head bullets at close-range targets in limousines along the mega-rich Las Lomas and Las Diagonales roads, the most secure district of Medellín, lined with fine trees, art galleries and luxurious mansions.

Medellín ruled as the murder capital of the Americas, with an average of seven killings a day and twenty-five per weekend. Group massacres were popular, especially during church services and funerals.

By the early 1990s US judges were handing out long sentences and the crack market was flooded with tons of South American coca, so the price had sunk. US-based Yardies therefore switched their crack focus onto Europe, especially the UK, where the Yardie ganja network was already well established.

In order to speak to Yardies active in the crack trade, which Columbo and James were not, I received excellent advice from Detective Superintendent John Jones, the boss of Operation Dalehouse, set up by the Met in 1991 to deal with the Yardie crack menace. In their first year his team, based in Croydon, made 270 arrests in South London alone for murder, kidnaps, drug dealing and armed robbery. Knife crimes were being overtaken by handgun killings. Dalehouse operators were informed by Marie Burke, a Jamaican official at the US Embassy's London visa office, that one of her colleagues was illegally providing visas to help Jamaican illegals move about more easily between the USA, the UK and Jamaica.

Marie was about to give key evidence to Dalehouse when she was strangled to death at her home in Central London. A torture much favoured by Yardies to punish suspected female informers was to run a hot steam iron over their nipples, breasts and cheeks.

The news of such intimidation within the Yardie community spread to all criminals from elsewhere who dealt with them. One result was that Operation Dalehouse officers who were investigating murders in public places, which had been witnessed by hundreds of people, were utterly frustrated when the known killers escaped prosecution again and again, because key witnesses refused to give evidence or withdrew their testimony at the last moment due to the terror of what they knew would thereafter befall them and their loved ones.

Another police officer, John Brennan, an expert on Yardie crime, explained to me the history of the invasion of London in the early 1980s by dealers and hitmen from Jamaica. In 1980 the two main political parties in Jamaica had vied viciously with one another, one supporting left-wing policies and hand in glove with Cuba, and the other supported by Washington.

Each party held power in clearly defined municipal fiefdoms, where the politicians gave guns to hitmen to enable them to murder opposition leaders and supporters. After the change of government following the 1980 election, many hitmen from the losing party, fearing now for their own lives, fled abroad, especially to Britain where many had relatives. Some 800 politically motivated murders were committed in Jamaica before and during the 1980 election. By 1990 immigration officials counted over 30,000 known Jamaican drug-dealing posse members operating in North America.

I met up with two crack addicts at Kings Cross station following an introduction by the Croydon police to a JA drugs baron. I paid the Jamaican £50 for allowing me to interview the addicts. One needed £1,000 a week to satisfy his cravings. He approached rich-looking individuals on crowded Tube platforms in broad daylight and casually asked them for 'Cash . . . Now!' as he briefly showed them his stiletto-shaped knife and his aerosol can of acid. He said that it took nerve but crack made him fear nothing.

He described the result of a crack hit as an emotional gearstick. Sometimes he would feel hyper-aggressive and ready to knife anybody who happened to annoy him. He carried a double-bladed Stanley knife, which he showed me with pride.

He explained how he never took crack without a supply of heroin to hand to deal with the miserable feeling of deep depression that invariably came after the magic 'better than the best sex' initial crack euphoria.

When he wanted another hit – and he always did – he would break into cars or homes with a tailor-made iron bar with which to 'tap' any dog or inmate who tried to stop him. If other such money sources were not quickly to hand and he was at the time in the flat of an acquaintance or relation, he would take whatever of value was available.

To experience the atmosphere in the so-called Front Line of Brixton, I got to know the Jamaican Brit, Tony Stepper, and his white wife Louise, who owned a multi-ethnic wine bar on Rushcroft Road. Tony had come to London aged eight and was the only black boy among 900 white students at Teddington Secondary School. Aged seventeen, he joined Chelsea's Youth Football Team, and then moved on to DJ and club work in Brixton. He and Louise bought Steppers as a reggae bar, but Yardie fights threatened his licence and he switched to pop. Yardie hard-men still visited, but they kept their open aggression to the nearby Vox club and other such crack dives.

Louise knew all about the crack scene and understood how a person's birth traits were exaggerated by its use. If you were naturally aggressive, then you might well become murderous when crack-high or on the hunt for your next fix. She also knew many women, three of whom she had saved from suicide, who lived in fear for their lives because of Yardie mule-masters for whom they transported drugs from Jamaica and elsewhere using condoms filled with cocaine pushed up their vaginas. There were many such mules who feared the agonising death (which they risked if the cocaine leaked from the condom) far less than they feared the punishments from their dealer-bosses if the transport service between Kingston and Gatwick should fail in any way. If, when away from home, they were tempted to run away with their 'cargo', they knew that their parents, sisters or children would be tortured and murdered. So they stayed in harness or killed themselves.

Colombian and Nigerian drug carriers preferred to swallow crack-filled condoms rather than using vaginal storage, but stomach juices sometimes corroded the condom skin, and this led to leakage, convulsions and kidney failure.

At the Lewisham NCE (Nigerian Crime Enterprise), known as the Ark Club, which was one of seventeen such NCEs in Britain, the Yoruba tribe held sway. Welfare fraud was their expertise alongside drug smuggling. Self-styled teachers taught club members and others the methods of the mules. Pupils learnt how the body can effectively conceal over a hundred cocaine-filled condoms. First the prospective mule has to prime his or her gullet by gulping down large grapes covered in honey, then it was best to expel as much air as possible so as to prevent the condoms floating in stomach juices, which were highly corrosive, rather than passing through the digestive system. Bowel-blocking pills were also a must to ensure no lavatory was needed before clearance of all airports.

In 1982 Ibo and Yoruba NCE sub-barons had established two schools, one in London and one in Birmingham, specifically to instruct NCE apprentices in the skills of documentary fraud, and the intricacies of the British welfare system and how to milk it. The schools' locations were highly mobile.

NCE members became officials at Petty France to obtain passports, and baggage handlers at Heathrow to steal consignments of blank credit cards and birth certificates, and by 1985 they were well established in local government and the Post Office.

The police attempted to form a specialised Nigerian Crime Squad, but this idea was abandoned because it was likely to prove racially provocative. Informers were few and far between, because NCEs were tribally based and would-be snouts feared for their families back in Nigeria. As a general rule, and unlike the IRA, NCEs did not punish their own turncoats, but hired Yardie enforcers for the task.

At Ark Club meetings the current chairman would often open proceedings with a reading, known as the 'Money Prayer', from the international NCE gospel:

> By the Father within, and all the powers that be, I believe it is the Lord's good will that I enjoy an abundance of money. God is King and, as his heir, I claim joy, peace, health, love and all the money I can use. The voice of God in me screams of wealth in abundance. The Money Prayer will help me achieve divine prosperity. Thanks be to the Father.

Together, the influx of the Yardies, the NCEs and Colombian crack increased by several notches the element of fear that emanated from the inmates of London's great concrete housing estates like some foetid swampland stench.

I learned of the fear of poor Asian families on the mega-estates, many of whom were among the 10,000 inmates of Woodberry Down. Sara had two cousins who were brothers and they ran a post office in Birmingham. In September 1985 they were burnt to death by local West Indian drug dealers, and as a result their surviving family moved down to London's Broadwater Farm Estate. But there, too, they suffered constant threats from bad elements, black and white, who hated the Asians. Another of her cousins told Sara:

> The black drug dealers rule us and the police daren't touch them. Most of the time there are only four police on the entire estate and they're as frightened as us. I am alone now with my mother, and her mind is not as it was. I keep her in the flat all the time, like a dog who might otherwise be run over. It's no life for her and there are so many other terrified old people waiting hour on hour for the next hammering on their door . . . dog mess or flaming newspapers through their letter box . . . hate messages.

The Broadwater Farm Estate had witnessed see-saw troubles between blacks and the police for five years. This was partly due to a small knot of criminals whose activities led to firm reactions from the police, which were labelled as racist aggression. The police then increased their patrols and arrests of any young blacks, which, in turn, irritated many innocent members of the black community. Individual beat bobbies in Tottenham were over the years attacked and stabbed, and the whole estate achieved a notoriety that tended to make police response to cries for help from estate inmates, like Sara's cousin, both slow and inadequate.

Taff's colleague, Detective Constable Clive Mills, admired the generation of Jamaicans who had arrived in London from the West Indies in the 1950s. He knew they were now as distressed as anyone by the vicious criminality of so many of the British-born Jamaicans of later generations.

Sara's cousin took to wearing a big black shawl in order to look as unattractive as possible, for gang rape was common on the estate. She carried no handbag and only minimal cash in her shoe to cover the shopping. She speculated as to whether honest folk back in the assassin districts of Dacca in Bangladesh, where she had been born, lived in such a state of fear as she and her mother did in London.

My police friend Taff Jones told me of the many times he had, in plain clothes and from a covert surveillance spot in an empty flat on the fifth 'deck' of Broadwater's Tangmere Block, observed a suspected amphetamine laboratory. Once, when he was in hiding there, two uniformed bobbies had been brutally stabbed and beaten senseless following a bogus rape call from the fourth 'deck'. He had been powerless to intervene and still boiled at the memory.

He had often watched a police van cruise by in the narrow street below Tangmere and be virtually ignored by the dealers he was observing. Inside the van, Taff knew, eight frustrated Special Patrol Group officers stared out of the wire-reinforced windows. They were on a 'high-profile' patrol, but they were well aware, as were the local cocaine dealers, that current police policy and prevailing inner-city tensions made it highly unlikely that they would leave the van for anything short of a murder perpetrated right under their noses. For Taff and the seven other plainclothes constables in his group from the St Anne's station, life was especially hazardous. Many local criminals knew them by sight. They could easily be cornered by a ruse or by a false phone call.

The construction of Broadwater Farm started in 1967 and ended in 1973, a twenty-one-acre estate of ten four-, five- or six-storey blocks and two eighteen-storey monsters. Most of the units were built on stilts because the River Moselle, which flowed across the site, was prone to flooding. The Department of the Environment gave the estate an award for 'good housing' and the planning committee's chairman, Roy Limb, told the press, 'Broadwater Farm will be an everlasting memorial to my committee.' For a short while the first tenants were content, but the arrogance of the money-not-tenant-orientated planners and architects was soon shown up. Rain and wind battered their monstrous blocks, roaring with katabatic violence through concrete tunnels and passageways.

No thought had been given to the weak and elderly, nor to police access to catch rapists, muggers and thieves preying on the tenants. Cars were vandalised and stolen, their drivers beaten up in the dark car ports of the basements. Flat roofs and burst pipes in upper storeys flooded flats. Lifts and heating systems broke down and were not repaired, window frames rotted and doors hung off their hinges. Ventilation systems gave easy access to flats for germs, cockroaches, rats and exotic varieties of flea.

Lighting was poor and broken bulbs were seldom, if ever, replaced, and most of the public lighting had been vandalised. Condensation and fungal slime skeined concrete walls that never dried out. Privacy was non-existent and the corridors amplified noise so that the sounds of footfalls on the walkways, neighbours snoring, screaming, and radios playing were magnified and transmitted day and night into the flats.

Refuse chutes were too narrow to take full rubbish bags, so they jammed and the stench filled the passageways. Fearful of entering the lifts and corridors below, tenants threw their bulging refuse bags off balconies to the rats at ground level, or left them in the walkways to rot.

Urine covered the ground, and excrement and used needles lay about like autumn leaves. Old folk had been killed by young motorcyclists playing chicken along a tenth-storey walkway. Waste areas between blocks were heaped with litter, glass and the faeces of dogs kept by tenants for company and protection.

The safest place for the lonely and the ill was to stay double-locked in their prison-like flats, but this was impossible because the planners had allowed for minimal community services. Vandals terrorised postmen and milkmen. Nothing was delivered and nobody would come to do repairs, thanks to Broadwater's fearful reputation and its air of alien menace. Nothing could be left outside a door, otherwise it would soon be smashed or stolen. To buy milk or bread, to collect a newspaper or post a letter meant a long journey through the corridors of fear.

No minicab driver would risk a visit nor, after a bad experience, would friends or relations. Shopkeepers in neighbouring suburbs gave no credit to 'Broadwater people', such was the stigma of the place as a 'sink' estate. Nobody wanted to live there, so the council increasingly used it as a dumping ground for drug addicts, the mentally and physically ill, alcoholics and 'ethnics'. The bullies reigned supreme. Neighbourliness, once a strong point among Farm people, fell away as individuals grew wary of one another. Feelings of hostility were so pronounced in some quarters that new residents preferred to remain anonymous to avoid the possibility of confrontation.

At any one time eight unarmed policemen, in four pairs, were meant to patrol the nightmare acres of the Farm. During the fortnight before Goodman's arrival in Tangmere, four of these constables had been assaulted and three were badly injured. They could not protect themselves, let alone the tenants. The authorities became scared of provoking racial conflagration, and JA drug dealers were quick to use resulting police no-go policies to their advantage. The law of the Broadwater Farm Estate quickly developed into the law of the jungle.

By standing back from a normal patrol presence and speedy reaction to calls for help from the innocent, and usually elderly, estate dwellers on such estates as Broadwater, the police were, in fact, following a different, but also racist path, since a great many black innocents were now horribly exposed to crime without the police protection that they would expect in a 'white' area.

The reality was, of course, that a great many West Indians of all ages and backgrounds were model British citizens; they hated crime and wanted only to live good, clean, successful lives in a loving family circle, like most of us, black, white, or whatever, wish to do. Trapped on these sink estates from hell, they hated the Yardie dealers who so tainted their Jamaican identity, in much the same way as most Germans regretted the Nazi connection to *their* race.

11

Third-party Fear

> *I was like a frightened little dog waiting for its master to lash out and kick it across the room with the toe of his boot.*
>
> Sophie Hayes

This book does not deal with the fear felt by animals and birds, but Alex Goodman's nemesis, 'Badger' Blackledge, the killer of his wife and daughter for whom he hunted for a decade, was addicted to the cruel sport of badger-baiting with trained dogs. In the course of tracing Blackledge's past, I met a very brave boatbuilder on the Isle of Wight called Paul Martin.

Having dabbled for a while on the edge of badger-baiting, Paul became horrified by the cruelty and violence of a visiting group of baiters under Blackledge who, during a dig that Paul was hosting in his local woods, discovered that a couple of students apparently keen on badger-baiting were, in fact, RSPCA stool pigeons. Blackledge was about to torture them when Paul, seeing the error of his ways, cleverly invented the imminent arrival of a police patrol, thereby saving the students and putting himself at great risk.

Not long afterwards Blackledge and his gang were convicted in court and Paul, who had by then realised the truly cruel nature of badger-baiting, agreed to be a witness to Blackledge's activities on the Isle of Wight.

In 2015 I wrote to ask Paul's wife if she could recall whether

Paul had suffered fear before or after the case, since he knew the vengeful reputation of Blackledge and his crew towards RSPCA informers. She wrote back to say that since those days she and Paul had opened to the public the Haven Falconry on the Isle of Wight, and that:

> Paul well remembers an episode following the conviction of the badger diggers . . . After the court case the defendants initially said that they would appeal against the conviction, and soon after that Paul was driving and noticed that he was being followed by a car. This car overtook him and pulled up. Paul soon realised that he was 'sandwiched' between two cars. Two men got out of the front car and one asked Paul to wind his window down. They were rough sorts. Paul did not recognise either of them. Paul wound the window down a little way and one of the men said, 'Oi, Martin, you're due to go to the appeal coming up, but you are not going to be there, are you?' Paul felt blood drain from his face and felt his pulse and adrenalin pumping. He did not at that moment know what to say, but then he said, 'Yes, I'm going. Why?' The threatening reply from this man was, 'If you try and turn up we'll have your kneecaps!'
>
> Fight or flight came into play for Paul at this stage, not sure whether to get out of the door on the passenger side and run, or get out of his door and take his chances, as Paul is not easily intimidated! The two guys from the car behind him got out and Paul had an instant feeling of helplessness, looked around for anyone else close by, and decided it was safer to stay in the car. 'I'm telling you, don't turn up . . . you've been warned!'
>
> Paul's adrenalin was pumping really hard, and he was feeling scared by this, and consequently did not have the presence of mind to take note of the cars or their registration plates as they drove off.
>
> The next morning we found both of our own cars outside our house vandalised badly; obviously their final warning to Paul.
>
> Fortunately, the appeal never took place after all!

When my book was published, I printed in its foreword an explanation to identify its genre. 'This book is a fictionalised account of the story told me by Alex Goodman. How much of the story is true I cannot say. Any similarity between fictional characters and real people is entirely coincidental.'

However, on publication the media made a point of querying the allegations made against certain characters whose photographs I had used in the hardback edition. One of these was of Blackledge himself, with whose imprisoned killer I had later become friendly. The result, which I had certainly not foreseen, was a series of 'anonymous' telephone threats against me and my wife that I assumed were from the friends or family of Blackledge.

I contacted the police, who suggested that when I left home for the well-publicised book-promotion tour, I should definitely not leave Ginny alone on Exmoor. However, because of the cattle, she could not be away from home, so I telephoned the sponsor of my currently planned expedition, James Dyson of the vacuum cleaner company, and he kindly sent two of his ex-Special Forces security staff to live in our farmhouse all the time that I was away.

For a long while, and particularly whenever I was away from home, I lived in fear for Ginny of what we called the Blackledge threat. I corresponded with the man who, due to his own fears, had shot Blackledge and was serving fifteen years for manslaughter. He warned me that anybody who had been involved with Blackledge's demise or had subsequently besmirched his reputation, should be advised to 'watch their backs'.

This third-party fear, whereby the threat of revenge against loved ones at an unspecified date can ruin the lives of those under threat, is favoured by many criminals. Let me give two examples.

In July 2015 in the Salford district of Manchester, a veteran local criminal, the so-called Mr Big of Salford, returned to his suburban home, parked his BMW in his driveway and was shot by a hidden gunman. He cried out for help but died within minutes, leaving a wife and five children.

The dead man, Paul Massey, told the BBC back in the 1990s, 'I could be shot dead anytime . . . I am prepared to face that. I know the stakes.' He later survived an attack by a man with a machine gun, after which he told the local press, 'I pity the bastard who did it.' In 1998 he was jailed for fourteen years for knifing a man in the groin, and when released he started up a firm providing security for pubs, building sites and blue-chip companies. After his death, one of his colleagues said, 'Massey had control of nearly all the pubs in Salford and those landlords who refused to cooperate with protection rackets would have their premises burnt down.'

Chief Superintendent Mary Doyle of the Greater Manchester Police commented on Massey's killer, 'These are the type of people who don't care for human life.'

As investigators hunted for Massey's killer, local sources speculated that he may have died at the hands of 'trigger-happy' young gangsters, eager to steal his reputation as the area's most formidable gangster. Police said they had received less information than expected in the investigation into his death, adding that the attack may have been carried out by one of his 'old enemies'. 'We would expect to get some intelligence and we're not getting anything at all. It's hard to say whether it is through fear,' said Doyle. She added, 'Witnesses may not be willing to come forward because of a "no-grass culture" in the area. There will be an element of fear with this, but we have no intelligence yet to suggest that there will be any reprisals.'

Contrary to this optimistic assessment, Massey's murder sparked off a series of revenge killings between local drug gangs in suburbs west of Salford.

Two teenage killers turned up one evening at a quiet suburban home in Swinton, Eccles, a couple of miles from the centre of Salford and the BBC's flagship Media City. They knocked on the door, which was answered by a twenty-nine-year-old housewife, Jayne Hickey, and her seven-year-old son.

When the two men, pointing guns at Hickey, did not get

immediate answers to their questions, they opened fire without delay at point-blank range, hitting Hickey twice in her leg and once in her son's leg.

Neither men were caught in the subsequent police hunt, and again, as with Massey, all those who knew the identity of the killers were too scared to tell the police, even anonymously.

This tactic of control by threat to a person's loved ones, who are usually defenceless, works well not only for powerful gangsters but equally well for a single, evil individual with no gang connections. All that is needed is the ability to persuade the victim that, if they fail to obey your instructions, their nearest and dearest will suffer. Take the example of Sophie Hayes from Leeds.

Sophie was a teenager when, out of nowhere, fear came her way and began to close in on her little world. You can write to her today via www.sophiehayesfoundation.org, the website she set up to help others suffering the same nightmare that she had gone through.

Sophie's father was a successful businessman, who lived in a comfortable suburban home in Leeds with his wife and five children. He was an abusive bully who showed no love to his family and, on the contrary, enjoyed humiliating them in public. When, in an angry moment, he head-butted his eldest son for arriving home late one night, his wife began seriously to consider leaving him. Soon afterwards she learned of his ongoing serial adultery, and they divorced.

Sophie's childhood had, of course, suffered from the cold tyranny of her father, but she was saved by a loving relationship with her mother and her brothers and sisters. Although her mother had submissively accepted her husband's constant criticism of her, she had always tried to defend the children against their father's frequent tirades.

At the age of eighteen, a year after her parents' divorce, Sophie left school and, well spoken and intelligent, soon found a good office job in Leeds along with a conveniently located flat. At weekends when she didn't go home, she and an old school friend,

Serena, enjoyed shopping, drinking coffee and dancing at a local club. Sophie avoided superficial relationships with boys, but she enjoyed dressing up and club gossip so long as Serena was around.

Then, at work, she grew fond of a colleague named John and moved in with him. After three years their initial ardour cooled off and, though still friends and flatmates, they led separate social lives. Sophie still went to her old club with Serena and often joked about a group of Albanians who were also regulars at the club. One particular man had spent much of his time over the years ogling Sophie and every now and again he had tried to inveigle her into dancing or merely having a coffee with him. Sophie resolutely turned down his advances, but she was intrigued by him, as he seemed different in some indefinable way when compared with his compatriots.

By the time Sophie was twenty-one, Serena had fallen in love and moved away, so Sophie's visits to the club stopped and for a while she saw no more of her Albanian admirer, whose name she had learned was Kas. Then, out of the blue, he texted her from Albania, and for many months the two developed a friendly, long-distance relationship by text and phone calls. Kas initially corresponded from his Albanian home and later from Italy.

As Sophie's relationship with John deteriorated, her correspondence with Kas flourished. He became like a father-confessor to her, and then, eventually, a 'big brother and best friend'.

After slowly and amicably breaking up with John, Sophie met and fell in love with a Leeds barman named Erion. After texting Kas about her new love, she was surprised when his reaction was less than enthusiastic.

'Why,' he snapped, 'would you think that it would make me glad to know that you're going out with someone?'

In a while she realised that her 'best friend' was clearly jealous. Even though she had thought that their long-distance friendship was entirely platonic, he apparently did not. For two years Sophie lived with Erion, but when he was deported for a while back to

Albania, having been an illegal immigrant in the UK for ten years, she eventually made up her mind not to marry him.

Kas, clearly delighted, phoned to invite her for a 'weekend break' with him at his new home in Italy. 'No worries,' he assured her, 'no stress.' The weekend went well. Kas made no advances, was kind and considerate, and when they said goodbye at the airport, Sophie felt greatly recovered from the Erion break-up.

But, back in Leeds in her flat, all the misery and loneliness returned. When Kas phoned a few weeks later from Italy inviting her to stay for a holiday, Sophie booked a few days off work and flew out to him. Romance was in the air, and after dinner at a five-star café by a beautiful lake, they made love for the first time in the five years since Kas had first stared at her back in the Leeds club.

On her second night in Italy, as Kas let them into his flat, Sophie felt 'an almost physical contentment'. She reached up to kiss his cheek and then went into the bathroom. When she came out and saw him staring at her, it was as though, in an instant, Dr Jekyll had become Mr Hyde, and Sophie was utterly bewildered by the metamorphosis. It was as though her bullying father had suddenly entered the room. She felt the same dread, the same desire to cower away. Yet this was just Kas, her very best friend and digital confidant of over four years.

He pointed at a kitchen chair. She sat down. His eyes cold as grey water, he told her, 'I have a debt to pay, and that is why you are here. *You* are going to repay this debt for me. I have always been there for you, and now you are going to do something for me. This is why I asked you to come to Italy. I've had a drugs deal that went wrong. The dealer wants his money.'

Sophie protested that, much as she would want to help Kas, her job would hardly produce enough money to pay off a drug debt. Kas sneered, 'You will earn the money *here* . . . on the streets.'

When she tried to mutter some protest, Kas grabbed her by the hair and, using foul language for the first time since she had met him, threw her to the floor.

'Do you think that you are the only woman who has ever worked on the streets for me? Your pussy will be a goldmine.'

When Sophie became hysterical, Kas exploded with fury. He followed her into the bathroom and in a low voice informed her that he knew every detail of her home and her family in Leeds, where he had friends who did his bidding. If ever she let him down in any way, he told her, her little brothers would suffer.

Sophie looked at him in horror as the full realisation of the deadly trap in which she was now ensnared sank in. He snapped with anger, 'How dare you look at me with disrespect.' He held her by her hair and slapped her face. 'Do you think anyone will listen to you? You are now just another woman on the street. Italians like most of all the three Ps . . . pussy, pizza and pasta.'

In the morning he drove her a few hundred metres down the road from his flat and turned off on a dirt track into a patch of scrub. 'You wait by the road. Then when a car stops, you fix a price and take the money. Get in his car and tell him to drive up this track. Nobody can see you here. Thirty euros for fifteen minutes, and Italians only. You work all night. When, and only when, a customer has paid you, you ask him, *Bocca* or *Fica*? Mouth or pussy?'

Kas took away her passport, credit cards and all the personal contents of her bag. These he replaced with tissues, baby wipes and condoms.

Sophie had learned to be utterly terrified of her erstwhile best friend . . . she was as mesmerised by him as by the gaze of a python. He kept up a constant stream of criticism, instructions and warnings. 'Never do it without a condom. Never anally. No black men. No Russians. Above all, you do as I say. You keep this mobile always on. Moroccans and East Europeans may try to kidnap you, steal your earnings and rape you.'

He made her phone her mother and stood over her as she lied that all was well and that she was enjoying herself. She ached to tell her mother that she was trapped and wanted to be rescued but, terrified, she merely said, as instructed, 'I've decided to stay here with Kas. We will travel about so I won't be home for a while.' She fought back her tears in order to make her voice sound normal.

He took Sophie to a cheap clothes shop and made her wear a short, shiny black skirt, a tight vest, knee-high boots and stark make-up. Then he drove her to the roadside and introduced her to another girl. 'Cara will show you what to do for a couple of nights. Then you're on your own.'

The night was cold and her revealing clothes were thin. When the first car stopped and the driver asked, 'How much?' Sophie's teeth were chattering with fear and she clasped her arms together in a vain attempt to stop herself shivering.

Her first few clients wanted *bocca*, not *fica*. She had never in her life put a condom on anyone. Yet on that first night of hell, Sophie, the nice, shy girl from Leeds became Sophie the back-street whore, opening her mouth and her legs to unwashed strangers for a few euros.

She had come to Italy to visit a man she thought of as a good and trusted friend, but he had turned out to be an evil bastard involved in forcing girls into prostitution through threats.

Life for Sophie now became ruled by fear and revulsion. Utter disgust at the minutiae of her new night-time job, and in Kas's presence by day, in a permanent state of rabbit-like fear of him. He would collect her from her workplace up the track at 5 a.m. each morning seven days a week, count her takings and punch her if they were less than an expected average. Twenty clients a night was sometimes the minimum acceptable. One night she was paid for satisfying thirty-four men, but she still received no positive comment from Kas. He controlled Sophie by behaving without rationale and by remaining at all times utterly unpredictable.

After slamming her up against the kitchen wall for spilling something, he would smile, speak gently and, kissing her lips, tell her that she was 'such a pretty little mouse'. Then his mood would reverse and Sophie would quake with apprehension. Her body was bruised from his punches, but he took care not to disfigure her face.

He allowed no 'days off' for menstrual, or indeed any, reasons. After a fortnight and risking a beating, Sophie said, 'I feel ill and weak. I can't breathe properly.' His reply was that she was only sick because she never ate enough. It was true that she was losing weight in an alarming way, and she knew it. She felt that she was punishing herself for 'doing the disgusting, horrible things' she was doing each night. Kas often forced food into her mouth and slapped her if she failed to swallow it. But her weight still dropped below 100 pounds (45 kilograms).

After the first month of working seven nights a week from 8 p.m. till 5 or 6 a.m., Sophie averaged twenty-five customers a night. She could refuse nobody unless they came into one of the categories blacklisted by Kas, for she knew that he had informers. He constantly told her that she was being watched. She could trust nobody, even the police who from time to time told her to move away or even took her briefly to the police station for a warning. Even they might be in league, she feared, with Kas.

As she stood by the roadside each night she would half-wish that no cars would stop, but her greatest fear was that by the following morning she would not have earned enough and when she handed over the euros stuffed down her boots, Kas would shout at her and beat her. He expected a daily minimum of 800 euros from Monday to Wednesday and over 1,000 on Thursday to Sunday.

One night he threatened her with a carving knife, another with a gun he thrust between her teeth, and once he took her to the side of a river and told her how easy it would be for him to drown her.

In his flat where he kept her, Kas would punch her for the smallest reason. She never spoke unless she was spoken to, and she learned not to look at him, after one outburst of, 'How dare you look at me sideways like that? How dare you disrespect me?

How fucking dare you?', after which he had thrown her to the floor and kicked at her in a fury.

Her body was covered in bruises and her neck hurt if she needed to raise her arms for any reason, which was due to his habit of smashing her head against the wall.

Some three months after her life as a sex-slave began, he suggested that she should offer drugs for sale to customers. But when she refused, he did not, for once, force her into obedience for fear, she guessed, that she would make a mess of it and he would end up in trouble through her stupidity.

Sophie lived in a constant state of apprehension when in the flat with Kas. 'I was like a frightened little dog waiting for its master to lash out and kick it across the room with the toe of his boot.'

After a few months Kas drove Sophie to a cheap hotel in southern France and left her there for a week, picking a workplace for her at random in a busy street. He had business in Holland. He would expect her to make good money in his absence.

As soon as he was gone, Sophie was attacked by other street-girls who worked the area and she was badly beaten up by a bald, fourteen-stone woman working with Bulgarian transvestites.

Despite death threats from this terrifying woman, Sophie's fear of not earning enough money for Kas was even greater, so she stayed in the town and was again attacked, this time by Albanian street girls. Despite all this, she never considered escape whilst Kas was away, for her fear of him ruled her entire world. Any wrong move by her would, she was certain, mean the murder of her loved ones back home.

Returning to Italy and with thirty men to satisfy every night, Sophie's health broke down. She felt sick and dizzy and the nights were cold, but Kas kept her in revealing clothes.

Some years before, Sophie had been operated on for a twisted bowel. Whether or not this problem recurred, she now started to experience severe stomach pains. One night the pain was so bad when she had sex that it felt as though a red-hot poker was being pushed up inside her. Next morning she dared to tell Kas, 'I can't do it any more. I can't bear the pain.'

He told her that it was a simple urinary infection and that she should try to do more oral. Utterly desperate, when Kas was briefly out of the flat Sophie limped along the road to a local hospital, where the doctors ordered her to stay on the ward. Conditioned as she was, she phoned puppet-master Kas and, of course, he was incandescent with rage. How dare she go there without his permission? He reminded her that he had her passport and said she must leave the hospital at once.

When she pointed out that she had a drip in her arm, he hissed, 'You think a fucking drip is a problem? I'll rip it out of your arm myself if I have to . . . and don't even think of phoning your mother.'

What he did not know was that Sophie's acute pains had proved to be the final straw that had at last, like pent-up flood water, provoked her into calling her mother and telling her that she was ill, in hospital and without a passport.

Sophie's mother had married again, to a good man named Steve, who had long suspected that something sinister lay behind his stepdaughter's long and unexplained absence.

Her mother had, on the phone, posed the critical question, 'Is he violent towards you?' and Sophie had uttered the key word at last. 'Yes,' she said.

Her mother then assured her, 'We're coming, my darling. We're on our way. Do not under any circumstances let him take you out of the hospital.'

Sensibly Steve then called the British Embassy, who spoke to the hospital staff. For once Sophie's luck was in and her mother and Steve arrived as Kas was in the act of coercing her to leave the hospital.

Sophie's mother had no idea what had happened to Sophie, but she was convinced that she must somehow get her daughter away from Kas, for she suspected that he was an evil criminal who had some form of influence over her. She could see that Sophie was not just sick and horribly thin, but that she was also living in fear.

So she and Steve played a cat-and-mouse game and managed to defeat Kas's attempts to lose them in the local traffic on the way from the hospital to collect Sophie's few belongings from his room.

At some point Kas appeared to accept the fact that he could not stop Sophie being taken home to recuperate. But whilst collecting her passport, her mother and Steve waited outside and Kas, slapping Sophie, pulled her head close to his and hissed, 'Don't even *think* about not coming back. I will find you.'

Such was his utter control over Sophie that, as he handed her passport back to her, he clearly believed she would never tell a soul what he had done and intended to continue doing to her. And that, once her stomach trouble was dealt with, she would come right back out of fear of his retribution.

That night on the way home, she and her parents, for she thought of Steve as the proper father-figure that she had never had, shared together the love and laughter so utterly absent during the six months of her enforced prostitution.

For weeks back home Sophie told nobody what had happened to her. Kas kept calling her asking when she would be back. Then a call came from someone calling himself Kas's brother, who said that Kas was in prison on a drugs charge. So Sophie told her family the dreadful truth, and the healing process began. Knowing that Kas, once free from prison, would come looking for her, the family contacted the local Vice Unit.

Sophie's world as it had been before had now ceased to exist for her due to the all-pervasive shame that she now lived with. She felt dirty. She told her mother, 'I hate myself. I don't want to be in this world any more. I don't want to have to go on living.'

She forced herself to find a job and a flat in Leeds, as she knew that she must not give in to the overwhelming temptation to stay at home, the only safe place in the world, and hide away from people. Bravely she told herself, 'Pull yourself together. It's over. It's in the past. Move on.'

She had tests for sexual diseases and cried with relief when she was found to be clear. An officer from the Vice Squad called Robin showed her an album of faces of Albanian criminals. Kas, it turned out, was wanted in Leeds for an attempted drugs-related shooting.

'When he gets out of prison in Albania,' Sophie told Robin, 'he'll come after me.'

'No, he won't,' Robin reassured her. 'He knows that he'll go to prison if he shows up here. If you want him prosecuted internationally for what he's done to you, we could put him away and save other girls like you from his evil ways.'

Sophie's raw fear returned in a wave. 'No!' she shouted. 'He would kill me, or send someone to do it.'

Robin was sympathetic. He had seen it all before. The terror on the faces of victims unwilling to face up to their traffickers was the reason why his unit so rarely managed to prosecute the vicious men behind the modern slave trade in Britain.

By chance Sophie met up again with Erion, her partner of over two years. But, even with him, she found no real happiness.

Then, some months after her return home, Kas was released from prison in Albania and he traced her new work address. Emails then came in thick and fast and all in the same threatening mode: 'You motherfucking police bitch. You have no idea how easy it would be for me to be there in just a few seconds. How dare you talk to the police.'

Sophie told Robin. She answered none of the emails. The police confirmed that Kas was out of prison. 'His emails make him technically guilty of harassment, but we can do nothing unless *you* press charges.'

Sophie refused. She said, 'He'll kill me. He would never forgive me. Even if he went to prison as a result, he'd be released one day and then he'd come after me. For the rest of my life it would never be over.' She had only to close her eyes and he was there, the source of all fear.

Exactly one year after her return to Leeds a letter addressed to her flat arrived, which stated that he was on his way. She told Robin and, with his help, moved at once to another flat.

On her way home from work soon afterwards, she was about to board a bus when she felt a hand on her shoulder. She stifled a scream and turned to look into the cold eyes that had haunted her nightmares for so long. He had somehow found out details of all the changes she had made in order to throw him off her scent – her email, her mobile number, her workplace, and her flat.

He told her that he had found a room in Liverpool from where she could again get to work with her legs open and once more be his gold mine. He gave her a date to agree to this or, he said, he would have her drugged and taken abroad.

That same evening, in terror, Sophie told Erion, who told her mother, and Robin immediately activated the Vice Squad. Sophie was sent to a safe house in Germany whilst the police closed in on Kas. They knew from an Albanian source in Leeds that Kas had been seen talking to a long-distance lorry driver, which was a likely preamble to having Sophie 'exported'.

Three days after Sophie's arrival in Germany, the police arrested Kas in a red-light district of Leeds. He was carrying several passports in different names and his existing charge of attempted shooting was flagged up. He was given a year in prison to be followed by deportation to Albania.

Sophie still lives in fear of his shadow, never knowing when he or his colleagues might come for her again. But she has tried to fight her fear and redeem some self-esteem by using her own terrifying and degrading experience to help others avoid such a fate.

She has set up the Sophie Hayes Foundation in the hope of being able to increase awareness and raise funds to assist the NGOs (e.g. groups like Stop the Traffik) who work so hard to combat human trafficking and to support survivors of this terrible crime.

To me there can be no better example of the lengths to which humans will go, out of fear for their loved ones, than Sophie's story.

12

The Ultimate Regime of Fear

Anyone with their eyes and ears half-open could see the sinister writing on Jewish walls.

Albert Einstein

After writing the story of Alex Goodman, I helped Ginny to expand her pedigree cattle herd and we showed the best cows and heifers at agricultural shows and her bulls to buyers who visited the farm. I would walk them around a concrete pen whilst Ginny extolled their virtues (and their value).

Bovine tuberculosis, unfortunately, closed in on our part of Exmoor and we waited on tenterhooks, fearing every phone call whilst the results of our annual TB test were checked out. Sadly they proved positive at the farmyard where Ginny kept the prize bulls. This, luckily, was ten miles away from the rest of the herd, so when all the bulls were killed, the main herd was spared.

At that time the farm was costing more than it produced, so I decided to write a book based on a diary I had found in a deserted British Antarctic science base in Antarctica, whilst I was lecturing on a cruise ship down there in the mid-1990s.

The resulting story was that of Ruth Jacobs, a German of Jewish extraction from the village of Jösnitz near Plauen, a textile town in the former East Germany, detailing her experiences during the Nazi Holocaust. Ruth's fate was shared by many millions of German Jews between the rise of Hitler in 1933 and the end of the Second World War in 1945: twelve years of fear as the Nazi net slowly but surely closed in.

I have read the stories of many disaster survivors, of horrific experiences ranging from tsunamis to Ebola, but none have, in my opinion, yielded so much pure-grade fear as did those years of persecution by the Jew-hunters of Germany.

That I was able to experience the faded echoes of that fear, fifty-five years later and at the age of fifty-five, was largely thanks to my German friend, Mike Kobold of Frankfurt. He helped me to trace the surviving SS guards involved in Ruth's story and, despite considerable procrastination from the German and Austrian authorities, also to obtain relevant war criminal records, which he translated for me. He then accompanied me to many interviews with survivors and witnesses in Sudetenland.

I have gazed at the sprawled heap of emaciated corpses in the great black-and-white photographs on the walls of the concentration camp at Belsen and wondered just how many days and years of terror each of those raddled cadavers had faced before their final grotesque, but merciful, release.

Ruth's family had lived in Germany for over 1,900 years, having arrived there at the time of the Roman legions. By 1910 when she was born, her family's original Jewishness had become almost nominal, certainly liberal and diluted. None of her family in pre-First World War Plauen bothered with kosher food, Jewish skull caps or dutiful synagogue visits. The Jacobs family thought of themselves as middle-class Germans with a Jewish history that was an irrelevance to their daily lives, certainly nothing that made them any different to the other German townsfolk of Plauen, where the buoyant textile trade ensured that what mattered in that town was money, not the manner in which you worshipped God.

Like many Germans with some Jewish blood, Ruth was blonde and looked Aryan. Her father had served with distinction in the German army during the First World War and was a lapsed Jew who had married a local Lutheran.

Just as, being brought up in South Africa to the age of twelve, I never noticed the rule of apartheid and, indeed, I had many black friends as playmates, so young Germans of Ruth's age, like most other young Europeans, were usually ignorant until their teens of negative Christian views of Jewry in general.

When Ruth was sixteen and taken to watch a Passion play in Bavaria, she noted that the actors playing Jews had black hats with devil horns, and she overheard a neighbour in the audience as they filed out of the playhouse commenting, 'Why do we allow these Christ-killers into our country, never mind let them run the law and the economy?' This was the very first indication of inbred German hostility to Jews that Ruth had ever experienced.

The Christian concept of Jews as the killers of Jesus Christ had led them to promulgate hatred and destruction of Jews over the next eighteen centuries. In the Middle Ages, a time of great cruelty and violence all over Europe, Jews were a favourite target, especially during the Christian Holy Week. During the intermittent pogroms, Jews cowered in their blazing ghettos and hid from screaming mobs of hate-filled Christians.

Anti-Semitism remained in Germany even after the medieval exterminations left a mere scattering of Jews there, certainly less than 1 per cent of the population, but for seventy years in the nineteenth century the level of hatred had dropped to a mere background simmer. Jews like Ruth's grandfather worked hard and did well, especially in finance.

When Germany lost the First World War, the Kaiser was given the boot and the democratic Weimar Republic was forced to kowtow to the French and British victors with crippling reparations that worsened the effects of the Depression. Ultra-nationalists and war veterans seethed with humiliation and vented their fury against the Jews, most of whom were ardent supporters of the Weimar Republic.

Marxism was, at the time, the great expanding ideology of Europe and its most influential leaders, including Marx himself, were Jews. Fear of this Red menace, resentment at defeat, and

Charlie Burton rushes to my aid. Immersion due to unstable ice was a constant fear. The Arctic Ocean, 1986.

The Greenland Ice Cap trials taught us a great deal about the do's and don'ts of polar travel on land-based ice with crevasse dangers.

Fresh tracks of a polar bear . . .

Survivors and the fuselage of the plane which crashed in the Andes in October 1972. Suffering from cold and starvation, three of the least weak men made a desperate nine-day trek over high mountains to seek rescue.

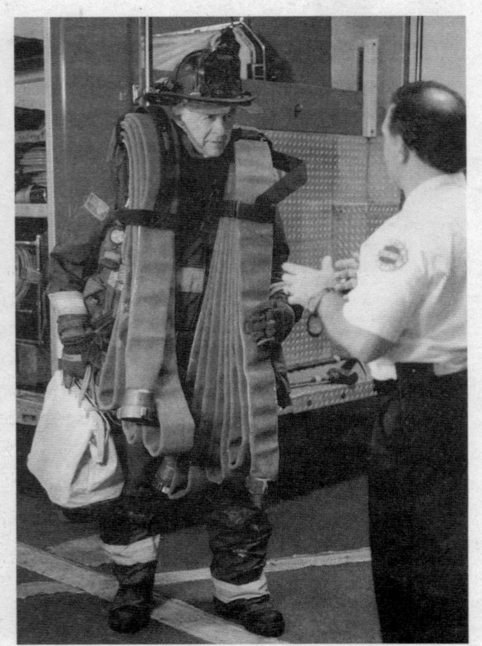

I tried on a 'standard load' at a Chicago fire station. Fire fighters carry 100lbs of gear each which makes their performance when the Twin Towers were destroyed even more extraordinary.

Apollo 13 launch, 11th April, 1970. A malfunction of vital electrical circuits during the flight caused the mission to be immediately aborted. The world held its breath in fear of the heat shield having been damaged as the stricken craft re-entered the Earth's atmosphere.

Aron Ralston with his father in May 2003. A rock climbing accident forced him to amputate his trapped arm below the elbow or face certain death.

Learning the ropes on a 'small' climb of the Old Man of Hoy in the Orkneys, I try to confront my greatest fear, that of falling into a void, a phobia I have suffered from since childhood.

'A proper Alpine climb', the North face of the Eiger. There's a drop of 3,000 feet from this overnight ledge known as Death Bivouac.

The summit ridge of the Eiger. I had felt more raw fear than at any time in my life and I knew I had failed to shake off the curse of vertigo.

Stalin ruled through his 'Reign of Terror' operated by his Secret Service, the NKVD, the predecessor of the KGB. His first purges began in 1930.

Under the 1975-79 regime of the Khmer rouge, Pol Pot had people killed and tortured at random.

General Ratko Mladic, Commander of the Bosnian Serb Army. The International Court of Justice ruled in 2007 that the 1995 massacre of nearly 8,000 Bosnian Muslims in Srebrenica was genocide.

Vlad III Prince of Wallachia, 1431-76, later known as Vlad the Impaler, became notorious for his inhuman cruelty.

Teloloapan, Mexico, May 2016. The last couple to remain in the town after a massive displacement of families due to drug trafficking violence, extortions, kidnappings and crime.

The People's March, London, September 2008. Demonstrators against increasing knife crime.

Lake Poopo, Bolivia, now dried up entirely. Climate Change worries more and more of us as its worst consequences are felt in increasing numbers of world regions.

Messages of support to those affected by the nightclub mass shooting in Orlando, Florida, on 12th June, 2016.

rage at poverty from unemployment were all taken out on the Jews by most of the German population.

The Weimar Republic, a weak democracy, witnessed bloody killings, largely by fanatical Conservatives, of left-wing politicians, and one of these fanatics, an Austrian army lance-corporal named Adolf Hitler, while wounded and in hospital on the Western Front in 1918, had a 'vision' that Germany's Jews were responsible for the Fatherland's humiliating defeat. So he resolved to exterminate them. Within a year, for he was a spellbinding street orator, he had attracted a band of talented disciples and, unimpeded by a weak government, formed his serpents' nest in Munich with a mission of mass murder.

This self-styled *Führer* had then made a public Christmas speech, including the words, 'Christ was the greatest fighter who ever lived. His teaching is fundamental in *our* ongoing fight against the Jew, the enemy of humanity.' And it soon became clear that Hitler would not stop at pure Jews; he would relentlessly persecute 'hidden Jews' masquerading as Christians. People like Ruth.

Even in 1921, 'anyone with their eyes and ears half-open could see the sinister writing on Jewish walls,' to use the words of the German Jew Albert Einstein. As a precaution, Ruth's father had her and her four brothers and sisters baptised as Christians.

By the end of 1928 a great many German Jews were suffering from the anti-Semitic propaganda of the ever more influential Nazi party. Since 1921 the assassins of Hitler's secret death squad, 'Cell G', had used murder, sexual blackmail and financial fraud on a grand scale against their political opponents on the left. Four hundred of Germany's best and bravest journalists and politicians were gunned down, drowned, strangled or knifed.

Hundreds of thousands of Germans voted for the Nazis, even after Hitler's hitherto secret 'final solution' plans were disclosed by the *Munich Post*'s brave surviving reporters. They revealed that, if not voted in, Hitler planned to seize power in a coup.

All members of the Socialist, Democratic and Catholic central parties would then be arrested and sent to labour camps. Trade unionists, homosexuals, cripples and gypsies, to mention just a few of Hitler's pet hates, would join all Jews and Communists as non-desirables to be eradicated.

By early 1932 Nazi sympathisers and informers, an early version of the Stasi, were everywhere and paid for by the Gestapo, Hitler's brutal goons.

Ruth's little sister Anna, aged ten in 1932, had been warned, as had all the family members, to make no mention to any outsider anywhere at any time of the family's past Jewishness, so her school was unaware of it. However, two of Anna's friends, Heidi and her brother Sandor, were known Jews, although until that year this had not been an issue in the class. But things began to change with the arrival of a new history teacher who held radical Nazi beliefs. He encouraged the children to participate in supporting 'the great *Führer*', and to join the Hitler Youth, if they had not already done so. Since free, very smart brown uniforms were available on joining, the children flocked to sign up. The anti-Semitic message soon spread among them like some hideous virus.

Heidi and Sandor, being Jews, could not of course enrol, and Anna watched from the sidelines as her two Jewish friends, both amicable, bubbly children and previously popular with everyone, began a slow and painful descent into a state of anguish. They were pushed about and called *Saujude*, Jew-filth, by their erstwhile school chums. The Nazi history teacher made Heidi stand in front of the class and compared her features with the official Nazi outline of a typical Jewish type that he had pinned to the board. Heidi had to stand there with tears pouring down her cheeks as his cane prodded her nose, her ears and her slightly frizzy black hair.

Anna was lucky that, at the time, nobody questioned her own Christian status. But the strain of subterfuge slowly gnawed away at her, for she was a naturally honest child. Each time she went out on a limb to be friendly to Heidi and Sandor, she risked discovery and denunciation.

Ruth married early in 1933 and a year later her son Uschi was born, a third generation Christian. Ruth's cousin, a reporter on the anti-Hitler *Munich Post*, came to her home (shortly before he was murdered) to warn her parents that Hitler was about to announce his plans to 'exterminate all Jews and *Mischlinge* (half-Jews) in Germany'. To claim non-Jewish identity would involve proof of three full generations clear of any Jewish taint on both sides of the family. Their cousin advised Ruth's father to emigrate as soon as possible and meanwhile to hide any trace of his parents' Jewishness.

On 30 January 1933 the Weimar Republic's President Hindenberg resigned in favour of Hitler, so the openly professed Jew-killer now had absolute power. All over Germany hundreds of thousands of Jews and other enemies of the Nazis felt, more than ever, the fear of the hunted fox.

Hitler's first victims were his political opponents and those representatives of the law who might be in positions to oppose or control his agenda. Within two months of his accession, 25,000 Communists had been arrested and sent to Dachau, a newly built concentration camp.

All Jewish businesses were then forced to close and all Jews were forbidden to enter public facilities such as hospitals, police stations, restaurants, cinemas or parks. Jews now had nowhere to hide and nobody in authority was prepared to protect them.

Ruth remembered the feeling of real fear running through the family kitchen on that dreadful spring day, when the coarse rant of Adolf Hitler's voice followed that of the radio announcer. His new Enabling Law gave his government complete freedom of action with *no* constitutional limitations. Nonetheless he inspired love, yes *love*, in the hearts of many millions of Germans. All over Germany houses were hung with great red flags and swastika pennants; village and town bands blared and oompahed their pride and joy. Men in brown, green or black uniforms goose-stepped in threatening columns, and cheering crowds lined the pavements.

In response to Hitler's spellbinding oratory of hatred, German citizens in schools, universities, factories, hospitals, and even in prisons, rose to their feet, their hands upraised in the Nazi salute and their voices united in a deafening cry of adulation, *Sieg Heil! Sieg Heil!* Ruth's father visited a genealogist in Munich, and he produced an impressive family tree going back many generations, which demonstrated that his Jewish ancestors had long ago married into Lutheran stock, and clearly 'proved' that his family were Christians. The cost of all this was exorbitant, but lives were at stake. Ruth's father had no doubt that if he did not provide the authorities with such evidence of 'clean roots', then the Gestapo would direct their 'bloodhound' researchers to the relevant birth and parish records.

Time ticked fearfully by for Ruth's family as the Nazi net closed in. Each knock on the door was potentially fateful. In the summer of 1936 the family doctor, a non-Jewish friend, warned them that the Gestapo had asked him if Ruth's father was circumcised. The good doctor had lied by saying that he had carried out the cut purely due to a local infection. In March 1933 Nazi thugs destroyed the offices of the *Munich Post* and arrested the staff. After two days of torture, all the paper's journalists, including Ruth's cousin, died in agony, suspended from meat hooks in a Munich cellar. At that point every last German media outlet was *gleichgeschaltet*, or brought into line by the Nazis.

Ruth's sister Anna married a Christian in 1938, and this increased the family's ever-present fears that their grandparents' Jewish link might be unearthed, since all new marriages were being closely inspected to check for racial impurity on either side, and the law for the Protection of German Blood was rigidly enforced. Many German Aryans were flung into prison just for flirting with Jews, Negroes or Gypsies. The 'aliens' involved were sent to concentration camps. The law's interpretation of intercourse included any act which 'satisfied a person's sex drive' and even kissing led many to prison.

Throughout the country, faithful churchgoers, both Catholic

and Protestant, expelled from their congregations fellow Christians they had worshipped with for twenty-five years and more, purely because of some real or imagined Jewish connection. Conversion to Christianity, or even having Christian parents when you were baptised, was not enough to transform a Jew into a German, any more than a black could ever be made white. In Berlin, Goering boasted, '*I* decide who is a Jew and who is not.'

Soon after the wedding, a plumber, the long-time tenant of a small cottage owned by Ruth's father, somehow heard a rumour of the family's Jewishness and used blackmail to refuse tenancy payments. When Mr Jacobs went to confront him, the plumber grew aggressive and knifed him to death.

The murder's subsequent investigation led to gossip of the family's 'suspected' status, which spread like wildfire. They were descended from Jews. They *were* Jews. As though overnight the family had broken out in plague spots, neighbours began to avoid them. Friends they had loved for years shunned them. Fear took away all memories of friendship and old times.

Shopping in the village became a trial of cold, hard stares, theatrical behind-your-back whispers, and aggressive shoves off the pavement, often by folk who had been acquaintances, or even friends, since childhood.

In October 1938 the bank accounts of the Jacobs family (and of all known Jews) suddenly closed without explanation. Then a Gestapo unit arrived at their home in a van to confiscate all items on a list, which included telephones, wirelesses and anything electrical. If any listed item was not handed over at once, the entire family would be arrested. Two days later the family car was likewise confiscated.

On 9 November the family's loyal gardener, Alfred, sneaked up from the village to warn Ruth and Anna of an impending visit by a mob of Jew-hating villagers. He said that this was happening all over Germany on orders from Goebbels. All Jews were to be beaten up, their properties destroyed and their synagogues burnt to the ground. The mob duly arrived at the Jacobs' house soon after midnight with screams of hate: 'Cursed Jews! Jew mongrels! Christ-killers!'

Ruth had hidden her aged grandparents in the chicken shed, but they were incinerated when local Hitler Youth yobbos set fire to the outhouses. Anna's husband was knifed to death when he tried to save her grandparents, and Ruth's four-year-old son Uschi was seized by one leg and thrown into the flames. A Hitler Youth teenager laughed as the child disappeared into the inferno of the chicken shed. *Huhnebraten!* he shouted. 'Roast chicken!' Ruth and Anna were both raped. The last building to be ignited was the house itself, before the mob headed off, singing and laughing, back to the village.

Ruth and Anna survived the subsequent Jew hunts only thanks to Alfred, who hid them in his own threadbare home and managed to alert Ruth's psychiatrist uncle, who then hid the sisters in a cellar of his clinic throughout the war. This was only possible because his clients secretly included two high-ranking Gestapo officers from Berlin who had children suffering from a schizophrenic disorder, officially termed as unacceptable to German society. Ruth later learned that Goebbels had personally ordered the anti-Jew violence all over Germany that fateful night. It became known as *Kristallnacht*, due to the crystal-like glint of the smashed window glass of Jewish homes all over the country.

Because of their uncle's Gestapo patronage, his clinic was never searched. Anna's son, Derek, was born there in August 1939. But whilst Ruth, Anna and little Derek remained safely hidden in their cellar for the next five years, millions of Jews were systematically rounded up and murdered.

When I visited Belsen in 1963, eighteen years after Hitler's defeat and in the uniform of the 'army of occupation', I was given fact sheets about the Nazi prison system.

There were 10,002 positively identified and named camps and ghettos, with a further 900 destroyed to the point of obliteration by the Nazis just before the war's end, which were thus unidentifiable. Of those that had been identified, 1,600 were labour camps reserved for the killing of Jews through overwork. There had been 51 main concentration camps with 1,200 satellite camps.

An average of one guard to every hundred prisoners was standard SS practice, so at least half a million German or ethnic German citizens, in addition to a number of anti-communists from countries like Latvia, were involved in the vast killing machine. Of these guards, only some 4,000 were executed or imprisoned after the war, so a huge number of sadistic murderers were able to live out their lives after the war entirely unpunished.

In 1939 Himmler sent a special Jew hunter–killer unit, the Order Police, into Poland behind the front-line troops. Their job was simple. Eradicate all Jews. The suffering they caused was unimaginable. Week after week for three years as the Nazi war machine devoured new regions of Eastern Europe, the Order Police continued their human cull, killing up to 30,000 people in just one massacre.

A *single* death pit that the Germans prepared in Poland was designed to take 28,000 bodies. In November 1941 an especially hard winter helped many Jews survive longer because the pits were too difficult to dig. The official estimate for Jews who were buried *alive* in the mass killings was 2 per cent. There were many thousands of lesser mass shootings all over Eastern Europe and over 4 million prisoners died in the camps.

Ruth's uncle kept her and Anna up to date with the world outside the clinic thanks to the Bund, a rescue pipeline for prisoners who had escaped from concentration camps, some of whom he temporarily housed at the clinic. One of these, a non-Jewish closet homosexual, had spent time in Auschwitz before being sent, thanks to his engineering skills, to make Messerschmitt fighters' wings at Flossenberg Camp, from whence he escaped and contacted the Bund.

As a place of real human horror, Auschwitz was, in my opinion, honed to perfection and difficult to beat. For Ruth and Anna in their cellar it would have been better *not* to have known what lay in wait for them, should the clinic's existence be leaked to the Gestapo at any time.

The Nazis created Auschwitz as one of six large killing camps inside Poland. The camp covered sixty-four square kilometres and was situated on a damp and swampy plain. It housed Jews from most of the occupied countries of the Reich.

The secret of Nazi success in achieving an efficient mass-murder system at Auschwitz was in keeping the world from discovering that the camp's specific purpose was to *kill*. Jews had to be persuaded to think that it was merely a *work* camp with food and accommodation for families. That way, since anything seemed preferable to starving in a ghetto, they flocked there willingly and unwittingly led their children to their deaths.

Sooner or later a deportation order would be delivered to each and every Jew with a known address in all Nazi-occupied lands, (as it would have been to Ruth and Anna had they not 'disappeared' into the clinic). On receiving his or her deportation order, a Jew (and all the family) would then have a few hours in which to report to the Gestapo at a designated railway station. There they waited (sometimes hours, often days) in the cold or heat without shelter, ringed by guards and leered at by passing German citizens. No water was available, nor toilets. Eventually a train hauling boxcars arrived, emanating a powerful stench of chlorine.

SS guards then forced the Jews into the boxcars. Some children screamed in fear. People were jammed in so tight that there was only standing room, and as more and more people were crammed in it became difficult to breathe. Shots were fired to encourage the last few passengers into the carriages. Then the heavy steel doors were slammed shut.

In each boxcar there was no window, just a single, barred ventilator slit. There was only one bucket. No doctor, although many people were already sick. People wet themselves and were frozen with embarrassment, for there was no privacy. All were degraded and stripped of their dignity and self-confidence. There was no straw on the wooden floor and no way of lying down . . . you would be trampled on.

In the morning after the first ghastly night, the death count was usually high. There was no water and the toilet bucket was soon full. The ventilator slit was too small to use to empty the bucket, so its contents were poured into one corner, which then ran all over the floor. People had to soil themselves after that. The stench by the second day was no longer just of chlorine.

When stopped in sidings without the slight draught caused by the train's motion, the air became almost impossible to breathe, and more people died or fainted. Some trains took eight days to make the journey to Auschwitz, and fewer than a dozen out of a hundred passengers survived.

On arrival the boxcar doors were slid open. Blinded by light, the survivors were assaulted by the sound of barking dogs and yelling guards: *Raus, Judensheisse!* 'Out, Jewish shit!'

People behaved like animals. 'Water,' they croaked, pulling each other by the hair and tripping over corpses. Prisoners in striped clothes pulled them down from the wagon, showing no sympathy, only fear of the SS guards behind them. Large dogs snarled and jumped against their handlers' chains.

New arrivals were then formed into two lines, male and female regardless of family ties, and were whipped at any sign of delay in following the constantly shouted orders. An SS man flipped his cane to the left or right and divided male prisoners, without a word, into two groups. Another officer across the yard was doing likewise with the women. Some people panicked as they clung to a daughter or sister, but they were beaten apart and forced into separate lines.

The men and women who remained behind when the lorries roared off were usually all over the age of eighteen, generally strong-looking and none wore glasses. A day later this group learned from other prisoners that their loved ones had been taken away to be gassed and then incinerated, as the Germans burned all those too feeble to be used for labour. The smoke that those selected to live could smell and see belching from the chimneys was all that remained of their parents, wives, husbands and children. And new freight trains kept coming, bringing more human fuel for the incinerators.

The first process for individuals selected for work, not gassing, was simple and efficient. All were rushed into a shower hall under the lash of whips. Lysol disinfectant was poured over their recently shaven body hair to kill lice. Screams resulted as this liquid ran into shaving cuts and eyes. Women were then searched gynaecologically in front of sneering guards for hidden valuables. Long, grey shirts were then doled out to pull over wet, shivering bodies, which made a mockery of the showers and disinfectants for they were soiled with the blood and excrement of their previous, now dead, owners. And they crawled with lice.

Those new arrivals designated for labour were at night jammed onto plank platforms, packed in like sardines and too scared to relieve themselves, since even after a brief absence they could never reclaim a place on the platform. The barracks were unheated, even in winter, but the overcrowded platforms at least gave the comfort of some body heat from the other bony-ribbed occupants.

At four-thirty every morning they were beaten out of the barracks and had to make a mad dash to a nearby open area where they were lined up in ranks of five. For four or five hours they would then wait for the SS to count them and everybody else in the main camp too. In winter it was cold, *very* cold. Bald heads, no underclothes, no socks in crude clogs and no body fat for insulation. Freezing winds, drenching rain, and sometimes snow. In summer, great heat, thirst and sunstroke. They were not allowed to stand at ease, much less to move or to faint. If they had diarrhoea, too bad. *Any* movement led to their death or a severe beating. Many people collapsed, some died.

It was *truly* miserable. Humans who have not lived in a camp like that do not even begin to understand the meaning of the word 'misery'. In that place people were always frightened. If a day went by without physical pain, suffering and mental anguish, then that was a minor miracle. There was never a moment of privacy. You could not defecate or do anything at all unobserved.

As for washing, that was a luxury no prisoner experienced, not even those assigned to latrine or litter duty. The 'litter' consisted of corpses which, like cigarette ends in a city, were constantly replaced by new arrivals. Assigned prisoners dragged the bodies to collection points and stacked them neatly in rows of six and layers of five. Many were not yet dead, but they soon would be. Rats and crows and cockroaches attended to the stacks, and in summer the stench of rotting flesh competed even with the smell of the chimneys.

Auschwitz prisoners lived in a state of acute fear, for they knew every detail of the dreadful death that awaited them at a moment's notice. The SS kept the gassings as economical as possible by cramming naked prisoners tightly into each chamber, and 780 at one sitting was the record. Babies and small children were often among the last entrants, and they would be tossed onto the heads of the assembled adults just before the doors were closed and sealed.

Whenever the Zyklon poison-gas supplies failed to keep up with the constant influx of Jews from all over the Reich, the SS turned to *direct* usage of the furnaces as a means of extermination. This entailed thousands of prisoners being burned alive.

Thanks to their psychiatrist uncle at the clinic, who had a well-hidden wireless, Ruth and Anna were able to keep in touch with outside events through the long years of 1942 to 1944. Sitting huddled around the squat black box, they would give heartfelt cheers as they learned from the BBC of any new German setback in North Africa or in Russia.

Germany still dominated most of Western Europe however, and Hitler's ability to exterminate all Jews, including *Mischlinge*, had increased hugely when three specialist killing centres came into full operation in late 1942. These were Treblinka, Sobibor and Belzec; all designed for wholesale mass murder. Hitler must have known he was going to lose, and he was now racing to kill as many Jews as he could before he was ousted.

On 26 March 1945, Ruth and Anna's sixth year at the clinic, disaster struck. Their uncle received a mere six-hours' warning from his Gestapo patrons that they were closing down the clinic. This was because of ever-increasing Allied bombing raids on the nearby VOMAG factories, which produced more than 20 per cent of the Reich's entire tank force. So the Gestapo men's schizophrenic children were in danger, but without them the clinic would soon become a death-trap for any fugitive Jew.

With Bippi, one of their uncle's Bund fugitives, Ruth and Anna and Anna's six-year-old son Derek escaped from the clinic during a bombing raid and, moving by night, headed for the comparative safety of the Czech border. But in mid-April, and less than two days from the border, they were stopped by a Nazi patrol who were hanging army deserters from trees.

Bippi escaped into the forest, but the two women were taken by passing SS guards to join a column of several hundred starving, lice-ridden, ex-Auschwitz Jewish women being forced to walk away from the advance of the Allied forces. The Americans were approaching fast from the west and the Soviets from the east. Literally hundreds of such death marches took place during the closing months of the war and involved nearly a million prisoners from the camps. Over 600,000 were killed at that time.

Only two days after Ruth, Anna and little Derek were forced to join the death march, Himmler sent out orders to the march commanders to release their prisoners. This was due to the fact that he had begun negotiations with the Allies. At that time the leading American forces were only fifteen kilometres away from Ruth's particular death march and they were closing rapidly on the nearby Czech border.

In June 2001, with a German friend and using 1945 maps, I retraced the route taken by Ruth's death-march group during the last month of the war.

As I learnt from the war records of the American army unit

who caught up with the death-march survivors after their captors had fled, some two dozen of the least feeble women were taken over the Czech border near Prachatice by three of the guards, in order to ensure that any passing SS patrol would identify the three of them as prison guards and not as deserters. On 2 May, with the American advance line a mere eight kilometres away, these three guards shot all but four of the women. Ruth, shot through the arm, pretended to be dead and survived the war.

After months of searching and with the help of a Canadian truck driver in the US Fifth Infantry Division, she eventually traced her son, who was in a Displaced Persons Camp. She married the Canadian and emigrated with him to Montreal. After months of research into the 1945 US war records, and the Auschwitz survivor accounts, and retracing the route of Ruth's death march, I wrote *The Secret Hunters*.

I later traced and interviewed the other three surviving women. Lola Lehrer, now Krispow, in Los Angeles; Jadzia Goldblum, now Kichler, in Toronto; and Luba Federman, now Dzialowski, in Tel Aviv.

In June 2001, with advice from the Austrian Nazi-hunter, Simon Wiesenthal, my German friend and I tracked down one of the worst death-march guards, Michael Weingärtner, to his home in the prosperous Austrian town of Wels, not far from Vienna and in an area much favoured by retired Nazis. The local government there was well known for its neo-Nazi views.

We confronted Weingärtner, but he showed no sign of remorse. 'I killed nobody,' he said, and slammed the door.

We tried to have the case against him reopened, but we failed. I know of no regime that caused so many humans to suffer so much fear for so long as did the Nazis, and many individuals like Weingärtner, who were an integral part of that terror machine, are still alive and still unpunished.

In the twenty-first century, right-wing European racial and religious fears switched from Jews to Muslims, and from the

Nazis and the Soviets to the Jihadists. This metamorphosis was encapsulated in 2011 in a Spanish newspaper article written by the popular journalist Sebastian Vilar Rodrigez under the heading, 'European Life Died in Auschwitz'. Rodrigez wrote:

> I walked down the street in Barcelona and suddenly discovered a terrible truth – Europe died in Auschwitz . . . We killed six million Jews and replaced them with twenty million Muslims. In Auschwitz we burned a culture, thought, creativity, talent. We destroyed the chosen people, truly chosen, because they produced great and wonderful people who changed the world. The contribution of this people is felt in all areas of life: science, art, international trade, and, above all, as the conscience of the world. These are the people we burned.
>
> And under the pretence of tolerance, and because we wanted to prove to ourselves that we were cured of the disease of racism, we opened our gates to twenty million Muslims. They have blown up our trains and turned our beautiful Spanish cities into the third world, drowning in filth and crime. Shut up in apartments they receive free from the government, they plan the murder and destruction of their naive hosts.
>
> What a terrible mistake was made by miserable Europe.

Rodrigez carefully, or pointedly, omits to mention the word Germans. The author of a 2015 book, *The Paradox of German Power*, and a Fellow of the German Marshall Fund, Hans Kundnani, wrote of Germany's post-war identity, 'This identity was in large part informed by a sense of responsibility and contrition for the Nazi past and the Holocaust.'

As the leading advocate of the idea of 'constitutional patriotism', the philosopher Jürgen Habermas once wrote, 'In Germany it was only after Auschwitz – and in a sense only because of the shock of this moral catastrophe – that democracy began to take root.'

This implied that there was no sense of national identity

available to Germany, other than one based on the lessons of 1945 . . . Moreover, from the creation of the Federal Republic onwards, the pride in their country that many citizens felt often came, not from the German constitution or from dealing with the Nazi past, but from economic success.

In his 2008 book on German myth, *Mythen der Deutschen*, the political scientist Herfried Münkler wrote that, 'against the background of the post-war *Wirtschaftswunder*, or economic miracle, the Mercedes badge had replaced the Iron Cross as a symbol of German national pride . . .'

While intellectuals identified with the idea of a post-national identity, or what has even been called 'a Holocaust identity', ordinary Germans instead took pride in the extraordinary economic success of the Federal Republic. The tension between these two versions of post-war identity was expressed most clearly in the statement allegedly made by the Bavarian Democrat leader, Franz Josef Strauss, who declared, 'a people that has achieved the economic success that we have has a right to hear nothing more about Auschwitz.'

To me this suggests a mild form of Holocaust denial. The vast pall of sheer terror and misery caused by Hitler's Nazis, who were voted into power by German citizens, should *never* be eclipsed by latter-day watchwords, such as *Vorsprung durch Technik*.

Prior to my studies of Auschwitz, prompted only by the necessity of research, I had no reason to nurse any attitude towards Germans and, indeed, have had a number of good German friends, but I now find myself reacting aggressively against even the faintest whiff of Holocaust denial. To the extent that I found myself inwardly grinning when I recently passed a van with a handwritten sign on its rear window (following the Volkswagen/Audi emissions scandal) which read: *VORSPRUNG DURCH FRAUD*.

That, I felt, should put Strauss in his place.

13

Conquering My Greatest Fear

Fear is essential. It is like a drug.

Luis Miguel Dominguin, Spanish bullfighter

When I was sixty, and for no particular reason, I had a massive heart attack whilst sitting on an aircraft about to take off from Bristol Airport. The cardiologist said later, 'Out of the hundred thousand people in the UK who have a cardiac arrest like you, the first and only warning they get is the attack itself, and only a very few are lucky enough to be near a defibrillator and someone who knows how to use it.'

After three days on a life-support machine and with various attempts made to shock my heart into ticking on its own followed by a double-bypass operation, I woke up to find Ginny beside my hospital bed. She had sat by my side day and night since the attack. We managed to kiss despite the various nose and mouth tubes.

Sixteen weeks later, with my habitual polar-expedition partner, Dr Mike Stroud, I ran seven marathons on seven continents in seven consecutive days. Being a 'world first', this made a great deal of money for our charity, the British Heart Foundation, but the day I returned home to Exmoor Ginny was suffering severe pains in her stomach. She had aggressive cancer and died three months later. For some time afterwards my life was hell, pointless and miserable. To escape my state of self-pity, I determined to shock myself back to life by scaring myself to death.

I would try to confront my greatest fear, which was that of falling into a void, a phobia I had suffered from since childhood. There are, I have learned, several names for the condition, including acrophobia, altophobia, hypsiphobia or, more commonly, vertigo.

When parachuting in my army days, I had disobeyed the instructor's severe warnings with regard to the dangers of closing one's eyes when leaving the aircraft. Doing that, he had stressed, has in the past led to many accidents when two or more jumpers collided just after their chutes deployed.

Back at school I had enjoyed the excitement of scaling the tallest college spires by night, knowing that I could never have done so by day, when I could see the drop below. A South African friend, Sibusisu Vilani, had invited me to climb Everest with him a year before Ginny's death, and I had turned him down due to my vertigo problem. But now I told him that I was keen to go with him, and he told me how to join the Everest guiding company (not their commercial title) who would organise our summit attempt.

Because of my age, cardiac history and, due to previous frostbite, seriously short finger stubs on one hand, the guiding company said that I should complete an Alpine fortnight and a ten-day volcano-scaling course in Ecuador before they would agree to accept me as Sibu's climbing companion on the Tibetan side of Everest.

So I went off to train in the Alps with the sole aim of scaling Everest in order to confront, and hopefully vanquish, my vertigo phobia. This new goal did help haul me out of my personal morass of misery by introducing me to another emotion hitherto absent from my life, as it is from the lives of the majority of people: that of fear. I studied the statistics of climbing on Everest, and I found them to be distinctly off-putting. Here are a couple:

- Everest, at 29,029 feet, has a so-called Death Zone, where the oxygen level falls off significantly at 26,000 feet.

- By 2015, there had been some 12,000 registered summit wannabes, of whom 4,000 failed to summit and 250 died.

Even the greatest climbers can experience fear. Stephen Venables was a friend of mine, whom I rated as one of Britain's most accomplished mountaineers; he had climbed Everest by horrific routes and had broken both his legs after long, bouncing falls from remote cliff faces, and still fought against his personal fears before big climbs. He admitted to me that, despite his many vertical successes, he still retained a deep fear of death by falling. Stephen helped me up various ascents, including a sea stack in the Orkneys called the Old Man of Hoy, and on various parts of the Eiger in Switzerland. Because he sympathised with my obvious nervousness, he was a great help in soothing it.

There were no memorable scares in the Alps and the guide gave the company boss a satisfactory report of my fitness for the follow-up Ecuador course. The local guide Pepé Landazuro took me up to the 19,000-foot (5,897 metres) summit of Cotopaxi, a dormant volcano that for many years was thought to be the second-highest mountain in the world.

'Tomorrow,' Pepé told me, 'I will take you south to Chimborazo, the big one.' If I survived Chimborazo in terms of my fitness at altitude, I would be allowed to sign up for Everest, since Chimborazo's summit is only 9,000 feet lower than Everest's.

Chimborazo sits about halfway between Cotopaxi and the spectacular volcanic ice-covered cone of Sangay. On reaching Chimborazo's summit, I listened to Pepé's stories of climbing disasters, of his fellow climbers sizzled by lightning strikes or struck by falling rocks. I could see the outline of Sangay some forty miles to the south and I thought of an old friend, Richard Snailham, who had nearly died there.

Richard was a member of a 1976 British Army expedition to study volcanic behaviour patterns and collect rock samples from (hopefully dormant) Andean volcanoes. With five others, Richard was at 16,000 feet (4,800 metres) and not far from Sangay's summit crater when the worst happened with terrifying consequences. As described by Richard, there was:

> a deafening crack and roar somewhere just above and slightly to the left of us. For five or six seconds the sky reverberated and a thunderous din prevailed . . . An avalanche of black rocks and boulders, some as big as dustbins, rained down from the luridly lit sky, rocketing down the icy slopes towards us, through us and over us.

The six men ran, fell and slid down the mountainside, experiencing raw panic for the first time in their lives. Richard's right arm, held over his head for protection, was smashed by a rock. All the men tumbled over 2,000 feet before reaching a ledge. All were badly hurt and lay bruised and bloodied, two of them with severe head wounds.

Weeks later in an Ecuadorean hospital, Richard noted down his memory of the realisation that he had survived the initial disaster with only a broken arm:

> As I looked almost dispassionately at the battered bodies of my friends lying on the snow, I felt only a detachment, a deadness, a matter-of-fact acceptance. I suppose this was partly the result of shock: the full realisation of what had happened was to be borne in on me later.

Four of the men were eventually rescued, but two died slowly of their injuries on the slopes of Sangay.

Pepé sent a favourable report, in terms of my altitude performance, back to the UK, so, early in 2005, I arrived with Sibu at the Everest base camp in Tibet confident that, if I could climb the highest mountain in the world, I would gain sufficient self-confidence to lose all fear of lesser heights.

Being over sixty, I had to show proof of insurance to the guide company. The cardiologist who had fixed my double bypass back in 2003 warned me to keep my heart rate low at all times, and an expert lung specialist diagnosed that the oxygen flow in my airways was 80 per cent of what it should be at my age. This, he warned me, would be an important limiting factor in my ability to carry on at 7,000 metres and above.

Two weeks before arriving in Tibet and a year after Ginny's death I had married Louise, a lovely lady I had met at a lecture in Chester, and we honeymooned at the Everest Base Camp. One night in our tent, Louise dreamed of me falling somewhere high on the mountain 'due to a problem with a rope'. I have never forgotten this and have taken great care with any and all ropes thereafter.

At the Tibetan base camp many of us suffered appetite loss, lethargy and severe headaches, so one of the other summit hopefuls, Dr Fred Ziel, gave us Diamox tablets, an altitude-sickness prevention drug. Fred, on a previous Everest attempt, had been forced back with severely frostbitten fingers and nose.

We spent two weeks in the base camp acclimatising at 5,200 metres (17,000 feet) and keeping fit by trudging up and down local slopes many times. We knew that our chances of summiting were largely dependent on the weather's behaviour during the short seasonal weather window in May. Some years there is no suitable weather and nobody summits, although there are always those who stupidly try in bad weather and often die as a result. The annual death rate at that time was one in every ten attempts.

An extremely fit Irish friend of mine, who was in a different travel group but camped nearby, headed upwards to the Advance Base Camp prior to our group doing so. He arrived back a day later with a Sherpa holding him steady on either side. At a certain height the blood vessels behind his retinas had burst. He was guided back off the mountain at once to avoid permanent blindness. I began to feel distinctly apprehensive.

When it was the turn of our group to climb to the Advance Base Camp, I discovered that I suffered from an ailment called

Cheyne–Stokes which prevented me from sleeping, or even dozing, from about 17,000 feet. Above that height I could only sleep when attached to an oxygen bottle.

Two months after my arrival in Tibet and poised for the final ascent, I finally found myself in the so-called Death Camp at over 28,000 feet. During the past month five climbers on our route had died. There was a frozen body, that of an Italian climber, in a nearby tent as we camped for the final push. Sibu left in our faster group, which did reach the summit. On his way back down he ran out of oxygen and became hypoxic. For some hours he was reported on our walkie-talkie system as missing. Then a Sherpa found him behind a rock mumbling to a 'resting' climber (who turned out to be a dead Canadian).

At 10 p.m. with my Sherpa I switched on my head lamp and, fixing my ascendeur (ascender clamp) to the main ascent rope, set out up a steep ice slope knowing that the summit was but eight hours distant and with a fixed rope all the way.

Quite suddenly I began to breathe heavily, despite many rest-halts hanging off the rope. Some forty minutes of ascent after setting out, a general feeling of disorientation, lung constriction and alarming dizziness led to a stabbing pain in my chest around the area where the metal wire (that had held my ribcage together since my bypass operation) led from my navel to my neck.

I felt a surge of panic in the sudden awareness that I was having another heart attack, this time with no nearby defibrillator and a long drop below my dangling boots. For a few seconds a mind-numbing fear and feeling of utter impotence grabbed me, for there seemed to be nothing I could do but hang there in the freezing darkness and wait for death. Then I remembered the glyceryl trinitrate (GTN) tablets that my wife had made me carry, despite my lifelong aversion to all pills other than painkillers. With my free hand, the one without frost-bitten fingers, I managed, despite my oxygen mask and backpack straps, to locate the little bottle of GTN pills and crammed a handful down my throat.

I was lucky to survive. That same night at the same height on the other (Nepal) side of Everest, an accomplished Scottish climber, forty-nine-year-old Robert Milne, died of a heart attack and was buried under the snow on a ledge. I assume that he had no GTN pills.

On Easter Day 2006 my daughter Elizabeth gave her first yell. Like her mother Louise, she was blonde and beautiful.

Despite my failure on Everest, our charity, Marie Curie, raised £2 million on the back of the attempt. They said that they could make the same again if I could only reach the summit, so I decided to try again at some point.

I had not achieved my main aim in attempting Everest, which was to confront and beat my vertigo phobia. On the route up Everest to the Death Camp all the way to my turn-back point I had noticed no great terrifying drops anywhere, merely white slopes rolling away with no suggestion of a beckoning void. The mountain had clearly failed to provide any realistic test to confront my fears.

One of the guides on my Alpine course had been Kenton Cool, and he had climbed Everest many times. I had mentioned to him my desire to fight vertigo and he had commented at the time that Everest was not, in his opinion, the most sensible mountain to use to rid myself of a fear of heights; firstly because of its lack of dizzy drops on the standard Nepali ascent route, and secondly because it cost so much in time and effort to get to the Himalayas. 'Why not,' he suggested, 'check out your fears in the nearby Alps? I could teach you to rock-climb on vertical walls there.'

Contemplating Kenton's suggestion, I read again the great book *Mountains of the Mind* by the talented Scots author and avid mountaineer Robert Macfarlane. From it I learned that, although the Alps were a mere nothing in altitude when compared with Everest and the Himalayas, they deserved cautious respect. Even the hills of Scotland, given bad weather, can kill. And as I write this in the spring of 2016, BBC Radio 4 tells me that 'a couple of young, but highly accomplished, climbers have been found dead on Ben Nevis over the weekend.'

Every year, Macfarlane noted, hundreds of people die on the world's mountains and many more thousands are injured. Mont Blanc has killed over 1,000 people, the Matterhorn 500 and, just in 1985, nearly 200 died in the Swiss Alps alone.

By 2003, when Macfarlane wrote about the mountains, his ardour had clearly dimmed a touch. He wrote, 'I'm scared more easily, too; my fear threshold has been sharply lowered. That fizzing, nauseous, faintly erotic feeling of real terror grips me more quickly these days. Edges that five years ago I would happily have walked along, I now keep my distance from.'

So, after learning the ropes on small climbs like the Old Man of Hoy in the Orkneys, the Dent de Géant (the Giant's Tooth) in Chamonix and numerous frozen waterfalls in Italy, I finally followed Kenton and his expert climbing partner of many years, Ian Parnell, to the base of a 'proper Alpine climb' known to Germans as the Mordwand or Murder Wall, the north face of the Eiger above the Swiss village of Grindelwald.

Not long before arriving in the village to await the prediction of a four-day window of good weather, I made the bad mistake of reading a book by the famous Austrian climber, Heinrich Harrer who, in 1938, achieved the first-ever ascent of the Mordwand.

His book *The White Spider* detailed the deaths of many of the fifty or so highly capable international climbers who had died on the face of the wall. He wrote:

> Any climber who dares to tackle the North Face must have examined and proved himself a hundred times in advance. And how about a climb of the North Face as a counterbalance to hysteria? An hysteric, an unstable character, would go to pieces at the very sight of the Wall, just as surely as any mask would fall away in the face of this menacing bastion of rock and ice.

Since, in terms of rock-climbing up walls, I was clearly what Harrer would classify as an 'hysteric', this was not good news. So I turned to the opinions of more modern famous climbers.

Joe Simpson of *Touching the Void* fame described the Wall as, 'The seminal mountain, a metaphorical mountain that represented everything that defines mountaineering – a route I had dreamed of climbing my entire adult life.'

Jon Krakauer, the most famous of American mountaineering journalists, wrote of the Wall:

> The trickiest moves on any climb are the mental ones, the psychological gymnastics that keep terror in check, and the Eiger's grim aura is intimidating enough to rattle anyone's poise . . . The names of the landmarks on the face . . . are household words among both active and armchair Alpinists from Tokyo to Buenos Aires; the very mention of these places is enough to make any climber's hands turn clammy. The rockfalls and avalanches that rain continuously down the Nordwand are legendary . . . Needless to say, all this makes the Wall one of the most coveted climbs in the world.

For my particular quest, to find a vertigo-confrontation wall, the Mordwand did indeed sound ideal, and Marie Curie fixed for the *Sunday Times* and ITN to cover the climb in order to raise £2 million to go towards the training of their nurses.

I decided to read Joe Simpson's books. In 2000 Simpson and his climbing partner were some way up the Wall and having a snack on a ledge, when two climbers (whom they'd met the day before in Grindelwald and who had set out before them) fell off the face directly above their ledge and dropped past them.

Simpson wrote, 'I thought of their endless, frictionless fall, numbed in their last minutes of consciousness by the full enormity of what was happening . . . I stared down thinking of them lying there tangled in their ropes, side by side. We didn't hear them go. They didn't scream.'

I spent eighteen anxious days in Grindelwald at all times aware of the great dark 8,000-feet-high Mordwand looming over the village. At last, on the nineteenth day, a long enough weather window was forecast and we caught a train to the foot of the Eiger.

I kissed my wife Louise and baby daughter Elizabeth goodbye and followed Ian and Kenton to the hostel. I could not sleep on that last night for I was extremely apprehensive. I remembered countless similar sleepless nights before big polar challenges, but those fears were dulled by an inner confidence born of experience. This was different, for I feared my own inadequacies and being revealed as a coward. Would the vertigo that lurked, buried deep in my karma, erupt at some horribly exposed place up there? To calm my worries I read again Joe Simpson's assurance that a fall to your death is not necessarily riven with terror.

He recalled his exact feelings as he had once fallen to his apparently certain death:

> Deprived of the ability to imagine the future you are fearless; suddenly there is nothing to be scared about. You have no time to ponder on death's significance . . . In the cataclysmic violence of the accident you lose not only the future but the past as well. You lose all possible reasons for fear . . . Time is frozen for you into the present events and sensations . . . I'm crashing. I'm falling fast. I'm about to die. This is it. In truth you have far too much on your mind for such frivolous luxuries as fear.

Unfortunately, I could not follow the rationale of this philosophy. To me, such a fall was highly likely to give me red-raw moments of ultimate terror. And, desperate to avoid such a nightmare, I might well find myself unable to move on some slippery cliff face, simply frozen with fear and thereby risking the lives of Kenton and Ian. Never mind the ridicule, bearing in mind that our every move would be reported for the *Sunday Times* and filmed by the telescopic lenses of ITN.

We set out in pitch darkness with Kenton leading. Ian recorded, 'For Ran, although he hid it well, Everest had been a failure. This time round we were to attempt the Eiger North Face and, while we didn't have the barrier of altitude, to my mind this was a much tougher challenge.'

Looking up at the towering wall to the starlit sky above, I felt a powerful desire to withdraw as Kenton bade me fix my crampons. I was, I realised, already shaking with fear. Only the greater fear of ridicule kept me silent.

The first 2,000 feet of the climb provided the landing area for the dozens of bodies that had fallen from various parts of the Wall above. We slept the first night on a tiny ledge known as the Swallows Nest, and the second night on another named Death Bivouac, where in 1935 four of the world's top climbers had found two frozen bodies not long before they too died in an attempt to traverse to the porthole drilled in the face of the mountain by railway engineers. One of the four fell and dropped free to the valley below, one was strangled by the rope, a third froze to death, and the youngest, a top German climber, dangled for twenty-four hours a mere 100 metres above the tunnel porthole but just out of reach of rescue, until he also froze to death.

When Heinrich Harrer made the first successful ascent he followed the same route as that located by the four dead men, known as the Hinterstoisser Traverse, and he wrote of it, 'The rocks across which we now had to traverse were almost vertical, plunging away into thin air.'

The world-famous climber Walter Bonatti wrote of the Wall in the 1960s, 'The aura of fatality and blood that hangs over this killer mountain . . .'

On our third day on the Wall the ITV film crew called Kenton with the good news (from the point of view of their movie content) that they had filmed an avalanche of rock and ice roaring down a dramatic feature known as the Ice Hose, below which they had filmed us ascending the previous day.

As we inched our way up the Second Ice Field, Kenton watched an ice axe whistle by him on its way down the face. He failed subsequently to identify its owner. I dreaded the thought of losing one of my two axes at any point on this mountain.

Late in the evening of the third day I had a bad time mentally on a rock section known as The Ramp. Ian told me that Adolf Mayr, an Austrian climber with a brilliant repertoire of ultra-severe Alpine ascents, had negotiated the earlier parts of The Ramp but, on the traverse of a slippery gulley, he missed a foothold and fell 4,000 feet.

Ian climbed ahead of me and wrote of The Ramp, 'There is no ice which would give good purchase for the axes, it's only rock. It's very steep in places and it's also overhanging. That pushes you out and, with the rucksack, all the weight is on your arms.'

On the morning of the fourth day I woke with a dry mouth knowing that the Traverse of the Gods, my greatest fear, lay immediately ahead, and I had made the mistake of reading Joe Simpson's professional description of it:

> For four hundred feet the points of protection, weak, damaged pitons, battered into shattered downwards-sloping cracks, are marginal to say the least. Most climbers would prefer not to weight such pitons statically, let alone to fall on them . . . and the drop beneath the climber's feet is 5,000 feet of clear air . . . The hardest climbing comes right at the end of the traverse around a protruding prow of rock and close to the edge of the White Spider.

In the valley below, the famous British climber and my friend, Stephen Venables, reporting for the *Sunday Times* wrote, 'Ran had to tread with steel points on snow, ice and bare rock. Terrified of damaging the shortened fingers of his left hand, he kept his mitts on, gripping as best he could. He knew that if he fell, he would go for a huge swing over the void before the rope held him.'

As I edged out onto the wall, I found the rock to be brittle and flaking and, in my mind, the piton screws along the traverse were highly unlikely to hold me if I fell. I envisaged my falling weight tearing away the pitons, along with Ian and Kenton, who were attached to them.

The Irish climber, Paul Harrington, wrote, 'There were no positive handholds . . . it was a psychological passage.'

We were glued to the sheer wall merely by our fingertips and booted toes like flies on the side of a skyscraper's window.

Ian, a rock-climber of many years' experience and with a record of hairy first ascents around the world, wrote, 'It's dramatic, nervy climbing for experienced climbers but, for someone like Ran who suffers from vertigo, it can easily become a complete nightmare. The rock here is loose, covered in verglas in winter and frighteningly exposed. In fact, at one point your heels overhang the whole drop of the Wall to the snows of Kleine Scheidegg below.'

It was, in fact, at that point that I lost my nerve and felt more raw fear than at any time in my life. Ian, perched precariously behind me, watched me go to pieces and lose my cool with Kenton who, himself in a highly tricky position, reacted angrily and had what Ian described as a 'kentrum'.

Ian recorded, 'The issue seemed to be that, caught out of rope, Kenton had been forced to take a belay on two pathetic rotting bits of tat. Ran, swinging round to the second half of the traverse, felt the full impact of the sickening exposure and suffered an attack of the vertigo he had so far successfully kept at bay. Reeling in their worlds, a frank exchange of views followed.'

Somehow I reached the end of the Traverse and followed Kenton up the White Spider, the Fly and the notorious Exit Cracks, where the Italian climber Longhi fell 100 feet onto a ledge on which, after waiting five days for rescue, he died. His body dangled from his rope for the next two years, ogled by telescope tourists from their Grindelwald hotels.

On the final steep snow face between the Cracks and the

summit ridge, I made a bad mistake with the rope fixture to Ian, who was then leading. Ian, unseen above me, slipped and slid and picked up speed towards the cliff edge. In the nick of time Kenton, beside me, spotted my error and in an instant correctly anchored Ian's rope.

Ian recorded, 'Kenton luckily heard my screams, yelled at Ran and, thankfully, my downwards journey was brought to an abrupt halt.'

We spent the night in a snow hole only 300 metres below the summit, and I remembered that, only two years before and again with Ian, I had camped a mere 400 metres below Everest's summit ridge, but I never made it to the top.

At 10 a.m. on the fifth day of our climb we reached the summit, and Kenton pointed to the south where evil-looking dark-grey clouds eclipsed the horizon. They were rushing straight towards the Eiger.

Marie Curie raised over £2 million from our ascent, but I swore never to rock-climb again.

I knew that I had failed to shake off the curse of vertigo, but nonetheless the Eiger experience made me realise that routes like the standard Everest ascent in Nepal were mostly exposure-free. So, in 2008, I returned to Everest with Kenton.

Due to passing a number of dead bodies above the Death Zone and through sheer physical exhaustion, I turned back within three hours of the summit. In 2009 I finally reached the top, guided by Tundu Sherpa, and raised our charity total for Marie Curie to £6.3 million.

In 2015, the exact same spot where my tent had been pitched in the Everest Base Camp in both 2008 and 2009 was struck by a great avalanche caused by the Kathmandu earthquake. Many tourists and Sherpas were wiped out in Base Camp that day.

But Everest, in terms of difficulty and danger, is a mere pussycat compared to some of its neighbouring giants, the 'Eiger' of which, in terms of a fearsome reputation as a killer, is known simply as K2. I had done a bit of climbing to try to get rid of my irrational fear of heights, but there is no way that I would climb horrific rock or ice faces *for pleasure*. Yet there is a whole world of what are known as adrenalin sports in which practitioners are addicted to scaring themselves silly again and again.

Reading *Mountains of the Mind* by Robert Macfarlane, I found that some two-and-a-half centuries ago it was realised that risk-taking could bring its own reward through the sense of physical exhilaration, which we now know comes from the effects of adrenalin. Macfarlane quotes a famous English playwright in the 1680s who, having enjoyed a guided tour in the Alps, wrote to a friend as follows:

> We walk'd upon the very brink, in a literal sense, of Destruction; one Stumble, and both Life and Carcass had been at once destroy'd. The sense of all this produc'd different motions in me, viz., a delightful Horrour, a terrible Joy, and at the same time, that I was infinitely pleas'd, I trembled.

Macfarlane explained why mountain climbing can be so addictive. 'Hope, fear – this is the fundamental rhythm of mountaineering. Life, it frequently seems in the mountains, is more intensely lived the closer one gets to its extinction: we never feel so alive as when we have nearly died.'

The famous Spanish bullfighter, Luis Miguel Dominguin, described it well in 1971: 'Fear is essential. It is like a drug. Fear makes you think you will die. For that reason each minute has intensity. It is a kind of purification.'

Despite Macfarlane's favourable comments on the enjoyment to be had from fear, I came away from his book determined to go nowhere near the appalling hazards of K2.

In August 2008, halfway between my two visits to the Nepalese side of Everest, a group of experienced mountaineers set out to scale K2. I thank God I was not with them.

K2, astride the Pakistan–China border, is 800 feet shorter than Everest, but infinitely more hazardous to climb, even by the so-called 'standard' route. The highest camp, from which the summit is usually attempted, is known as Camp Four and it is situated at about 26,000 feet, some 2,000 feet from the summit.

On that August day a number of climbers from eight separate teams and from different countries all tried to summit K2, having set out more or less together. The month of August is considered to be the best weather season for K2, just as May is best for Everest some 550 miles to the south. But K2's ascent route is much steeper and more exposed to avalanche danger than Everest's, and, as a result, serious mountaineers prize the bagging of K2 far higher than that of Everest.

By 2008 over 3,000 people had stood atop Everest, compared to only 278 on K2. Sixty-six climbers had been killed scaling K2, most of them due to various hazards existing *above* Camp Four.

The key to summiting K2 safely is to leave Camp Four very early in the morning using fixed ropes pre-positioned by your Sherpas during the previous hours (or, ideally, days), in order to reach the summit by about midday, so that you have a good chance of returning to Camp Four before dark.

When the various groups woke up that August morning in 2008 the weather was fine, though very cold, but due to a mix-up, some of the ropes above Camp Four were yet to be fixed. This caused a short but fatal delay.

The biggest and slowest team was that of the South Koreans, fifteen in number. Other teams came from France, America, Serbia, Norway, Holland and Italy, plus a solo Basque climber. All were well aware of K2's death toll, including thirteen from avalanches in 1986, and in 1995 seven killed in a single storm.

From Camp Four there is a long ridgeline known as the Shoulder, which leads to a steep ascent up a gully known as the Bottleneck. This is overshadowed by a crumbling serac, or hanging glacier, that often cracks due to changing temperatures and sends catastrophic avalanches down the gulleys, which can kill any climbers there at the time.

Two American climbers noted by 10.30 a.m. that morning that, largely due to the slow rope-laying of the large South Korean group upfront, *all* the climbers would be lucky to reach the summit by 3 p.m. which, in their opinion, would lead to a lethal descent in the dark. So, very sensibly, they and some others heeded their growing fears and turned back down to Camp Four. A total of twenty-seven climbers carried on, determined to reach the summit. Out ahead of all the rest, including the slow South Koreans, was the solo Basque climber, Alberto Zerain.

Once above the Death Zone at around 25,000 feet most people need oxygen, and many climbers have died due to hypoxia – oxygen starvation – when their oxygen supply runs out because of some delay or other.

Three Serbians, fearful of their rapidly depleting oxygen supplies, tried to overtake the slow climbers fixed to the main rope, a dangerous manoeuvre. One of them, Dren Mandic, became tangled with a well-known Norwegian climber, Cecilie Skog, and fell 200 feet to his death. His two colleagues turned back at that point.

A Swede and a Pakistani porter named Jehan Baig agreed to help the two Serbs drag the body of their dead colleague back down to Base Camp. But Baig himself, increasingly hypoxic, lost his senses and ended up sliding away over a precipice to his death.

From then on things went from bad to worse. Apart from Zerain, who reached the summit in good time to return to Camp Four in daylight, all the others summited dangerously late. In fact, an Italian and a Dutchman did not leave the summit until after dark.

Over the next few hours the visibility and conditions on the mountain worsened considerably and a series of sudden avalanches, icefalls and roping accidents swept several more climbers and porters to their deaths as they tried to descend in the darkness.

Back at Camp Four, as the lone survivors limped back there, the two Americans did their best to treat their injuries and frost-bite. Each new explosive echo from above caused them to flinch, for they were increasingly apprehensive of the mounting death toll.

Only two days after twenty-seven climbers had set out hopefully from Camp Four, eleven of them were dead and their supporters in Base Camp were telephoning their loved ones with the news of their deaths.

K2, like the Eiger, had lived up to its reputation as a mountain to be feared.

14

Ruling by Fear

I was sweating with fear. My mouth was dry.

John Peters

For several years back in the 1980s and '90s I had hoped to secure the so-called Grand Slam. Back in George Mallory's day, Mount Everest was described within the mountaineering community as the Third Pole, and the coveted Grand Slam involved reaching all three 'Poles'. I was beaten to this achievement by the Norwegian Erling Kagge, but the next and considerably more difficult challenge, which became the next Grand Slam, was to cross both of the world's ice caps via their respective Poles and scale Everest. At the time there were three individuals in the world who had completed the crossing of the ice caps, and the other two, apart from me, were Børge Ousland from Norway and Alain Hubert from Belgium. I was lucky to finally succeed on Everest before either of the other two, and thus to hold the Grand Slam for Britain.

After this climbing interlude I agreed to participate in a television documentary suggested by BBC Wales, which would hopefully produce enough income to help Louise and me with the Arab horse business she was planning.

The documentary was titled *Top Dogs* and it involved three individuals, all in their late sixties, who specialised in different professions, teaching each other their 'trades'. Robin Knox-Johnston, Britain's most famous single-handed sailor, took John

Simpson, the BBC war correspondent, and me around Cape Horn in his yacht to teach us rough-sea sailing. I then took Robin and John manhaul-sledging in the Canadian Arctic, and John taught Robin and me how to be a war correspondent in war-torn Afghanistan.

For this latter episode we interviewed President Karzai and various ambassadors and generals and travelled with armed guards through high-danger zones between Kabul and the Khyber Pass.

One night on a camp bed under a starry sky and surrounded by Afghan police machine guns, we looked down on the Tora Bora caves, one-time home of Osama bin Laden and still often haunted by Taliban groups.

On my return home, and needing further funds for our horse business, I was contracted to complete an article for a South African magazine on successful terror regimes of the past century. Reading it now, I would still rate Hitler and the Nazis at the top of my power-by-terror list, but Stalin comes a close runner-up. Hitler luckily had no nuclear weapons at his disposal unlike Stalin and his successors, who did. Throughout my lifetime the result of this has meant that there has always been the constant background fear of the potential obliteration of the human species. I well remember, aged thirteen in Sussex, digging a nuclear-fallout shelter into the side of a steep slope in the local wood. Six other lads from our village helped with the digging. It may well still be there.

When truly evil individuals reach positions of unassailable dictatorship, they can and do cause misery and terror to millions. On top of this, the human tendency, which can hardly be blamed on Darwinian theories, to fear and to wish to crush others who are racially, religiously or ideologically different, has killed tens of millions in the last century alone.

Stalin ruled through his Apparatus of Terror operated by his Secret Service, the NKVD, the predecessor of the KGB, and his first purges date back to around 1930. These were aimed at the extermination or deportation of all *kulaks* (farm owners and entrepreneurs who opposed his policies of collectivisation) and caused severe famine, especially in the Ukraine.

In the summer of 1932 Stalin became aware that opposition to his policies was growing. Some party members were publicly criticising him and calling for the readmission of Leon Trotsky to the party. When the issue was discussed at the Politburo, Stalin demanded that the critics should be arrested and executed. Sergey Kirov, Stalin's intended successor, who up to this time had been a staunch Stalinist, argued against this policy. When the vote was taken, the majority of the Politburo supported Kirov against Stalin.

Stalin no doubt began to wonder if Kirov was willing to wait for his mentor to die before becoming leader of the party. He was particularly concerned by Kirov's willingness to argue with him in public. So that December he had Kirov assassinated and then he accused the 'party's enemies' of killing Kirov. Hundreds of people were executed without trial.

From the 1917 October Revolution onward, Lenin had used repression against perceived enemies of the Bolsheviks as a systematic method of instilling fear and facilitating social control, especially during the campaign commonly referred to as the Red Terror. This policy continued and intensified under Stalin. A distinctive feature of the Great Purge was that, for the first time, members of the ruling party were included on a massive scale as victims of the repression.

In the years 1936–8 three very large Moscow trials of former Communist Party leaders were held, in which they were accused of conspiring with fascist and capitalist powers to assassinate Stalin and other Soviet leaders and to dismember the Soviet Union and restore capitalism. These trials were highly publicised and extensively covered in the outside world, where people were mesmerised by the spectacle of Lenin's closest associates confessing to the most outrageous crimes and begging for death sentences.

It is now known that the confessions were given only after great psychological pressure and torture had been applied to the defendants. From the accounts of a former OGPU officer, Alexander Orlov, and others, the methods used to extract these confessions included repeated beatings, simulated drownings, making prisoners stand or go without sleep for days on end, and threats to arrest and execute the prisoners' families. After months of interrogation and torture, the defendants were driven to despair and exhaustion.

Eventually almost all of the Bolsheviks who had played prominent roles during the Russian Revolution of 1917, or were in Lenin's Soviet government afterwards, were executed. Of the six members of the original Politburo during the 1917 October Revolution who lived until the Great Purge, Stalin himself was the only one who remained in the Soviet Union alive. Four of the other five were executed. The fifth, Leon Trotsky, went into exile in Mexico after being expelled from the party. Even previously sympathetic observers, who had stomached the earlier trials, found it hard to swallow these new allegations as they became ever more absurd, and the purge expanded to include almost every living Old Bolshevik leader, except Stalin.

It was at this time that Stalin personally intervened to speed up the whole process, and he replaced his security boss Yagoda with Nikolai Yezhov, who quickly arranged the arrest of all the leading political figures in the Soviet Union who were critical of Stalin.

According to the declassified Soviet archives, during 1937 and 1938 the NKVD detained 1,548,366 persons, of whom 681,692 were shot – an average of 1,000 executions a day. The Kulak Operation was the largest single campaign of repression, with 669,929 people arrested and 376,202 executed, more than half the total of known executions.

In the period of the Yezhov terror, when the mass arrests came in waves of varying intensity, there must have been times when there was no more room in the jails, and to those still free it looked as though the highest wave had passed and the terror was abating. After each show trial people sighed, 'Well, it's all over at last.'

Wild inventions and monstrous accusations had become an end in themselves, and officials of the secret police applied all their ingenuity to them, as though revelling in the total arbitrariness of their power.

The principles and aims of mass terror have nothing in common with ordinary police work or with security. The only purpose of terror is intimidation. To plunge the whole country into a state of chronic fear, the number of victims must be raised to astronomical levels, and on every floor of every building there must always be several apartments from which the tenants have suddenly been taken away, and this will cause the remaining inhabitants to be model citizens for the rest of their lives. This was true for every street and every city through which the broom had swept. One essential rule for those who rule by terror is not to overlook the new generations growing up without faith in their elders, and so to keep on repeating the executions in a systematic fashion.

In 1937 the Commander-in-Chief of the Red Army and seven leading generals were shot. In 1938–9 all the admirals and half the army's officers were executed or imprisoned. In the same period thousands of religious leaders were imprisoned and churches closed. The purges affected not only those who openly opposed Stalin, but ordinary people as well. During Stalin's rule of the country over 20 million people were sent to labour camps, where nearly half of them died.

The following categories were systematically tracked down: 'ex-kulaks', who were previously deported to 'special settlements' in inhospitable parts of the country, such as Siberia, Urals, Kazakhstan and the Far North, members of the clergy, persons deprived of voting rights, former members of non-Bolshevik parties, ordinary criminals like thieves who were known to the police, and various other 'socially harmful elements'. However, many were also arrested at random in police sweeps or as a result of denunciations, or simply because they happened to be relatives, friends or just acquaintances of people already arrested. Many railwaymen, workers, peasants and engineers were arrested in the course of the Kulak Operation just because they had the misfortune to be working in, or near, important strategic factories, railways or building sites.

At the time when the NKVD was killing members of national minorities, many of its leading officers were themselves members of such minorities. In 1937 and 1938 NKVD officers, many of whom were of Jewish, Latvian, Polish or German nationality, were implementing policies of national killing that exceeded anything that Hitler and his SS had as yet attempted. Then in the summer of 1938 Yezhov was relieved of his post as head of the NKVD, and he was eventually tried and executed.

As an ex-prisoner himself, Stalin knew very well that jails and places of exile were the 'universities' of the revolutionaries. Events had taught him to take no risks with those already incarcerated. All political discussion and activity in prisons and places of exile was mercilessly suppressed; and prisoners were, by privation and hard labour, reduced to such a miserable, animal-like existence that they were incapable of the normal processes of thinking and of formulating views.

With the start of the Second World War, Stalin's terror transformed into the extermination of war prisoners and 'traitors'. The largest of several simultaneous executions of prisoners of war – the infamous Katyn massacre – took place in April and May 1940 in Smolensk region. It was a mass execution of Polish nationals, which was prompted by Lavrentiy Beria's proposal to execute all members of the Polish Officer Corps. This official document was approved and signed by the Soviet Politburo, including its leader, Joseph Stalin. The number of victims of Katyn is estimated at about 22,000. Of the total killed, about 8,000 were officers taken prisoner during the 1939 Soviet invasion of Poland, another 6,000 were police officers, with the rest being Polish intelligentsia arrested for allegedly being 'intelligence agents, gendarmes, landowners, saboteurs, factory owners, lawyers and priests'.

Torture was commonly used to extract 'confessions'. An example of typical proceedings was described in a letter from prison written by theatre director Vsevolod Meyerhold before he was shot in 1940:

> The investigators began to use force on me, a sick sixty-five-year-old man. I was made to lie face down and was beaten on the soles of my feet and my spine with a rubber strap . . . For the next few days when those parts of my legs were covered with extensive internal haemorrhaging, they again beat the red-blue-and-yellow bruises with the strap, and the pain was so intense that it felt as if boiling water was being poured on these sensitive areas. I howled and wept from the pain. I incriminated myself in the hope that by telling them lies I could end the ordeal. When, after eighteen hours of interrogation, I lay down on the cot and fell asleep, knowing I had to go back in an hour's time for more, I was woken up by my own groaning and because I was jerking about like a patient in the last stages of typhoid fever.

Following the collapse of the Soviet Union, numerous mass graves filled with executed victims of the terror were discovered. Some, such as the killing fields at Kurapaty near Minsk, and Bykivnia near Kiev, contained up to 200,000 corpses.

Given the lack of complete data, it is difficult to establish the total loss of life brought about by the Stalinist terror. An average estimate is that in the Soviet Union as a whole, about 500,000 were executed in the period 1937–9, and somewhere between 3 million and 12 million were sent to labour camps.

The Terror finally burnt itself out late in 1938, and at the Party Congress in March of the following year Stalin announced the end of the era of mass purges. But the campaign had caused lasting devastation. The exact number may never be known, but most historians estimate that *millions* of Russians were either executed or shipped off to the dreaded Siberian gulags in the years 1936–8. The Soviet psyche itself suffered damage as the entire nation and its attendant culture sank into a deep-seated paranoia and a frightened submission to the state, the effects of which are still being felt in Russia today. The generation who survived the fearful times of the Stalin era became conditioned to avoid all independent thinking.

Over in China a similar terror regime was installed by Chairman Mao, and I was lucky enough in the summer of 1973 to interview Ahmad Deblaan, a Dhofari PFLOAG defector some two years after I shot the commissars in Dhofar. He had volunteered to learn English, and the Omani Government had sent him to Bournemouth for an English language course. It was there that I met him to record his memories of his indoctrination course in Peking back in 1968.

He remembered the endless lessons, which he was still able to repeat by rote:

> *What is the Koran and who is the Prophet, comrade?*
> The Koran, the Prophet and all other manifestations of Islam are inventions of the British imperialists who are running dogs and lackeys of the US.
> *Why did they spread about such inventions in Arab lands?*
> They wished to poison our society with the class-ideologies of religion. To cloud the Arab mind with Islamic ritual – leaving no time to ponder the injustice of our suppression . . . To make us place all inequalities at the door of a make-believe God, when in reality the British and their puppet Sultans were to blame. In Arabia, more than any other country in the world, religion is a tool used by the regime to terrorise and mystify the people . . .

Ahmad also recalled the guided Peking tours, and he told me that in the fields between the Forbidden City and the great compound of the military school, the peasants worked ceaselessly like ants. Barefooted in the dry, dusty fields, tilling the earth with ancient hoes and man-pulled ploughs, heaving and straining . . . and around them the red fluttering pennants.

Seated on hall floors in geometrical patterns of blue and serge, the political cadres listened and were exhorted, roared chorused quotations, and sang the revolutionary songs . . . and above them the wall placards featured the great Mao Zedong, Chairman Mao; godhead to the godless.

There were cheerleaders who asked, 'What do we do to the Black Gang and the bourgeoisie?' And from the body of the hall the massive chanting response, *Shah, shah* . . . 'Kill, kill.'

And the interpreter, in whose Warszawa saloon car Ahmad and two others were taken around, explained that the bourgeoisie were those selfish Chinese people who still considered themselves as individuals, who wore tapered trousers, applied scent to their bodies, kept a pet cat, wore long hair-tresses, and so on. That the Black Gang were the capitalist intellectual clique who dared to mislead the proletariat into thinking they were superior just because they were teachers and professors.

The interpreter explained that fortunately these menaces had largely been dealt with since 1966. That was when the great Chairman had begun a Cultural Revolution to purify the Republic of such filth. Throughout the vastness of the land they had been eradicated one by one, humiliated, vilified, beaten, and then executed by the elite corps of Red Guards specially formed from youths whose devotion to Mao was proven.

This 'cultural revolution' had known no bounds, purging the misguided, from the lowest workers to those in the upper echelons of power. Even the President, Lin Shao-Chi, and the Mayor of Peking, Peng Cheng, had been removed and disgraced. Mao had learned from Stalin that nobody, but nobody, must feel exempt from his Death List.

In much the same way in Cambodia, the 1975–9 regime of the Khmer Rouge under Pol Pot killed and tortured at random.

Pol Pot's secret police, the Santebal, used a number of imaginative ways to torture, maim and kill, since terror was their expertise. Schools were turned into Santebal torture centres and they killed teenagers with healthy livers and gall bladders, which they collected in sacks. Both of these body parts were thought to be excellent medicines for fevers and were often cooked and eaten by the Khmer Rouge cadres.

Killings without torture were rare. People were seldom shot as bullets were expensive, so after they had dug their own grave holes, victims were clubbed with *vay choul* hoes.

Fortunately, the Khmer Rouge's brutal reign was brought to an abrupt end in 1979 by an invasion of the Vietnamese Army, but this was not before Pol Pot had murdered an estimated 1.7 million of his fellow countrymen.

It is easy today to quickly dismiss such terrible happenings because it all happened some time ago and in remote, cruel countries, but the mass murders in Syria have continued into the age of the iPad, and the modern catchphrase of 'ethnic cleansing' stemmed from an incident that occurred under the so-called jurisdiction of UN troops in the heart of 1990s Europe. The process was honed by Serbian General Ratko Mladić, who simply wished to cleanse the region of Srebrenica in the Serb heartland of Bosnia of all Muslims. Such cleansing is merely a refinement of a particular form of inter-human hatred, whether religious, racial or doctrinal.

For many years of Soviet domination, General Tito had, like Saddam Hussein in Iraq, kept a lid on tensions between the various ethnic sections of the Federal Republic of Yugoslavia (where, incidentally, I spent my honeymoon in 1970) but, with Tito gone, the Serbs were the dominant power in the ensuing civil struggles in Croatia, Bosnia and Kosovo. In Srebrenica, and in so many other towns and villages, the Mladić cleansing process proved highly efficient and effective. The reason that Srebrenica stood out was not just the sheer numbers of Muslims murdered (some 7,000), but the fact that in modern, civilised Europe, a Hitler-type monster could, with impunity, ride roughshod over armed UN troops in order to carry out mass murder against innocent citizens.

The Srebrenica massacre involved a strong unit of the Serbian Army, with minimal heavy weapons, and a fleet of empty civilian buses that arrived at the target town, evicted the Muslim inhabitants from their homes, which were set on fire, and then separated the men from their families. The buses were then filled with all the men, including young teenagers, and they were sent off to pre-designated halls or open fields where everyone was shot and buried in mass graves.

In quick time and with minimal fuss and, initially, no come-back, Mladić had cleared the entire Muslim population from an area designated by the UN as a 'safe area'.

It was the very *absence* of fear due to the UN presence that helped Mladić to complete this ethnic cleansing atrocity by lulling the target population into a false sense of, at least partial, security.

Hitler's Gestapo used a lulling-of-fear process, known as *Nacht und Nebel* (Night and Fog), to persuade Jews to come from their ghettos to central collection points with the promise of improved circumstances. Once corralled on the death trains to hell, the poor Jews realised too late that they had been duped.

For the end aim of removing an unwanted group of humans from a given area by eviction, whether or not this involved murder or merely booting them out to other countries, maintaining a reign of terror is unnecessary. The more complex situation for a dictator is that of maintaining power over a resident population, many or most of whom would dearly love to get rid of him.

The answer down the ages and still true today is to instil mega-fear into all your potential enemies. Knowing that you will imprison them if they show any sign of opposition works well, but for the more troublesome you need to impress on them that truly nightmarish experiences await them should they make any trouble and fall into your hands. The name of the game is to publicise the practice of imaginative forms of torture.

Vlad the Impaler, the nickname of King Vlad III of Transylvania, was especially good at this sort of barbaric behaviour. He ruled a region of the Balkans, known then as Wallachia, where he became notorious for his inhuman cruelty for a thankfully short period in the mid-fifteenth century.

Although he experimented with various forms of torture, his favourite was that of impalement, which is and was one of the most gruesome, painful and slow ways of dying. Vlad used a horse attached to each of the victim's legs and a sharpened stake was gradually forced into the body. The end of the stake was usually oiled and care was taken that the stake not be too sharp, otherwise the victim might die too rapidly from shock. Normally the stake was inserted into the body through the buttocks and was often forced through the body until it emerged from the mouth. However, there were many instances where victims were impaled through other body orifices or through the abdomen or chest. Infants were sometimes impaled on the stake forced through their mother's chest. The records indicate that victims were sometimes also impaled so that they hung upside down on the stake.

The decaying corpses could be left for months. It was once reported that an invading Turkish army turned back in fright when it encountered thousands of rotting corpses impaled along the banks of the Danube. In 1461 Mohammed II, the conqueror of Constantinople, a man not noted for his squeamishness, returned to Constantinople after being sickened by the sight of 20,000 impaled Turkish prisoners outside the city of Tirgoviste. This gruesome sight is remembered in history as the 'Forest of the Impaled'.

Thousands were often impaled at a single time. Ten thousand were impaled in the Transylvanian city of Sibiu in 1460. The previous year Vlad III had 30,000 of the merchants of the Transylvanian city of Brasov impaled. One of the most famous woodcuts of the period shows feasting amongst a forest of stakes and their grisly burdens outside Brasov, while nearby an executioner cuts apart other victims.

My sister-in-law and Ginny's younger sister, Abbie, lives near Brasov and on a clear day she can see Vlad's castle from her mountain cottage.

Although impalement was Vlad Dracula's favourite method of torture, it was by no means the only method he used. The list of tortures employed by this cruel prince reads like an inventory of hell's tools: nails in heads, cutting off limbs, blinding, strangulation, burning, cutting off noses and ears, mutilation of sexual organs (especially in the case of women), scalping, skinning, exposure to the elements or to wild animals, and burning alive.

Vlad, despite his penchant for torture, was known to have a moral concern for female chastity and he tried to enforce this in his kingdom. Maidens who lost their virginity, adulterous wives and unchaste widows were all targeted. Such women often had their sexual organs cut out or their breasts cut off and were then impaled through the vagina on red-hot stakes.

No wonder that the Dracula novels of Bram Stoker were based on Vlad the Impaler. Evil though his methods were, they worked well and he maintained order through terror, despite turbulent times elsewhere in the Balkans.

A more recent example of torture involved the Afghan Mujahideen, many of whom later joined the Taliban, in their fight against the Russian invasion forces in the 1980s. Despite the considerable technical superiority of the Russians, their morale was greatly lowered by the knowledge of what would happen to them if they were captured by the Mujahideen.

Gaz Hunter was a British mercenary attached to a Taliban group, who witnessed his Afghan colleagues torturing a Russian prisoner to death:

> Four of them got round him, pulling his arms and legs apart until he was stretched straight out. Two more sat down on

his shoulders and kidneys. A third man sat on his backside, pulled the Russian's right leg up between his own, and held it so that the foot stuck straight up . . . at the same time forcing the heel up and out. He brought up the knife, rammed its point through the ankle behind the Achilles tendon, hooked back on the blade, and twisted it. The tendon snapped like a piano wire. The Russian let out a scream, a terrible high-pitched howling . . .

The group moved on, dragging the disabled Russian conscript with them. After a while they stopped, fed up with having to pull him along. God only knew what horror the boy was feeling . . . They got on top of him again, pinning him down so that he was utterly unable to move. One of them pushed the boy's eyelids apart with his finger and thumb, and stuck the point of his knife into the Russian's left eye. With a flick of his wrist he hooked out the eyeball, then stood back, leaving it hanging from its stalk. Our commander wanted the Russian's remaining eye left intact, not out of mercy or because enough was enough, but so that he'd see and understand exactly what they were going to do to him next.

Later they smashed all his fingers with their rifle butts. After that they slashed open his stomach, the cut just wide and deep enough to start his stomach contents bulging, so that he'd reek of his own blood and guts but live on for another six to twelve hours. Then, to stop him screaming, they had cut out his tongue . . . They'd left him like that, face down on the rock with his eyeball hanging down and his insides coming out, for the rats, the wild dogs and the mountain foxes.

They had their own logic for treating their Russian prisoners in that way. They did it out of hatred, for revenge and to break the enemy's morale. They wanted the Russians out of their country, and they would do anything to achieve that. Fear was their most potent weapon and Mujahideen had to make the Russians pay too high a cost.

The nerves of the Russian conscript soldier captured by the Mujahideen would already have been on edge and he would have expected a bad time, despite Kremlin media control back home in Russia, due to the horrific stories circulating in their barracks and, to a lesser extent, due to his own training.

During my own SAS training in the Cold War days of the early 1960s, I was among those subjected to 'Resistance to Interrogation' in an empty building in North Wales.

The make-believe enemy interrogators were men of the RAF Regiment who, judging by their streams of filthy language and abuse, would have loved to have been able to beat the hell out of us in a realistic manner. So the closest I ever came to glimpsing the terror of torture was in meeting and talking to Britain's best-known victim of torture, ex-Squadron Leader John Peters, who was shot down when on an RAF bombing mission in Iraq in 1991. He was twenty-nine years old at the time.

He recalled having been briefed that 'Saddam Hussein controlled the fourth largest standing army in the world, with over a million men permanently under arms.' He told me, 'Ours was to be the first, and the last, Tornado low-level daylight bombing mission of the entire war . . . In a matter of hours we went from a position of power in a Tornado GR1 as part of the largest air offensive in the history of mankind, to being blown out of the sky by a SAM [surface to air missile] and triple-A [anti-aircraft artillery] at 600 mph, 50 feet above the ground. We had ejected into the desert.'

John and his navigator, John Nichol, had tried to escape on foot, but they were shot at and caught within half a mile of their crash site. They were taken to Baghdad and imprisoned in a building that received a direct hit from a massive USAF air raid. So they were in an understandably shaken state when their interrogations began. Their dread of what they were about to experience was akin to that of the Russian conscripts when they were caught in Afghanistan. Even back in their UK bases, fighter crews all said the same thing: 'We don't mind being shot down and killed, but we don't want to be shot down and caught.'

By this time, horror stories had begun to emerge in the Western media about the things Iraq's ruling Ba'ath Party torturers were doing to the Kuwaiti people – like cutting off their ears and nailing them to the wall, or drilling through their eyes with a power drill.

John described disjointed memories of the nightmare that followed:

> The first fist splitting your lip open is a mind-numbing shock. Then they grabbed my hair and threw my head against the wall. With hands cuffed behind my back, I twisted to shield my balls they were whipping at. My left eye was extremely squelchy, like a wet sponge. The more it swelled, the more they concentrated on hitting it with wooden batons. Then the thick, plaited rubber strap thwacking across the face, the ear, inflicts a harsh, bitter, penetrating sting forming glowing red weals. The jarring shock from a wooden baton knocks you flying off the chair, sprawling heavily to the floor. The blood spurting from my nose was thick and grimy on my tongue and teeth. The atmosphere in the room is intense, narrow, dedicated.

John was kept blindfolded in his prison cell and described the regular interrogation and beatings by his Iraqi captors as like being in a medieval torture chamber:

> The interrogation process is designed to sustain and enhance the anxiety of capture, isolation, disorientation and vulnerability. It is intended to manipulate fear, uncertainty and doubt. The fight–flight response is systematically and deliberately enhanced by the process of beatings, sensory deprivation and solitary confinement. From the bag on your head to the constancy of violence, cold, hunger, sleep deprivation and dehydration. All designed and executed precisely to sap your resolve, isolate the senses and remove

> the capacity to process your surroundings. All designed to induce fear. All designed to subvert and control your will.
>
> The atmosphere was extremely hostile. When you're blindfolded you feel things more intensely. Your mind is constantly on edge, your nerves heightened, your body in constant tension. You mouth is dry and, despite the cold, you sweat with fear.
>
> The helplessness was a big part of it, humiliating, sordid, degrading. It preys on the imagination, works its horror. The psychological terror, the psychological torture, is just as great as the physical torture. You are shit-scared.

John was placed on starvation rations. He wrote that one USAF prisoner in a neighbouring cell shouted along the corridor, 'I got so hungry I picked the scabs off my arms and put them in the soup. I needed something to chew . . .' Everybody understood exactly how he felt.

In one prison with thick walls John suffered from sensory deprivation, whilst in another he heard:

> another man shrieking in the next cell. It was horrible, almost as bad as being beaten yourself, this extreme noise of another human being in violent pain, this fellow prisoner screaming his guts out . . . It preys on the imagination, works its horror. Whoever it was, he was refusing to speak. The noise went on and on, for what felt like hours. He was an English speaker. Occasionally the screams would flatten out and then rise into an extended repeated wailing, 'No-o-o . . .' of punctuated agony.
>
> The most difficult challenge is controlling one's own imagination running away with itself. The only thing to fear is fear itself . . . It is in between the beatings: the psychological, self-imposed pressures, where one's own imagination can wreak havoc. This self-induced fear from your own imagination imposes an impending sense of dread, humiliation and pain that seeps into your bones, saps the strength and sucks the will.
>
> The beatings were spaced out, with what felt like twenty

> minutes or so between each session. What I feared most at this stage was letting myself and my friends down: letting the side down . . . The various pressures can become overwhelming and, magnified by your imagination, you risk falling into a self-defeating spiral of fear . . . In particular, after a situation where I was stripped naked and thought I was going to get gang-raped, they threatened to shove knives up my arse. They did neither but, returning to my cell afterwards, I was shaking uncontrollably. I was so angry with myself that I could not stop my body shaking for half an hour. That moment was pivotal because then I realised that I had learnt about fear and each time the fear factor was pushed further, I became more able to deal with it. Each boundary I passed increased my resilience. I knew from that moment on that they were never going to win. I had learnt to deal with fear. I had found a strength I never believed I had.

Fortunately, John did not suffer PTSD, but recognises the importance of recognising its symptoms:

> PTSD can and does affect anyone and it is a syndrome not a disease. Its chief symptoms include violent outbursts, unwillingness to talk about experiences, unexplained changes in character, self-loathing for surviving when others did not, self-isolation, inability to readjust to normal life, inability to communicate with loved ones or to reciprocate love, the desire to be with others undergoing the same thing who will 'understand', and flashbacks and nightmares brought on by reminders of the trauma.

Anyone who suffers some or all of these symptoms is advised to be as open as possible with friends, family and, above all, with a PTSD specialist psychologist. To bottle everything up and tell nobody has led sufferers into madness.

As research progresses into the psychological effects of wars on their protagonists, more is known of the lasting mental effects of great trauma. More British soldiers killed themselves *after* the Falklands War due to PTSD than died during the actual fighting. The charity Help for Heroes is doing great things for the hundreds of injured soldiers with mental and physical war wounds of varying degrees of severity, but the personal courage of these soldiers remains a very real ingredient in 'making the best of a bad deal'.

Simon Weston, the Welsh guardsman who was badly burnt during the Falklands War and went on to become the patron of a number of charities that support military veterans and people living with disfigurements, is a fine example of just such inner spirit.

15
Fears of the Future

Age is an ugly thing and keeps on getting worse.
Diana Cooper

In 2006 Louise gave birth to our lovely daughter Elizabeth and the three of us travelled all over the world to conferences where I lectured about my expeditions. Apart from climbing and mounting a science-based vehicle expedition in Antarctica, I concentrated on raising a target figure of £10 million for Marie Curie nurses. I was diagnosed with prostate cancer and my old friend Anton Bowring, with whom I was still co-leading expeditions, was treated for cancer of the oesophagus.

In 2015 I became, at seventy-one, the oldest Briton to run the Marathon des Sables (Marathon of the Sands) in the Moroccan Sahara, and this raised over £2 million for Marie Curie. Their nurses are needed more and more as we all grow older and the number of terminally ill people without family or friends increases year on year.

I did finish the six-day marathon, often labelled as the hottest endurance race in the world, but for the first time I began to doubt my own physical abilities. I had to train much harder and for longer in order to stay even relatively fit, and my back, neck and legs began to remember old injuries. Worse still, chest and lung pains, coupled with dizzy spells, interrupted my standard jogging sessions, and I began to fear the creeping threat of old age. I decided to fight it, but recalled from an old history lesson the story of King Canute who, resting on a sandy beach, told the incoming tide to stay away.

I have so far been lucky enough to live my life in places where Fear is not in charge, whether in the form of a dictator, a rampant disease, terrorist activities, perennial natural disasters, or any of the other nasties described in this book.

I was born in a country which, at the time, was being bombed, but I never experienced an explosion. In the 1950s, when I was in my teens, we feared a nuclear war, and during the Cuban Missile Crisis in October 1962, the world trembled with tension whilst awaiting global annihilation, but I was more aware of the next impending school boxing match.

Following the fall of the Iron Curtain things got better, and East–West relations improved to a friendly status until the advent of Putin's aggressive phase, which continues to this day. Now capitalist, oligarch-led Russia, not Soviet Russia, is the new source of our military-based fears, and cyber warfare becomes an ever greater threat to our defences, including the likelihood that even our Trident nuclear submarines could be hacked into uselessness and then destroyed by drone submarine-hunters.

The nuclear threat has faded since its fear-laden peak in the 1960s, but is still with us and we would do well not to forget that the near nuclear squeak of the Cuban crisis was played out by two sensible world leaders, Khrushchev and Kennedy, who stepped back from the brink. Next time a nuclear confrontation could involve less clear-headed decision-makers from, say, Pakistan, North Korea or Iran.

And although a great many nuclear warheads were disarmed in the days of détente, stewardship of the ever-lethal nuclear components, plutonium and enriched uranium, was seldom thorough during the political turmoil of Russia in the early 1990s. It is quite possible that Chechen and other rebel groups in the ex-Soviet Union managed to obtain and secrete for a rainy day such powerful blackmail or jihadi ingredients. After all, they would not need a great quantity: two cricket-ball-sized chunks of enriched uranium if detonated in a big city in the rush hour would blow many thousands of people to bits.

Much less ambitious terror acts occurring at random all over the world have the desired effect of frightening normal people who are personally as harmless and politically uninvolved as so many hedgehogs. But they are, nonetheless, fearful of enjoying concerts, church services, football matches, greeting friends and family at airports, or even enjoying coffee in city centres. Because the media has warned them that any gathering of people whose limbs can be blown off and eyeballs blasted from their sockets may be the next target of the lone jihadist, or the sort of social misfit who kills women and children in Oslo, Tunis, Islamabad, Nairobi or Oklahoma on any day of the year.

To avoid major killing sprees, most governments enforce security measures for the storage of nuclear materials and dangerous viruses. But just one successful infringement of such security by those with evil in mind could end in widespread disaster. So we have every reason to feel as people do who live their lives below a dormant volcano.

In terms of biological or chemical attacks of the nature carried out by the Aum Shinrikyo terror group in 1995 on the Tokyo subway, the twenty-four-hour fear of everyone in a threatened area would be of lingering death and of the constant need to treat even good friends with suspicion lest they be already infected. Terrorists would, of course, favour a deadly virus for which no vaccine exists, perhaps a variant of AIDS that is transmitted like influenza, or a version of Ebola with a longer gestation period. Outbreaks of this dreadful contagious disease are usually contained because it acts so fast, killing its victims by eroding away their flesh before they have much chance to infect others. In contrast, it is the slowness with which AIDS acts that allows it to be effectively transmitted.

War is no longer, 'You attack . . . We defend'. Today, so-called hybrid warfare, such as Putin evolved so well in the Ukraine, blurs the dividing line between war and peace, shrouding acts of war in deniability and ambiguity.

At NATO's Command Centre operational HQ at Mons in Belgium, the Head of Cyber Security said, in 2016, 'Every single day we are operational, experiencing cyber attacks and defending against them.' They log some 300 serious cyber attacks against NATO's HQ and global bases every week. And he went on to say, 'We talk about wars that might take place in the future – cyber attacks are something we are dealing with right now.'

As for our big, white fear-deterrent, Trident, the Executive Director of the British American Security Information Council said that Trident subs are 'old technology. They are big and expensive, with very long lead times. The technology chasing them will be thirty or forty generations on by the time they hit the water.' He believes that the uncertainties about Trident are just one part of a much bigger revolution, in which missile submarines and aircraft carriers are being outpaced.

So our main Cold War weapon of peace-and-war, which for so long dulled our fear of nuclear war, as painkillers help to damp down pain, may well soon be made redundant. As for that grade of fear most often paired with war, that of terror, these days there are less massive terror regimes than those at the time of Stalin, Hitler, Mao and Pol Pot, but President Bashar al-Assad of Syria stands out as a contemporary repressive dictator, responsible by 2016 for the deaths of over 300,000 of his people and a huge quotient of fear among many of the survivors, who have become refugees in order to escape the killing, the hunger and the misery of civil war.

Time magazine worked out that 'if all the world's uprooted and desperate migrants, like the Rohingya people of West Burma (Myanmar), were to form their own country (as uprooted Jews once did in Israel), they would make up the world's twenty-ninth most populous nation – as big as South Korea.'

Christians are fleeing the Middle East in droves. In the decades before the Arab Spring many Christian leaders lent their support to authoritarian rulers in return for the protection of Christians. But the deal broke down when the dictators fell.

Boutros al-Rahi, Lebanon's Maronite Christian Patriarch, said in 2012:

> In Iraq when Saddam Hussein was removed we lost a million Christians. Why? Not because the regime fell, but because there was no more authority, there was just a vacuum. In Syria, it's the same thing, Christians do not love the regime of Bashar al-Assad, but they are afraid of what may come next.

Mosul, in northern Iraq, was once home to tens of thousands of Christians. Perceived as supporting the Americans, they were targeted by insurgents after the invasion. A wave of killings in 2008, including that of the local Chaldean archbishop, seemed to mark the low point for the community. Then came ISIS. When the jihadists entered the city in 2014, they reportedly tagged Christian houses with an 'N', for 'Nazarene', and gave the occupants of such houses a choice: convert, pay the *jizyo* (a tax on non-Muslims), or face possible death. Most fled. In July 2014 ISIS announced that the city was free of Christians.

Meanwhile, in many areas of Iraq, Syria and other parts of the Middle East, Shia Muslims kill Sunni, and Sunni kill Shia, often without knowledge of the actual differences between their separate beliefs, which are to an outsider as irrelevant and insignificant as the differences between those Catholics and Protestants who burnt, tortured and beheaded one another over many previous centuries.

The fear experienced by Jews living in Nazi Germany, or by the Yazidis in the path of an ISIS advance is far more rational than that of a school teacher dreading the chance arrival of a serial killer in the classroom, or of a Paris tourist sipping coffee outside a café and hearing a sudden roar from a car exhaust. Yet sudden terror events in hitherto peaceful settings are a new norm.

According to the US State Department, there were 13,463 terror attacks across the globe in 2014, which is 1,122 a month on average, or about thirty-seven per day, or roughly one every forty minutes.

SAS terror expert, David Lyon, defines *Terrorism* as 'the threat or use of violence to instil fear in order to achieve change'; *State Terrorism* as 'the pursuit of change by one country in another through the support of local groups. Iran's support of Houthis in Yemen, Hezbollah in Lebanon, Hamas in Palestine, and Assad in Syria'; *Non-State Terrorism* as 'Al Qaeda, ISIS, and Boko Haram individuals'; *Global Terrorism* as 'terrorism that in some way impacts on more than one nation'.

Past terror organisations include Weathermen, Black September, KKK, Red Brigades, the Irish Republican Army, and Timothy McVeigh – small groups or individuals mainly operating in a single country. Al Qaeda, Taliban and ISIS have all emerged over the last twenty-five years and have conducted more sophisticated operations across international boundaries, particularly Al Qaeda, than ever before.

Since 2014 ISIS has raised politically intimidating violence in the area it controls, and the publication of that violence internationally through social media, to ever new levels. It has initiated a number of small-scale attacks by individuals, such as that on the staff of *Charlie Hebdo* magazine in Paris and elsewhere in Europe. So what should we take into account when considering how terrorism, at home and across multiple states, may develop over the next decades?

Demographics are a key factor. Most developing countries are experiencing dramatic increases in the percentage of their populations under thirty years of age. Opportunities for employment for these young people have not matched those increases. There also remains substantial poverty across developing countries, but there has also been, as they grow economically, a significant increase in the number of middle-class families who have sent their children to be educated in the developed world. Some of these find that, post-education, there are no jobs for them, either at home or abroad, and they are unable to integrate into Western society with its cultures and values.

At the same time they react against the corruption in their own societies and find themselves in a spiritual vacuum. They see no positive future, no challenge to respond to, and they are vulnerable to the siren call of a cause. Fundamentalist Islam provides just what they seek, using great persuasive skill through masterful propaganda and individual targeting via the Internet. So the terrorists of the next decades will include increasing numbers of frustrated, middle-class, well-educated, technically competent, culturally experienced, sophisticated communicators.

They will provide the brains of terrorist organisations in a war of ideas. They go where the 'fight for the cause' goes, because that becomes their whole life. They are seldom welcomed by local populations, but they have learnt to know their weapons and how to fight. They represent a substantial long-term challenge, as their skills enable them to move from country to country, wherever demand and the money is highest.

The Internet and the spread of mobile phones and computers with the ability to communicate verbally and pictorially in real time at minimal cost, either on a large scale or with individual targets, is a growing opportunity. Terrorists have taken full advantage of this capability to instil fear, trigger overreaction by governments, recruit and organise attacks. Their propaganda is highly sophisticated strategically, tactically and technically. It is one of their most effective weapons. Western democracies are a soft target. But believing in freedom of speech and being generally antipathetic to the use of propaganda, we, in the West, have been slow to respond.

And *change* is everywhere these days. From caveman to Steve Jobs did not happen overnight. Mother Earth has existed for at least 4 billion years, but the wipe-out of the dinosaurs, probably by an asteroid strike, was a mere 65 million years ago. The extinction of subsequent species occurred at a rate of about one species in a million per year. Then, subsequent to our (Homo sapiens') arrival on this planet, the rate of extinction of other species increased to about one species per thousand every year as a result of their habitats being destroyed or the introduction of alien species to new habitats.

A continuing growing background fear is of our own technical advances placing ever greater pressures on our environment and that it, as well as society at large, will inadvertently be vulnerable to cyber-risks disrupting previous norms. Change is everywhere, and alongside resulting benefits lurks the fear of human-induced pressures on the environment that spark off even greater chain-reaction disasters than were ever caused by asteroid impact, earthquakes or volcanoes. The unintended consequences of scientific breakthroughs, however innocently conceived, could cause catastrophes.

And we increasingly fear advances in robotics, for there is nothing, it seems, to stop their ever-increasing superiority over the humans who build them. They can already thrash human chess champions. Once computers can watch and interpret their immediate environment as intelligently as we do through our basic senses, their ability to think and react more quickly will give them an advantage over us. Even now, robotics engineers are working on nanotechnology 'assemblers' capable of arranging atoms in machines with molecule-size components, in which information can be stored in memories a billion times smaller than what is possible today.

I was given a book titled *Our Final Century* by Professor Martin Rees, an international leader in cosmology and former President of the British Association for the Advancement of Science, in which he wrote me a personal note saying, 'in the hope that this book is too pessimistic'.

He writes that physicists aim to understand the particles that the world is made of and the forces that govern those particles. Hence the CERN particle accelerator in Europe and a similar experimental station in the USA. The aim of these units is to produce an intense concentration of energy and to accelerate atoms to enormous speeds, close to that of light, then crash them together.

Such atom-smashing experiments, like their nuclear equivalents of the twentieth century, *could* go wildly wrong. As Martin Rees points out, 'Some have speculated that the concentrated energy created when particles crash together could trigger a "phase transition" that would rip the fabric of space itself,' and 'likewise, a hypothetical "strangelet" [CERN-speak] disaster could transform the entire planet Earth into an inert hyperdense sphere about one hundred metres across.' He is quick to stress that 'these scenarios may be extremely unlikely', but they raise in acute form the issue of who should decide, and how, whether to proceed with experiments that have a genuine scientific purpose, but that pose a very tiny risk of an utterly calamitous outcome.

Quite apart from CERN-type explosions being an ever-present nightmare scenario of our times, we are increasingly at risk from some malfunction in cyberspace causing global havoc, either through some cyber-expert's complex error or by the scheming of a malign Dr No or jihadi madman. New sciences may soon enable a terror group, or even a lone-wolf psychotic, to blackmail governments with genuine cyber, nuclear or biological doomsday threats.

In June 2002 the US National Academy of Sciences reported that, 'Just a few individuals with specialised skills and access to a laboratory could inexpensively and easily produce a panoply of lethal biological weapons that might seriously threaten the US population.'

A feature applicable to all biological attacks is that they cannot be detected until it is too late to prevent their spread in these days of mass global travel and media coverage. The SARS epidemic, for instance, caused ever-spreading fear well in advance of the disease itself, as did the mere anonymous sending of anthrax-contaminated envelopes to two US Senators and to a few media editors. Five people died, but the resulting hysterical media coverage caused a 'dread factor' that, for a while, gripped the entire nation.

In the 1990s the Japanese terror cult group Aum Shinrikyo achieved worldwide notoriety and alarm by using chemicals as terror weapons. They managed to manufacture the nerve gas sarin, which they tested on sheep at a remote farm in Australia and on their victims in Japan in 1994. In June that year they released sarin in the city of Matsumoto, killing eight and injuring two hundred. Using a converted refrigerator truck, they also released a deadly cloud of sarin near the home of an anti-cult judge. Seven people were killed and five hundred were injured on that occasion.

In May 1995 Aum members set fire to a hydrogen-cyanide device in a Tokyo subway toilet, but it was discovered and extinguished. Scientists reported that, had the device been triggered, enough gas would have been released to kill 10,000 commuters. As it was, devices Aum left on five subway trains killed only thirteen and injured some nine hundred people.

Subsequent police raids on Aum properties reported finding explosives, chemical weapons, a Russian helicopter and biological agents, including anthrax and Ebola cultures. Also found were stockpiles of chemicals that could be used to produce enough sarin to kill 4 million people. They had apparently intended to use a blueprint of the Ebola virus with which to spread panic, but they were unable to obtain it. Today, however, such a group would find the Ebola genetic blueprint far easier to obtain, for it is archived and there are thousands of individuals worldwide with the skills to assemble it using commercially available DNA strands.

More fearful even than Ebola and just as contagious is smallpox. This virus was eradicated worldwide in the 1970s by the World Health Organization, but stocks were kept to help develop vaccines. A third of smallpox victims will die and the toll of an outbreak today would, given an international scenario, run into millions.

Geographical change is also a continuing factor, be it physical, economic or human. We are bombarded with arguments about the impact of climate change, but we are probably less well aware of the impacts of other geographical changes, except when we travel to a place after an interval of several years.

Particularly relevant to the future of terrorism is the growth of megacities, and particularly coastal cities where the risk of law enforcement vacuums increases. Such vacuums provide opportunities for criminal or terrorist groups to establish fiefdoms or cells, which are extremely difficult to eradicate, even in places like Brussels and Paris.

Improved Internet monitoring, target acquisition and armed drones have made life much more dangerous for mountain-based terrorists, so they are increasingly moving into towns and cities, where it is easier to live undetected and where the risk of causing collateral damage by killing innocent civilians is a substantial limitation to the use of drones. Large cities also provide attractive opportunities for spectacular or combined attacks by small groups, as in Mumbai.

Living, even today, as a vocal protestor against the government in Moscow, Peking, Cairo, Hong Kong, Istanbul, and a great many other cities, you have every reason to live in fear from dawn to dusk.

With today's sudden random acts of terror, only a tiny number of individuals will suffer and so very few need fear being in the wrong place at the wrong time. Like the risk of being struck by lightning, your chances of death, unless you choose to trek in the volcanic region of Peru during a storm, are minimal. When you fly on Malaysian Airlines (as was) or any airline that has attracted a lethal reputation, whether deserved or not, you may well feel a touch uneasy. But you are as likely to end up dead on a trusted German airline on a routine flight because the depressed pilot just happens to decide to commit hara-kiri on your particular journey.

When you spread your picnic out on a Tunisian beach in front of your luxury hotel, you do not expect the arrival of a lone jihadi with an automatic rifle seeking out tourists to murder.

Lone individuals, often with unhappy childhoods, can decide to murder innocent people to gain publicity for a cause they believe in, or merely because they are feeling suicidally depressed. How can the security forces be expected to prevent such loners from carrying out their deadly aims? Sometimes it is only by sheer luck.

Take the October 2015 case of the fourteen-year-old Blackburn Muslim schoolboy, 'Britain's youngest terrorist', whose parents were separated and who behaved badly at school, where he drew up a list of teachers he wanted to behead. The Government's deradicalisation programme 'Channel' tried hard to make the boy calm down, but he became an ISIS fan and, online, contacted a known ISIS jihadi recruiter, 'Al-Cambodi', in Australia, and this recruiter then introduced him to an eighteen-year-old wannabe jihadi hit man, 'Besim', who lived in Melbourne.

The two youngsters plotted together online to carry out the mass murder of police officers at a memorial parade on Anzac Day. Due to the Blackburn boy's suspect behaviour, his Channel caseworkers alerted the local police, who visited him and, through his hate-filled ramblings, learned about the Anzac Day plot.

At the subsequent Manchester Court hearings, the boy's defending QC explained that 'from an early age the boy was concerned for the Muslim community.'

Had the plot ever succeeded, Australian police would have been killed by an Australian Muslim following the urging of a teenage British Muslim whom he had never met. In a work of fiction, such a plot would probably be seen as too convoluted and far-fetched to be taken seriously.

For many years, when I was based in London in the 1970s, I travelled on the Underground on a daily basis and considered it, on the rare occasions that the thought crossed my mind, to be a considerably safer form of transport than a car or bicycle. But in July 2005, when I was just back from a very near escape from death on Everest, my car broke down en route to an imminent lecture I was contracted to deliver at the British Museum. After calling the AA, I rushed to the nearest Underground station, as I knew a taxi would take too long to get me to the museum on time.

As I reached the escalator descending to the Circle Line, I was struck, with no warning at all, by a sudden feeling that it would be utterly stupid to travel by tube. A few days previously (on 8 July) I had watched a TV report on the devastation caused when four terrorist bombs exploded on the London Transport system, killing 52 people and injuring another 700. I recalled that some of the most horrific scenes had been in the wreckage of a Circle Line train. Feeling ashamed of my unbelievable cowardice, I rushed back up to the street and caught a taxi, despite the risk of being late to lecture to 300 people.

Ten years on from that time I contacted two of the survivors of those bombs to ask if their memories were such that they would never again travel on public transport.

Professor John Tulloch was only six feet away from one of the Circle Line suicide bombers and was sitting diagonally opposite to him when the bomb detonated. All the passengers in the carriage near to John were killed or lost limbs, except for John himself, whose wounds were painful but not lethal. The suitcase that John was carrying saved his life. He told me:

> There's something about having been blown up in a terrorist attack that can bring you to tears at the most unexpected times. Sometimes I still just break down . . . At the time my glasses were blown away, so I couldn't see much. Now I'm grateful for that because of all the horror. There was a huge crater in the floor of the train with a man stuck in it.

John still suffers from PTSD as a result of his experience.

> I have one fear that comes when objects or people are very close to my face, and this is presumably a response to the things which damaged my head in the blast. For example, the

> other day I was reaching for my jacket on a coat stand when an empty coat hanger swung across my face. The resulting wave of fear was more about me being fearful and emotionally 'out of control' rather than a fear of the coat hanger hurting me. I gather it is a fear related to a response of the amygdala, but it has dire results for me since, family-wise, I need to take at least four long-haul flights between Sydney and London every year and I can only fly business class in order to avoid panic-inducing close-up contact with other passengers. I am retired now and not well off, so this is a major financial problem for me.

John struck me as an extremely rational and calm person, but he suffers from a specific fear of Piccadilly Line trains, because he had learned that their silhouettes are semi-circular and fit into the tunnel like a glove, and this was the reason for the greater number of deaths on the Piccadilly Line than occurred on the other lines, whose trains were box-shaped with more room in their tunnels for the blast effects to dissipate. So even when it makes him late for meetings, John will never travel on the Piccadilly Line.

Another passenger on a bombed train, Martine Wright, had far worse injuries than John, but ended up without residual PTSD fears. She does remember screams and smells and seeing that 'the train had crumbled into my legs'. She remembers feeling no pain, but a fireman later told her, 'You were conscious the whole time we were cutting you out of the train.' She was in a coma for ten days, her body so swollen that her family didn't recognise her. She remembers:

> When I woke up, someone said, 'Martine, you've been in an accident and we've had to take your legs away.' I remember looking at other victims in hospital and thinking, Why me? Why am I one of the worst injured? Why have I lost both my legs, and above the knee?

> The 'Why me?' was a big thing in the first year. But ten years on, I truly believe I was destined to get into that carriage and sustain those injuries. I'm strong and I have a wonderful, supportive family. I've always been a glass half-full person, so maybe I was chosen because I can deal with it.

Martine fell in love with wheelchair 'sitting' volleyball and she competed in the London 2012 Paralympics.

I never met Martine, but I did correspond with a third train-bomb survivor, whose profession at the time was ironically that of risk management. His name was Sudhesh Dahad. He sent me his views on the fear that follows close contact with a terrorist and survival through sheer good luck. He wrote:

> After escaping from a near-death event . . . psychologists and victims alike speak of 'survivor's guilt'. I often hear – and indeed speak of it myself – that we owe it to the people who didn't get off the three trains and the bus to make the most of our lives. This can lead to a sense of pressure and an additional source of guilt if we don't accomplish something with the second chance we've been given. Many of us endure our fears quietly, as we don't want to sound ungrateful for the continuing gift of life when it hangs by a thread for so many other people. Fear can fade away with life's little successes, but it can return with a vengeance with the failures.
>
> My estimate of *all* risks has been turned on its head since the bomb. I now have a tendency to overestimate the probability of being exposed to *further* bad events. Ironically, the resulting constant state of high alert (anxiety) is probably going to shorten my life anyway, due to the stress effect. Ten years of living in a state of hypervigilance is bound to take its toll on both physical and mental health . . .
>
> Before this event my minor fears were either about job security, domestic security (being burgled) or, as every parent experiences, a fear for their child's health every time they have even a hint

of a runny nose. But such fears did not dominate my life until 2005 . . .

After 7/7 that supreme confidence was shattered. I began to see every danger that would previously have seemed to be possible but unlikely as suddenly being highly likely. Risks became exaggerated in my head. For the rest of 2005 I was even afraid to leave the house, unless it was to get out into the countryside and away from crowds, because this might make me a potential target for further attacks . . .

With such an exaggerated perception of the threat, how does a survivor of terrorism return to normalcy? The short answer is that many rarely do. Few of them can truly be emotionally immune to such an experience.

The subsequent effects from their decidedly close dances with death on John and Martine and Sudhesh over a ten-year period were all different. Martine experienced little or no follow-up fears, and the other two were forever wary of very varied harbingers of lurking danger.

One Army survivor from an IRA bomb-blast told me that his therapist had cured him of his severe PTSD attacks, which were set off whenever he noticed any pub on a street corner, by making him deliberately visit such pubs as often as he possibly could. At first he hated doing so, but as he commented with a shrug of his shoulders, 'Familiarity breeds contempt . . . eventually.'

Virtual Reality headsets, some resembling space-age helmets, are now being tested and used to treat patients with PTSD and phobias. So, without having the psychologist's couch, a troubled war veteran can repeatedly experience a lifelike war situation such as that which caused his or her PTSD. A sufferer from vertigo can stand teetering on the edge of a skyscraper, or a snake-fear victim can bed down with a writhing mass of vipers and slowly learn to find them cuddly.

Suicide bombers believe that their acts of martyrdom 'for Islam' will render them worthy of a five-star afterlife and the assurance of an instant painless death. So their actions, very often killing and maiming other Muslims, are in a very basic way much easier to comprehend than the actions of killers with no religious aims and who, if they are caught, will spend the rest of their lives in prison. An example of one such terrorist is that of the Norwegian Anders Breivik, who in the summer of 2011 murdered sixty-nine people, most of them teenagers, on an island campsite close to the Norwegian coast and just after setting off a home-made car bomb in central Oslo, which killed eight passers-by.

Norwegians pride themselves on living in a land of peace, freedom and happiness, so the Breivik murders by one of their own, a tall, blond Nordic middle-class son of a diplomat, truly shocked the nation.

It soon became clear that he was by no means a 'normal' Norwegian. One Oslo reporter wrote of him: 'It is a ghastly story of family dysfunction, professional and sexual failure, grotesque narcissism and the temptation of apocalyptic delusions.'

Such mass shootings by a random, mentally unhinged killer are sadly common, for obvious reasons, in countries where automatic weapons are more easily obtainable, as in the USA. After one such tragedy where twenty little children were murdered at Sandy Hook Elementary School by madman Adam Lanza, the media reaction to President Obama's heartfelt appeal to tighten the gun laws was strident, but dependent on the pre-existing and stubborn views of individual US citizens.

American writer David Robertson wrote in *Vox* magazine: 'To the gun owner, another mass shooting is not an argument for getting rid of guns. It's a confirmation of his every instinct, another sign of moral and societal decay, another reason to arm himself and defend what he's got left.'

The comedian Bill Maher once likened the experience of arguing with American conservatives to getting your dog to take a pill. 'You have to feed them the truth wrapped in a piece of baloney, hold their snout shut, and stroke their throats. Even then, just when you think they've swallowed it, they spit it out on the linoleum.'

Especially when it comes to the emotional issue of gun control, Republicans who own guns are startlingly fact-resistant and reason-impervious.

In June 2015 thirty British tourists were shot by a lone, radicalised engineering student as they sunbathed on a Tunisian beach. And on the same day in Kuwait, twenty-seven Muslims in a mosque were killed by other Muslims.

The previous April, fear visited my own family when a cousin of mine, James Fiennes, was chatting to a friend in the Tapestry Tapas Bar in Mortlake and, for no known reason, a stranger produced a large pair of scissors and stabbed James to death. His wife Caroline has been a family friend and the sister of my god-daughter for many years. She wrote to me as follows:

> Just to clarify events from that dreadful night two years ago: the press continually printed that James was with a friend in the Tapestry. He was not. He was alone, sitting quietly with a beer, doing his emails after work. Hunter (the murderer) came in to meet a friend of his, and it was this friend whom Hunter initially threatened to murder. He then caught sight of the only other person in the bar, who was James, and beckoned him over. Being the wonderful, trusting and kind man that he was, James got up and went over. And was then attacked.
>
> I am sure you will appreciate that the constant disparity of what is written in the press when compared with the actual reality is a great source of annoyance, and hurt, to me.
>
> Fear is a scary thing – and it is extraordinary that we all react to things in different ways. I experienced real fear after James's murder, and it took many months before I could even walk down the street without fearing that a complete stranger was going to attack me for no reason, as this was exactly what DID happen to James. I would zigzag across the street so that

> I wouldn't have to walk past another human being. Even now, the sound of emergency vehicle sirens will ignite fear. I was driven from Dorset to London by the police on that awful night, and from the outskirts of London the sirens blared. This sound never fails to transport me back . . . you have to work very hard to conquer fear.

At about the same time, another Caroline Fiennes, the widow of Mark Fiennes, the father of the actors Ralph and Joseph, lived in terror of a cyber-stalker who texted her at all times, including when she went for walks in the country, telling her to slow down because he could not keep up. This was especially frightening for her. She called the Fraud Squad when her bank account was hacked and raided, but her stalker was never caught.

16

The Promotion of Fear

Let me assert my firm belief that the only thing we have to fear is fear itself.

Franklin D. Roosevelt

Individual acts of terror directly affect only a tiny percentage of people, but climate change is beginning to worry more and more of us as its worst consequences are felt in increasing numbers of world regions. Nay-sayers who believe that human behaviour is not to blame are finding their position increasingly untenable.

In November 2015 a headline in *Newsweek* ran, 'The climate talks in Paris this month could be the planet's last chance of survival'. The primary objective of the talks was to divvy up carbon cuts in order to reduce worldwide greenhouse gas emissions and cap global warming at 3.5°F over pre-Industrial Revolution levels by 2100. That's roughly the point at which, research suggests, the ice sheets in Greenland and Antarctica will start to melt at an unstoppable pace, prompting a catastrophic rise in global sea levels. Parts of the world will be hit by devastating floods, while others will experience severe droughts that will lead to famine.

The winter of 2015 saw the worst blizzards in living memory across the north-east of the USA, with eleven States declaring a state of emergency, whilst down south in Bolivia, Lake Poopó in the Andes which, two years before had covered 400 square miles, had dried up to mere mud as the Andean glaciers that supplied the water for the lake had receded . . . as have virtually all the glaciers on earth.

Air and water pollution is killing off thousands of Chinese people in industrial regions, and leakages of natural-gas methane, a more powerful gas than carbon dioxide, are occurring all over the United States. In California a natural-gas storage reservoir is leaking some 65,000 lb of methane per hour via a seven-inch hole in the ground which, in one day, warms the climate at a rate equivalent to driving 4.5 million cars for a day. This leak has caused thousands of Los Angeles residents to flee their homes with their children, who were experiencing headaches, bloody noses and vomiting.

Well-meaning efforts to reduce pollution can easily have the opposite effect. Take for example the ironic and sad fact that measures taken since the 1980s to reduce air pollution in Britain and the rest of Europe are, according to the results of a study undertaken in 2015, in fact accelerating the melting of Arctic ice. Sulphur dioxide, an air pollutant emitted by old power stations, vehicle exhausts and industrial processes, has a cooling effect by creating billions of tiny particles that scatter sunlight and cause clouds to form, shielding the earth from solar radiation.

European Union regulations have sharply reduced sulphur emissions and the fall in particles has magnified the warming of the Arctic by 0.5°C since 1980, according to a study by Stockholm University. Many of the particles were previously blown from Europe over the Arctic, where they had a direct cooling effect. The research suggests that the emission cuts have made Europe 0.13°C warmer, but have had a much greater impact on the Arctic. In February 2015 the area covered by sea ice in the Arctic was at its lowest level for February since satellite records began in 1979 – 450,000 square miles below the long-term average. Scientists talk with alarm about the risks of climate change causing 'runaway evaporation' of water from the oceans (water vapour being a greenhouse gas). But a far worse global danger is that of runaway methane, such as is happening from storage wells in many countries, for methane is twenty times more deadly as a greenhouse gas than is carbon dioxide.

In some countries, such as those of the Sahel Belt into which Saharan conditions are spreading, and those increasingly prone to drought, such as Ethiopia and Somalia, the lack of available food alongside overpopulation is causing panic, whereas in Japan, under-population is the big worry as the percentage of the elderly becomes unwieldy without enough young breadwinners to tax.

In all countries, whether dictatorships or benign democracies preside, the prime controller of public fears is the media, and this is increasingly true due to the advent of the digital age and social media.

There's no doubt that our culture *induces fear*, even among those nations who have no real day-to-day cause to be afraid, such as the USA. One of the best examples of this is the fear that has been created by the US government and reinforced by the media, that somehow an evil enemy is out there waiting to devour all Americans. The ironic thing is that the US is in many ways the least vulnerable to disaster of any country in the world, being a very powerful and rich country with an ocean on both sides that nobody is likely to invade, and yet fear is still created and was intense in the period following the Second World War, when the Soviet Union and communism were held up as serious threats to the US. That fear then enabled the government to take away the liberties of people, which led to many losing their jobs, and there was a hysteria about communism, including blacklists and witch-hunts in the culture and entertainment industries.

The 'spectre of communism', which Marx used in the first words of the *Communist Manifesto*, haunted the US and was spread very deliberately by the government, because it served a useful purpose – it enabled them to justify the expenditure of huge sums of national money on military weapons, including nuclear bombs. It also enabled them to use controls over what people did and what people said to intimidate them and distort their own behaviour in order to remain safe. When the Soviet

Union disintegrated in 1989 and there was no more genuinely serious threat from communism, it didn't stop the US government from maintaining an atmosphere of fear, sometimes to great lengths, including the wars in Iraq and Afghanistan, all because of the terrorist attack of 11 September 2001, which created a justification for going to war against an unseen enemy and terrorists who couldn't be identified.

Today the Nazis and their propaganda are long gone, and life is in many ways and for many humans vastly improved. Crime is way down. War is declining. Cruelty as entertainment, human sacrifice to indulge superstition, slavery as a labour-saving device, genocide as a means of acquiring land, mutilation as punishment, and the death penalty for misdemeanours were all features of life for most of human history, but today they are all but non-existent in the West and far less common elsewhere than they once were, and are widely condemned when they are known about.

We are also safer and healthier than ever and yet we are more worried about injury, disease and death. Why? In part it's because there are few opportunities to make money from convincing people that they are, in fact, safer and healthier than ever – but there are huge profits to be made by promoting fear.

We overestimate the likelihood of being killed by the things that make the evening news, and we underestimate those that don't. What makes the evening news? Murder, terrorism, fire, and flood. The particularly tragic death of a single child will be reported around the world, while a massive and continuing decline in child mortality rates is hardly noticed. Consideration of accurate and complete facts is not a central concern for those pumping out the messages. What matters is circulation, and if twisted numbers, misleading language and unreasonable conclusions can more effectively deliver better sales figures, so be it.

As the editor of *The Week* once noted, 'We all hate being frightened but love being scared. As long as it's imaginary (a thriller) or distant (a scary headline), we relish the threat of impending doom.'

The media are among those that profit by marketing fear – nothing gives a boost to circulation and ratings like a good panic, and the media also promote unreasonable fears for subtler and more compelling reasons. And they are not alone. Politicians promote fear to win elections. Police departments and militaries do it to expand budgets and obtain new powers. The opportunities for finding a fear, promoting it and leveraging it to increase sales are limited only by imagination.

Then there are the health-scare stories that sell newspapers like hot cakes and have sometimes caused mass panic. For example, the silicone breast implant scare involved countless tragic stories of sick women, who believed that their implants were to blame. Despite no medical proof that any or all implants were unsafe, thousands of women who had received implants lived in fear for years, thinking they would become sick. Eventually in the USA, the Food and Drug Administration Agency lifted a hastily imposed, media-driven ban on silicone breast implants, stating that although they could rupture and cause pain, there was no evidence that they posed a specific disease risk.

In the early years of the 1980s, reporting on AIDS was sparse, despite the steadily growing number of victims. That changed in July 1985 when the number of newspaper articles on AIDS published in the United States soared 500 per cent. The event that changed everything was Rock Hudson's announcement that he had AIDS, and his familiar face did what no statistic could do. 'The death of one man is a tragedy, the deaths of millions is a statistic,' said that expert on death, Joseph Stalin.

Horror headlines were everywhere and stress was laid on the fact that there was *no* treatment available. Get the virus and you were certain to die a lingering, wasting death. And there was a good chance that you would get it because a breakthrough into the heterosexual population was inevitable. 'AIDS has both sexes running scared,' Oprah Winfrey told her audience in 1987. 'Research studies now project that one in five heterosexuals could be dead from AIDS at the end of the next three years. That's by 1990. One in five.'

Surgeon General C. Everett Koop in the US called it 'the biggest threat to health this nation has ever faced'. A member of the President's commission on AIDS went one further, declaring the disease to be 'the greatest threat to society, as we know it, ever faced by civilisation – more serious than the plagues of past centuries.'

Like many other people, I believed that any contact at all with the blood of an HIV-carrier, which could mean virtually anyone, could very easily infect me. I thanked God that I'd had no extra-marital relations, did not inject myself with needles, nor had I received a transplant. I hoped that I would not need to visit any dentist and, when running marathons in the countryside, I took care to wear long leggings and a sleeved vest in case I brushed against a thorny bush that may have previously scratched another runner.

One night, driving home along an Exmoor road, I came across a car crash. There were four bodies and all appeared to be dead. Then one of them groaned. My immediate reaction was to cradle and comfort the person, clearly badly injured, and too late did I realise the ever-present theoretical danger of AIDS. The very next day I called the local doctor, but was assured that I had no need to worry.

Two years later the World Health Organization announced that HIV/AIDS was the fourth-biggest cause of death worldwide and the number-one killer in Africa. An estimated 33 million people were living with HIV and 14 million people had died from AIDS since the start of the epidemic.

The development of highly effective antiretroviral drugs represented a major turning point in the outlook of those who were infected, for they could now look forward to a good chance of living long and healthy lives.

As I write this in February 2016, the newspaper headlines include a new scare story, *Zika's Alarming Spread*, with a sub-heading of 'The Zika virus is spreading explosively across the Americas and could affect four million people by 2017, the WHO warned last week'.

The Zika-carrying mosquito, active in twenty-five countries in the Americas was, it was thought, likely to be infecting many more common varieties of mosquito, thus allowing Zika to spread globally.

My reaction to this Zika scare is very different to the dread that I remember feeling on first reading about AIDS. I do nowadays take most media fear-stirring headlines only at face value, which cuts out a great deal of unnecessary stress. But, back in the 1960s at the time I married Ginny I had read a number of media descriptions of difficult childbirths that scared me rigid, although Ginny never appeared worried at the prospect. One of the dismal statistics I remember well was that only sixty years ago fourteen per cent of all babies born in Britain died, mostly *at birth*. In fact, since 1970 birth-death rates have dropped everywhere, and in Germany by an astonishing three-quarters.

There were two reasons, according to the authors of my scaremongering articles, for the high rate of deaths of mothers and babies at birth. One was (and in developing countries still is, since 800 women there still die *every day* from childbirth or pregnancy problems) that we humans have developed such big heads. The downside of evolving ever bigger brains is the size of human babies' heads that jam in the mother's pelvis. So she feels danger and the amygdalan response wrongly makes her tense and starves her uterus, the main birth muscle, of power just when it most needs it, telling her body to 'freeze' and contract just when it should be relaxing.

A friend of mine in London, John Stewart, is a practising psychologist, who for the last sixteen years has been treating patients for mental stress. He listed for me, in order of occurrence, the main problems of his patients. They are:

Anxiety / Fear
Depression / Grief
Addiction / Abuse and Dependence
Eating Disorders
Trauma / Post-Traumatic Stress Disorder
Marriage and Relationship Counselling
Couples and Family Psychotherapy
Teenage Developmental Problems (16 years +)
Philosophical and Existential Emptiness

Within these general headings there are the odd individuals with immigrant-phobia, those scared stiff whenever their children are out of sight, some who hate their business colleagues but fear to lose their job security, along with others who detest their immediate family circle but love their home. And a great many other unusual hang-ups.

Not covered by descriptions of terror regimes, kidnappers, jihadists or nuclear dangers are those fears experienced by many millions of individuals from day to day, even in the most peaceful of settings with no impending war, sickness or poverty. This is the fear of things going (or gone) badly wrong with one's life.

Susan Jeffers, in her insightful book *The Feel the Fear Guide to Lasting Love*, stresses that dependency in a relationship creates some very unattractive side effects – anger, jealousy, resentment, clinging, nagging – all very unpleasant to live with. These self-defeating qualities are the result of a deep-seated fear of losing that which we see as the basis of our entire identity.

The family unit can, with luck, tolerance, compromise and, above all, *real love*, survive all manner of stresses, internal jealousies and strains, even a lack of communication due to no common interests or activities. But many fail when one partner's love dims and the result can too often end in bitterness, great depression and loneliness for one or both partners. Some men see their image based entirely on their success at their job, and should they ever find themselves dismissed for any reason, they feel utterly devastated, helpless and even suicidal. They are unable to fall back on their family's support as their whole life has been centred on work, promotional prospects and pay packets. There are women who have fallen into this trap, but there are far fewer of them.

When such individuals are forced to retire, many fall apart emotionally, as though their reason for living has gone. It is a medical fact that many men, healthy until retirement, soon become ill and die, deeply depressed and fearful of the dark, empty void they see as their future. There are women who similarly fall to pieces and succumb to deep mental depression when the last of their children leaves home for good.

Susan Jeffers sums it up in her bestselling book *Feel the Fear and Do It Anyway*:

> Fear seems to be epidemic in our society. We fear beginnings, we fear endings. We fear changing, we fear 'staying stuck'. We fear success, we fear failure. We fear living, we fear dying.

Jeffers advocates breathing and yoga-type exercises alongside specific, always optimistic, thought processes. In her audio book *The Art of Fearbusting*, her basic message is as follows:

> Until you fully understand that *you*, and no one else, create what goes on in your head, you will never be in control of your life. *You* are the cause of all your experiences of life, meaning that you are the cause of your *reactions* to everything that happens to you. If you can create your own misery, it stands to reason that you can also create your own joy . . . so . . . *constantly* fight that negative voice in your head. Do so repeatedly every day.

Many thousands of readers of Susan Jeffers' books swear that her advice has changed their previously fear-ridden lives for the better.

But nonetheless, with so many fears and with so many people living with depression, it is no wonder that a small percentage consider suicide, politely termed self-deliverance, as an easier option than an ongoing nightmare of pain, whether mental or physical.

In the USA with a population of 318 million, about 31,000 commit suicide every year. In the UK with a population of around 64 million, there is an average of 6,000 suicides annually. In developed 'wealthy' countries the main reasons for suicide are fear of illness, unemployment, financial pressures, loneliness, marriage troubles, mental health and, in middle-aged men, a loss of masculine pride.

In Japan, with its long Samurai tradition of 'honourable suicide', some 70 people commit suicide every day, of whom 71 per cent are male and their chief reason for killing themselves is depression. Their favourite self-killing ground is a deep forest near the foot of Mount Fuji, said to be second only to San Francisco's Golden Gate Bridge as a suicide location. Thirty thousand Japanese people commit suicide annually out of a total population of 127 million, which is well over double the US suicide rate.

Not included as suicides are the many cases of *passive euthanasia* or *pulling the plug*, where anybody can state in a legally prepared Advance Declaration or Living Will that, in the event that they become terminally ill, they do not wish to be kept alive by life-support equipment.

The science fiction writer, Isaac Asimov, opined, 'No decent human being would allow an animal to suffer without putting it out of its misery. It is only to human beings that human beings are so cruel as to allow them to live on in pain, in hopelessness, in living death, without moving a muscle to help them.'

And Betty Rollin, the author of *Last Wish*, wrote, 'Some people want to eke out every second of life – no matter how grim – and that is their right. But others do not. And that should be *their* right.'

When all is said and done, a great many individuals do live in fear of their future being unbearably disagreeable and without hope of relief. The only way out of that fear and of being able to avoid interminable years of living hell is, they believe, to opt out, preferably in some manner causing themselves and their families minimal distress.

Many of them, of course, may have made the wrong decision, but will never have a chance to change their mind through the wisdom of hindsight. For them the wise words of German Chancellor Angela Merkel, 'Fear has never been a good adviser, neither in our personal lives nor in society', will not be helpful.

A major reason for depression-linked suicides in Japan is the specific fear of being sacked and unable to find a new job. This is likely to worsen with the imminent rise of capable robots. Already in the USA there are algorithms that mark exam papers, computers that can manage share portfolios and fill out tax returns, wearable medical devices that do the basic jobs of health workers, and driverless cars and trucks that will soon render many taxi and lorry drivers obsolete.

At Singapore's Nanyang Technological University there is a receptionist named Nadine, utterly lifelike and pretty, who will greet you politely, make relevant small talk and, if she has met you before, remember your name. Robots like Nadine will soon be able to care for the elderly and do a great many routine office or factory jobs. Irrevocable change is just around the corner, and this will greatly increase the fearful results of unemployment, and not just in the suicide forests of Japan.

For many years, perhaps due to my Anglican beliefs from Sunday School as a child, I had a morbid fear of finding something horrible and hell-like at the moment of my death . . . Devils with red-hot pincers and *no* escape *ever.* My heart-attack experience thankfully left me with a decreased anxiety about this and about the whole mystery side of death. Nobody knows what happens to our soul or our 'self' when we die . . . Will there be some sort of unpleasant aftermath? Some sort of hellish pay-back for our bad behaviour? This uncertainty surely adds to our general fear of death.

But because I had been 'dead' for more than three days and nights during the period when the cardio team in Bristol had tried twelve times to start my heart ticking again, I concluded that my total lack of awareness whilst on their life-support machine would have remained, as it were, had all future attempts to make me 'tick' also failed. Therefore, my mental state in that three-day period had given me an insight, or at least a taste, of *real death*. Since the entire experience had merely involved a state of nothingness, during which I had seen no angels, devils or, indeed, anything other than *nothing*, I could safely assume that death, when it comes, will presumably be a carbon copy of such nothingness. Just like a good, dreamless sleep.

One of my worries is that of ageism. Am I, at seventy-plus, going to lose lectures to other, younger presenters? 'You are only as good as your last movie' is an old Hollywood saying, and my expeditions usually require a basic degree of physical fitness.

Back in 1995 I first experienced worries about fitness, and as a result I took on a trainer on a sponsorship basis. The resulting strains damaged my lower back, which was duly sorted out with deep injections of dextrose, glycerine and phenol solution into the ligaments on either side of my spine in the lower-back area.

Two years later I was manhauling in Alaska with a sixty-three-year-old Canadian, who I knew worked out daily in his gym and always kept himself fit. He neither smoked nor drank alcohol, but watching him floundering about in the snow set me thinking. I was, at fifty-three, some ten years younger than he was, and yet a mere eight hours of heavy manhauling in deep snow had rendered him exhausted. Soon, I felt, the ageing process would drag at me, and I too would gasp for breath, hold up colleagues and wonder whether it was time to learn to play golf or bridge. I glimpsed the future and did not like what I saw. A life without the prospect of any physical challenge would be no life at all.

Two decades on, such worries have, of course, increased, along with the slow deterioration of my physical abilities. These worries continued following my first heart attack in 2003, a six-hour prostate operation for cancer in 2007, and a diagnosis of pre-diabetes in 2013. Of these, the dread of resurgent cancer is a constant background threat, often well described as low-level fretting. Since one in four of us will die of this creeping killer, it is also a very common fear. One survivor of the disease wrote, 'It is a crab-like scavenger reaching its greedy tentacles into the life of the soul as well as the body. It destroys the will as it gnaws away the flesh.'

In the USA the Cancer Prevention Coalition in a 2007 press release printed up-to-date medical statistics that, 'Cancer strikes nearly one in every two men and more than one in every three women. It now impacts about 1.3 million Americans annually and kills 550,000.'

A cancer sufferer and friend with whom I recently corresponded, but who has asked to remain anonymous, wrote:

> Following the doctor's summary of my MRI scan, I felt a coldness that brought with it feelings of total and absolute isolation. For no matter how close my family and friends might be, I felt totally alone and lost . . . The fear I experienced was a deep-rooted dread of the unknown. For terror breeds in dark spaces, and central to the whole appalling business was my ever-increasing awareness of my own impotence and powerlessness in the face of the anonymous medical establishment, in whose hands I now was.
>
> As someone who had managed people all my life, I was now the one who was being 'managed'. I was fast losing control of everything – and all the everyday norms I had come to accept as second nature were up for grabs. For I had discovered that I wasn't invulnerable – something I had always considered myself to be. Yes, I had really felt that I would go on for ever – until experience changed my mind!
>
> Such things as cancer don't happen to people like me – or

> to those I love! Yes, that is the implicit belief under which most of us exist, and I was no exception. But it was overturned by a simple sentence from a man in a white coat! Overturned completely and utterly! My life, my hopes, my very identity – all vanished in seconds. And that is something that can only be understood by those who experience it – and believe me, it's not a pleasant place to be.
>
> My growing fear made me much more sensitive, too. For once the threat had been articulated, the word *cancer* came at me in ways I had never previously noticed. It sprang at me suddenly – out of the dark, and from every quarter. In newspapers, on the television, in conversations with friends who did not know my symptoms and who casually mentioned to me the name of someone we both knew who was dying in some appalling way; they would tell me the details with apparent heartfelt sincerity before moving on to relate their worries about immigration, their thoughts on a new film that they'd seen, or a new book they had just read . . .
>
> *Cancer* was everywhere – it was the last thing I thought about at night and the first thing to greet me with a cold chill when I woke – it was a constant presence at my side at almost every waking moment and it was persistent and insidious.
>
> Suicide does enter your mind – enters it not as something frightening, but as a positive alternative to what might be in store for you, as by taking that course of action one could at least be freed from the horrendous final stages of a truly terrible disease.

Cancer fears have led to many suicides, but other motives for a desperate desire to self-destruct include anxiety, which is the single largest mental-health problem in the USA. Drugs to treat anxiety are among the most widely used medicines in the world, with billions spent each year, and general anxieties haunt every human, irrespective of their background, intelligence quotient or success in life.

Two of post-war Europe's most intelligent and highly praised writers were Albert Camus and Jean-Paul Sartre. The latter stated that 'life is a useless passion, full of absurdity' and Camus wrote that 'men die and they are not happy', and that 'there is only one hell and it is on earth'. His punchline is blunt and undeniably clear. 'Life is without hope, and there is no sensible reason to believe that tomorrow or the day after will be any different from today. Therefore, live and try to die happy, or else the realisation of life's meaninglessness will compel you to suicide.'

Many people do not fear death *per se*, but the pain of a slow death that is beyond their control. Joanna Trollope, the bestselling novelist, said of the prospect of old age, and especially if she found herself in the early stages of dementia, 'I would absolutely hate to be a nuisance. Ideally I would be seen by a nice man with a pot of happy pills and a plastic bag to pop over my head.'

Then there are those, unlike Joanna, whose fears of tarnishing their posthumous reputation, turn down the option of suicide. In the words of Cyril Connolly, 'There are many who dare not kill themselves for fear of what the neighbours will say.'

Maybe we should all try yoga breathing exercises which, according to *Time* magazine in 2015, 'have been shown to help control blood pressure, improve heart rate, make arteries more flexible and activate the para-sympathetic nervous system which tamps down the body's fight-or-flight response to stress.'

Dr Andrew Weil, the founder of the Arizona Center for Integrative Medicine at the University of Arizona, believes that 'breath is the only function through which you can influence the involuntary nervous system.'

The Samaritans organisation has saved many lonely people from taking their own lives, as have many loving spouses. To live with someone that you love, so long as they love you back, is life-sustaining. People are hungry for love. There is nothing you can do to *make* somebody that you love return that love, but you make every effort because of the fear, above all, of rejection.

Nowadays divorce from a partner is common, but there are

also a great many individuals who only stay together through the fear of losing their children or their home. And there are those who would love to leave their job, but fear that they won't find another.

Then there are others who fear to spend money that they have stockpiled for 'a rainy day' that never comes, so they end up with lots of money in the bank, having lived an unnecessarily empty life.

Most people find their own little niche in life, a comfort zone in which they feel safe but from which, if they venture far, the exposure to fear may well begin, and many people are living lives that they don't want to live, just because they are imprisoned in safe comfort zones that they dare not exit for fear of failure, change, risk, ridicule, and so on. They dream of better jobs, happier relationships and fulfilment, but those goals are rarely attained, because lying ominously between fancy and fact is FEAR.

Pain, fear, exhaustion, boredom and low self-esteem will all gnaw away at our weaker links in order to make us quit and capitulate. Overcoming these elements will help to develop character, heighten self-esteem, and increase ability to respect fear but avoid panic.

Fear is a vital evolutionary legacy that helps us recognise threats. It is an emotion produced by the perception of present or impending danger. Fear girds our loins for rapid action in the face of an enemy and alerts us to perform well under stress. It helps us to fight, drive carefully, parachute safely, take exams, speak well to a critical audience, and keep a foothold when mountain climbing.

So we should most definitely say 'thank you' to our Creator for giving us fear, providing we *use* it rather than let it imprison us for, as Brendan Behan once said, 'Every man, through fear, mugs his aspirations a dozen times a day.'

To avoid this trap, I used to have two quotations on my desk when planning expeditions into known areas of lethal risk. One, by Ernest Hemingway, was, 'Cowardice, as distinguished from panic, is almost always simply a lack of ability to suspend the functioning of the imagination'. The other, by the poet John Milton, stated the warning that, 'Imagination can make a heaven out of hell or a hell out of heaven.'

Neither observation helped subdue my state of utter panic back in 2005 when suddenly attacked with cardiac pains near to the summit of Everest. But they did prove highly effective when, suffering as I did from phobic vertigo, I managed to scale the Eiger's 6,000-foot Murder Wall . . . constantly forcing myself to remember my guide's dictum, '*Never* look down and, more important, *never* allow yourself to THINK about what looking down would be like.'

Amazingly this worked which, given my extremely high degree of apprehension prior to the climb, convinced me of the truth of the age-old saying, 'It's all in the mind.'

Entire books have been written about ways of fighting fear, but my five decades of breaking world records through taking risks have convinced me that, with due respect to devotees of yoga, breathing and powerful drugs, successful control of your own mind gives you the best chance of winning the battle and even of achieving that most enviable of states . . . being a happy human being.

Appendix I

Excerpts from an Article on Fear by London Psychologist John Stewart

The reality is that we cannot survive without fear, as our evolution tells us. It is an integral part of our lives. As human beings we are very different from our animal cousins, yet still only five per cent up the evolutionary scale from chimpanzees! In a book by Robert Sapolsky, a distinguished neurobiologist, the author spells out clearly why we are so different. The title of his book is *Why Zebras don't get Ulcers*.

We experience fear-based episodes in our lives; zebras do more so as they are regularly chased by lions in the savannah, but their stamina usually allows them to outrun their predators. However, the zebras don't get ulcers! In other words, once the threat is over, they calmly revert to grazing and replacing the energy that was lost, as well as instinctively feeding themselves, not just because of hunger but to fuel themselves for future flights from predators.

We humans are very different. We respond as animals in either a flight, fight or freeze response, but differ after the incident. While zebras graze and chill out, we humans ruminate by thinking over and over what *might* have happened or what should have happened. Human beings are also very prone to assess what happened by thinking what they should or ought to have done, and they will check over and over how they could have avoided the situation. As a result they can start to obsess about the incident. Images and thoughts of fear can turn to shame, guilt, and horror about what *might* have happened. Fear of concrete incidents can morph into anxiety about non-existent incidents.

Zebras and all non-humans, except for some chimpanzee behaviour, do not have that capacity for self-reflection or rumination. Animals don't think as we know it, and they do not have the neuronal brain capacity to do so. The front part of our brains, the pre-frontal cortex, evolved further than that of animals like zebras, and we therefore assess in a cognitive (processing thoughts) way what could or should have happened. Sadly, though, this often leads to stress in our bodies and more serious and sometimes more fatal stress-related illnesses. Fear is our friend and saviour. Anxiety is not. Hence most psychiatrists, psychologists and psychotherapists have to treat anxiety disorders and not fear disorders.

By the beginning of the twentieth century, psychologists felt that the mind could only be studied through evidence of behaviour in controlled laboratory experiments. This was called Behaviourism and was begun by Pavlov. Behaviourists took no notice of the concept of the mind, such as thinking, feeling emotion and experiencing perception, for they saw the origins, explanation and insight into emotions, such as fear, as pointless. It took five new revolutions in psychology to understand fear more fully, and the theories came from psychoanalysis, evolutionary psychology, cognitive psychology, psychotherapy and neuroscience. These theories comprise a century and a half of psychological research and a lifetime of writing. It is important to touch briefly on some of these ideas in order to understand more fully the concept of fear.

Psychoanalysis was founded by Sigmund Freud in 1895, but some of his colleagues, such as Carl Gustav Jung and Alfred Adler, broke away to found their own schools of psychology, believing Freud to be too rigid and dogmatic. Freud's model was the first to highlight more about anxiety than fear. He talked of phobias in several case studies; usually his belief was that the fear of horses or other objects was the result of repressed sexual instincts from childhood. His theory was that childhood memories were repressed because they were sexually charged, and that the shame or guilt of these infantile feelings led to further repression, suppression, projection or displacement.

Fears are often 'displaced', and none are seen so widely and prevalently today as those associated with immigration and terrorism. We might look at a person in the street and immediately, in our cognitive attribution, think that they are members of a terrorist cell. Clearly this is absurd and neurotically irrational. But equally it is part of a frenzy of fear which leads to assumptions which, in turn, lead to 'catastrophisation'. We can be fearful of foreigners, and that fear leads to aggression. Equally, it can be converted into healthy displacement, such as love. Fear sublimated into love was evident during major events where fear was socially seeping under everyone's doors. Post 9/11 and *Charlie Hebdo*, and more recently after the appalling massacres in Paris, people from all walks of society were being altruistic, compassionate, generous, warm and non-judgemental. Love replaced fear.

The more hate increases, evolving not just to fear but to anger and to aggression, the more humankind engages in acts of war and terrorism. This is a dangerous game and one that seems to occur cyclically and repeatedly in the Middle East. The most common and most denied fear of all is that of death. Humans, unlike animals, know rationally that they are going to die. The problem that faces us is that we do not know *when* or *how* we are going to die. It is important, as existential therapists working from the texts and novels of Camus, Sartre, de Beauvoir and Heidegger will state, to be fully aware and accepting of the fear of death as normal and vital if we are to live freely.

If we can do that, then we can live fully in the here and now and accept our own mortality with grace and calm. Fear of death is a normal feeling. But terror and death anxiety is not and is deeply pathological, often blocking normalised relations with others and our natural creativity.

Appendix II

Comments on the Sensory Background to Fear as advised by John Stewart

Fear of two staring eyes is widespread throughout the animal kingdom. The more conspicuously eye-like the markings are, the more they deter.

When the context of a stare is neutral or ambiguous, it can be unsettling and provoke escape. In an experiment where a bystander either stared at drivers who stopped at a red light or gave them a quick glance of civil inattention, the drivers who had been stared at pulled away faster when the traffic light changed than those who had merely been glanced at.

In humans, hearing and vision are the dominant channels influencing the stream of behaviour. Human parents have an urge to rush to their baby's aid when it cries in fear or pain, and humans experience acute discomfort on hearing others screaming in agony or panic. The angry buzzing of bees instils panic in many people.

Contemporary research identifies the *amygdala* – two groups of nuclei located within the temporal lobes – as playing a critical role in the neurological process of fear. Below is a concise, simplified overview of the current understanding of the process:

- External auditory, visual, olfactory or somatosensory stimuli are relayed via the thalamus to the amygdala and cortex. There is an emotional intra-amygdala processing of the stimuli, which then activates the Hypothalamus, Lateral Hypothalamus, and Locus Coeruleus. Respectively, these areas are responsible for the release of dopamine, the regulation of respiration and blood pressure, and the release of noradrenaline (which increases heart rate).

- Through its processing, the amygdala also activates various mid-brain regions or nuclei that are responsible for different aspects of the fear–anxiety response: freezing or escape, increased respiratory rate, and startle response.
- Meanwhile, the prefrontal cortex processes more elaborate 'cognitive' information, and it modulates behavioural responses to the external stimuli via the amygdala. Like other emotions, fear is a package of reactions that tend to occur together simultaneously or sequentially. These include visible behavioural expression, an inner feeling, and accompanying physiological changes. In humans, as well as in animals, two obvious behavioural expressions of fear present a striking contrast. One is the tendency to freeze and become mute, which reaches its extreme form in death feigning. The opposite is to startle, scream and run away from the source of danger. Behaviour may shift rapidly from one pattern to the other when a frightened person first freezes and then suddenly scurries for shelter.

In moments of danger or confrontation the body releases chemicals from the adrenal gland that hit and go through the bloodstream like a speeding train, preparing the body for fight or flight, deeming it stronger, faster and partially, sometimes completely, anaesthetised to pain. The more demanding the situation, the bigger the build-up and adrenalin release, the better the performance (running or fighting). However, by the same count, the bigger the build-up and release, the harder it is to control.

Subsequently, because the adrenalin often lies unutilised in the body, it builds up like a pressure cooker and explodes into other aspects of our lives. This could be in the car as road rage, or in the home by shouting at your partner or children.

If the adrenalin is not pushed outward it often turns inward and becomes anxiety, a constant background shadow that can creep quite easily into depression. We become afraid of the feeling of fear, and the very act of feeling afraid triggers more adrenalin and more fear. You end up on a downward spiral of fear and adrenalin. This exhausts the mind and depression can be the result.

Appendix III

Phobias by Topic

Abuse: sexual – Contreltophobia.
Accidents – Dystychiphobia.
Air – Anemophobia.
Air swallowing – Aerophobia.
Airborne noxious substances – Aerophobia.
Airsickness – Aeronausiphobia.
Alcohol – Methyphobia or Potophobia.
Alone, being – Autophobia or Monophobia.
Alone, being or solitude – Isolophobia.
Amnesia – Amnesiphobia.
Anger – Angrophobia or Cholerophobia.
Angina – Anginophobia.
Animals – Zoophobia.
Animals, skins of or fur – Doraphobia.
Animals, wild – Agrizoophobia.
Ants – Myrmecophobia.
Anything new – Neophobia.
Asymmetrical things – Asymmetriphobia.
Atomic explosions – Atomosophobia.
Automobile, being in a moving – Ochophobia.
Automobiles – Motorphobia.

Bacteria – Bacteriophobia.
Bald people – Peladophobia.
Bald, becoming – Phalacrophobia.
Bathing – Ablutophobia.
Bats – Chiroptophobia.
Beards – Pogonophobia.
Beaten by a rod or instrument of punishment, or of being severely criticized – Rhabdophobia.
Beautiful women – Caligynephobia.
Beds or going to bed – Clinophobia.
Bees – Apiphobia or Melissophobia.
Belly buttons – Omphalophobia.

Bicycles – Cyclophobia.
Birds – Ornithophobia.
Black – Melanophobia.
Blindness in a visual field – Scotomaphobia.
Blood – Hemophobia, Hemaphobia or Hematophobia.
Blushing or the colour red – Erythrophobia, Erytophobia or Ereuthophobia.
Body odours – Osmophobia or Osphresiophobia.
Body, things to the left side of the body – Levophobia.
Body, things to the right side of the body – Dextrophobia.
Bogeyman or bogies – Bogyphobia.
Bolsheviks – Bolshephobia.
Books – Bibliophobia.
Bound or tied up – Merinthophobia.
Bowel movements: painful – Defecaloesiophobia.
Brain disease – Meningitophobia.
Bridges or of crossing them – Gephyrophobia.
Buildings: being close to high buildings – Batophobia.
Bullets – Ballistophobia.
Bulls – Taurophobia.
Burglars, or being harmed by wicked persons – Scelerophobia.
Buried alive, being or cemeteries – Taphephobia or Taphophobia.

Cancer – Cancerophobia, Carcinophobia.
Car or vehicle, riding in – Amaxophobia.
Cats – Aclurophobia, Ailurophobia, Elurophobia, Felinophobia, Galeophobia, or Gatophobia.
Celestial spaces – Astrophobia.
Cemeteries – Coimetrophobia.
Cemeteries or being buried alive – Taphephobia or Taphophobia.
Ceremonies, religious – Teleophobia.
Changes, making; moving – Tropophobia or Metathesiophobia.
Chickens – Alektorophobia.
Child, bearing a deformed; deformed people – Teratophobia.
Childbirth – Maleusiophobia, Tocophobia, Parturiphobia, or Lockiophobia.
Children – Pedophobia.
Chinese or Chinese culture – Sinophobia.
Chins – Geniophobia.
Choking or being smothered – Pnigophobia or Pnigerophobia.
Choking – Anginophobia.

Cholera – Cholerophobia.
Chopsticks – Consecotaleophobia.
Church – Ecclesiophobia.
Clocks – Chronomentrophobia.
Clocks or time – Chronophobia.
Clothing – Vestiphobia.
Clouds – Nephophobia.
Clowns – Coulrophobia.
Coitus – Coitophobia.
Cold or cold things – Frigophobia.
Cold: extreme, ice or frost – Cryophobia.
Cold – Cheimaphobia, Cheimatophobia, Psychrophobia or Psychropophobia.
Colour purple – Porphyrophobia.
Colour red or blushing – Erythrophobia, Erytophobia or Ereuthophobia.
Colour yellow – Xanthophobia.
Colour white – Leukophobia.
Colours – Chromophobia or Chromatophobia.
Comets – Cometophobia.
Computers or working on computers – Cyberphobia.
Confined spaces – Claustrophobia.
Constipation – Coprastasophobia.
Contamination, dirt or infection – Molysmophobia or Molysomophobia.
Contamination with dirt or germs – Misophobia or Mysophobia.
Cooking – Mageirocophobia.
Corpses – Necrophobia.
Cosmic Phenomenon – Kosmikophobia.
Creepy, crawly things – Herpetophobia.
Criticized severely, or beaten by rod or instrument of punishment – Rhabdophobia.
Criticism – Enissophobia.
Crosses or the crucifix – Staurophobia.
Crossing streets – Agyrophobia or Dromophobia.
Crowded public places like markets – Agoraphobia.
Crowds or mobs – Enochlophobia, Demophobia or Ochlophobia.
Crucifix, the or crosses – Staurophobia.
Crystals or glass – Crystallophobia.

Dampness, moisture or liquids – Hygrophobia.
Dancing – Chorophobia.
Dark or night – Nyctophobia.
Dark place, being in – Lygophobia.
Darkness – Achluophobia or Myctophobia, or Scotophobia.
Dawn or daylight – Eosophobia.
Daylight or sunshine – Phengophobia.
Death or dying – Thanatophobia.

Death or dead things – Necrophobia.
Decaying matter – Seplophobia.
Decisions: making decisions – Decidophobia.
Defeat – Kakorrhaphiophobia.
Deformed people or bearing a deformed child – Teratophobia.
Deformity or unattractive body image – Dysmorphophobia.
Demons – Demonophobia or Daemonophobia.
Dental surgery – Odontophobia.
Dentists – Dentophobia.
Dependence on others – Soteriophobia.
Depth – Bathophobia.
Diabetes – Diabetophobia.
Dining or dinner conversations – Deipnophobia.
Dirt, contamination or infection – Molysmophobia or Molysomophobia.
Dirt or germs, being contaminated with – Misophobia or mysophobia.
Dirt or filth – Rhypophobia or Rupophobia.
Dirty, being dirty or personal filth – Automysophobia.
Disease – Nosophobia, Nosemaphobia or Pathophobia.
Disease and suffering – Panthophobia.
Disease, a definite – Monopathophobia.
Disease, brain – Meningitophobia.
Disease: kidney – Albuminurophobia.
Disease, rectal – Rectophobia.
Disorder or untidiness – Ataxophobia.
Dizziness or vertigo when looking down – Illyngophobia.
Dizziness or whirlpools – Dinophobia.
Doctor, going to the – Iatrophobia.
Doctrine, challenges to or radical deviation from official – Heresyphobia or Hereiophobia.
Dogs or rabies – Cynophobia.
Dolls – Pediophobia.
Double vision – Diplophobia.
Draughts – Aerophobia or Anemophobia.
Dreams, wet – Oneirogmophobia.
Dreams – Oneirophobia.
Drinking – Dipsophobia.
Drugs, new – Neopharmaphobia.
Drugs or taking medicine – Pharmacophobia.
Dryness – Xerophobia.
Dust – Amathophobia or Koniophobia.
Dust – Amathophobia.
Duty or responsibility, neglecting – Paralipophobia.
Dying or death – Thanatophobia.

Eating or swallowing – Phagophobia.
Eating or food – Sitophobia or Sitiophobia.
Eating or swallowing or of being eaten – Phagophobia.
Eight, the number – Octophobia.
Electricity – Electrophobia.
Englishness – Anglophobia.
Erect penis – Medorthophobia.
Erection, losing an – Medomalacuphobia.
Everything – Panophobia, Panphobia, Pamphobia, or Pantophobia.
Eyes – Ommetaphobia or Ommatophobia.
Eyes, opening one's – Optophobia.

Fabrics, certain – Textophobia.
Failure – Atychiphobia or Kakorrhaphiophobia.
Fainting – Asthenophobia.
Fatigue – Kopophobia.
Fearful situations: being preferred by a phobic – Counterphobia.
Feathers or being tickled by feathers – Pteronophobia.
Faecal matter, faeces – Coprophobia or Scatophobia.
Female genitals – Kolpophobia.
Female genitalia – Eurotophobia.
Fever – Febriphobia, Fibriphobia, Fidriophobia or Pyrexiophobia.
Filth or dirt – Rhypophobia.
Fire – Arsonphobia or Pyrophobia.
Firearms – Hoplophobia.
Fish – Ichthyophobia.
Flashes – Selaphobia.
Flogging or punishment – Mastigophobia.
Floods – Antlophobia.
Flowers – Anthrophobia or Anthophobia.
Flutes – Aulophobia.
Flying – Aviophobia or Aviatophobia or Pteromerhanophobia.
Fog – Homichlophobia or Nebulaphobia.
Food or eating – Sitophobia or Sitiophobia.
Food – Cibophobia.
Foreigners or strangers – Xenophobia.
Foreign languages – Xenoglossophobia.
Forests or wooden objects – Xylophobia.
Forests – Hylophobia.
Forests, dark wooded area, of at night – Nyctohylophobia
Forgetting or being forgotten – Athazagoraphobia.
France or French culture – Francophobia, Gallophobia or Galiphobia.
Freedom – Eleutherophobia.
Friday the 13th – Paraskavedekatriaphobia.

Frogs – Batrachophobia.

Frost, ice or extreme cold – Cryophobia.

Frost or ice – Pagophobia.

Functioning or work: surgeon's fear of operating – Ergasiophobia.

Fur or skins of animals – Doraphobia.

Gaiety – Cherophobia.

Garlic – Alliumphobia.

Genitals, particularly female – Kolpophobia.

Genitalia, female – Eurotophobia.

Germans or German culture – Germanophobia or Teutophobia.

Germs or dirt, being contaminated with – Misophobia or mysophobia.

Germs – Verminophobia.

Ghosts or spectres – Spectrophobia.

Ghosts – Phasmophobia.

Girls, young or virgins – Parthenophobia.

Glass or crystals – Crystallophobia.

Glass – Hyelophobia, Hyalophobia or Nelophobia.

Gloomy place, being in – Lygophobia.

God or gods – Zeusophobia.

Gods or religion – Theophobia.

Gold – Aurophobia.

Good news, hearing good news – Euphobia.

Gravity – Barophobia.

Greek or Greek culture – Hellophobia.

Greek terms – Hellenologophobia.

Hair – Chaetophobia, Trichopathophobia, Trichophobia, or Hypertrichophobia.

Halloween – Samhainophobia.

Hands – Chirophobia.

Handwriting – Graphophobia.

Harmed by wicked persons; bad men or burglars – Scelerophobia.

Heart – Cardiophobia.

Heat – Thermophobia.

Heaven – Ouranophobia or Uranophobia.

Heights – Acrophobia, Altophobia, Batophobia, Hypsiphobia or Hyposophobia.

Hell – Hadephobia, Stygiophobia or Stigiophobia.

Heredity – Patroiophobia.

Hoarding – Disposophobia.

Holy things – Hagiophobia.

Home – Ecophobia.

Home surroundings or a house – Oikophobia.

Home, returning – Nostophobia.

Home surroundings – Eicophobia.

Homosexuality or of becoming homosexual – Homophobia.

Horses – Equinophobia or Hippophobia.
Hospitals – Nosocomephobia.
House or home surroundings – Oikophobia.
Houses or being in a house – Domatophobia.
Hurricanes and tornadoes – Lilapsophobia.
Hypnotized, being or of sleep – Hypnophobia.

Ice or frost – Pagophobia.
Ice, frost or extreme cold – Cryophobia.
Ideas – Ideophobia.
Ignored, being – Athazagoraphobia.
Imperfection – Atelophobia.
Inability to stand – Basiphobia or Basophobia.
Infection, contamination or dirt – Molysmophobia or Molysomophobia.
Infinity – Apeirophobia.
Injections – Trypanophobia.
Injury – Traumatophobia.
Insanity, dealing with – Lyssophobia.
Insanity – Dementophobia or Maniaphobia.
Insects – Acarophobia or Entomophobia or Insectophobia.
Insects that eat wood – Isopterophobia.
Insects that cause itching – Acarophobia.
Itching – Acarophobia.

Japanese or Japanese culture – Japanophobia.
Jealousy – Zelophobia.
Jews – Judeophobia.
Joint immobility – Ankylophobia.
Jumping from high and low places – Catapedaphobia.
Justice – Dikephobia.

Kidney disease – Albuminurophobia.
Kissing – Philemaphobia or Philematophobia.
Knees – Genuphobia.
Knowledge – Gnosiophobia or Epistemophobia.

Lakes – Limnophobia.
Large things – Megalophobia.
Laughter – Geliophobia.
Lawsuits – Liticaphobia.
Learning – Sophophobia.
Left-handed; objects at the left side of the body – Sinistrophobia.
Leprosy – Leprophobia or Lepraphobia.
Lice – Pediculophobia or Phthiriophobia.
Light – Photophobia.
Light flashes – Selaphobia.

Lightning and thunder – Brontophobia or Karaunophobia.
Lights, glaring – Photoaugliaphobia.
Liquids, dampness or moisture – Hygrophobia.
Locked in an enclosed place – Cleithrophobia, Cleisiophobia, or Clithrophobia.
Lockjaw or tetanus – Tetanophobia.
Loneliness or of being oneself – Eremophobia or Eremiphobia.
Looking up – Anablephobia or Anablepophobia.
Loud noises – Ligyrophobia.
Love, sexual love – Erotophobia.
Love play – Malaxophobia or Sarmassophobia.
Love, falling or being in – Philophobia.

Machines – Mechanophobia.
Mad, becoming – Lyssophobia.
Many things – Polyphobia.
Marriage – Gamophobia.
Materialism – Hylephobia.
Matter, decaying – Seplophobia.
Meat – Carnophobia.
Medicine, taking; or drugs – Pharmacophobia.
Medicines, mercurial – Hydrargyophobia.
Medicine, prescribing by a doctor – Opiophobia.
Memories – Mnemophobia.
Men, bad or burglars or being harmed by wicked persons – Scelerophobia.
Men – Androphobia or Arrhenphobia or Hominophobia.
Menstruation – Menophobia.
Mercurial medicines – Hydrargyophobia.
Metal – Metallophobia.
Meteors – Meteorophobia.
Mice – Musophobia, Murophobia or Suriphobia.
Microbes – Bacillophobia or Microbiophobia.
Mind – Psychophobia.
Mirrors or seeing oneself in a mirror – Eisoptrophobia.
Mirrors – Catoptrophobia.
Missiles – Ballistophobia.
Mobs or crowds – Demophobia, Enochlophobia or Ochlophobia.
Moisture, dampness or liquids – Hygrophobia.
Money – Chrometophobia or Chrematophobia.
Moon – Selenophobia.
Mother-in-law – Pentheraphobia.
Moths – Mottephobia.
Motion or movement – Kinetophobia or Kinesophobia.
Moving or making changes – Tropophobia.

Moving automobile or vehicle, being in – Ochophobia.
Muscular incoordination (Ataxia) – Ataxiophobia.
Mushrooms – Mycophobia.
Music – Melophobia.
Myths or stories or false statements – Mythophobia.

Names or hearing a certain name – Onomatophobia.
Names – Nomatophobia.
Narrow things or places – Stenophobia.
Narrowness – Anginophobia.
Needles – Aichmophobia or Belonephobia.
New, anything or novel – Kainophobia, Kainolophobia, Cenophobia, Centophobia, or Neophobia.
Newness – Cainophobia, Cenophobia, Centophobia, or Cainotophobia.
News: hearing good news – Euphobia.
Night or dark – Nyctophobia.
Night – Noctiphobia.
Noise – Acousticophobia.
Noises, loud – Ligyrophobia.
Noises or voices, speaking aloud, or telephones – Phonophobia.
Northern lights – Auroraphobia.
Nosebleeds – Epistaxiophobia.
Novelty or anything new – Kainophobia or Kainolophobia.
Novelty – Cainophobia or Cainotophobia.
Nuclear weapons – Nucleomituphobia.
Nudity – Gymnophobia or Nudophobia.
Number 8 – Octophobia.
Number 13 – Triskadekaphobia.
Numbers – Arithmophobia or Numerophobia.

Objects, small – Tapinophobia.
Ocean or sea – Thalassophobia.
Odour, personal – Bromidrosiphobia, Bromidrophobia, Osmophobia or Osphresiophobia.
Odour, that one has a vile odour – Autodysomophobia.
Odours or smells – Olfactophobia.
Official doctrine, challenges to or radical deviation from – Heresyphobia or Hereiophobia.
Old people – Gerontophobia.
Old, growing – Gerascophobia or Gerontophobia.
Open spaces – Agoraphobia.
Open high places – Aeroacrophobia.
Operation, surgical – Tomophobia.
Opinions – Allodoxaphobia.
Opinions, expressing – Doxophobia.

Others, dependence on – Soteriophobia.
Otters – Lutraphobia.
Outer space – Spacephobia.

Pain – Algiophobia, Ponophobia, Odynophobia or Odynephobia.
Paper – Papyrophobia.
Parasites – Parasitophobia.
Parents-in-law – Soceraphobia.
Peanut butter sticking to the roof of the mouth – Arachibutyrophobia.
Pellagra – Pellagrophobia.
Penis, erect – Medorthophobia.
Penis, esp. erect – Phallophobia.
Penis, erect: seeing, thinking about or having – Ithyphallophobia.
Penis, losing an erection – Medomalacuphobia.
People – Anthropophobia.
People in general or society – Sociophobia.
People, deformed or bearing a deformed child – Teratophobia.
Philosophy – Philsosphobia.
Phobias – Phobophobia.
Phobic preferring fearful situations – Counterphobia.
Pins and needles – Belonephobia.
Pins – Enetophobia.
Place: locked in an enclosed place – Cleithrophobia, Cleisiophobia, or Clithrophobia.
Place, being in a dark or gloomy – Lygophobia.
Places, certain – Topophobia.
Places, crowded public – Agoraphobia.
Places, open high – Aeroacrophobia.
Places or things, narrow – Stenophobia.
Plants – Botanophobia.
Pleasure, feeling – Hedonophobia.
Poetry – Metrophobia.
Pointed objects – Aichmophobia.
Poison – Iophobia.
Poisoned, being – Toxiphobia, Toxophobia, or Toxicophobia.
Poliomyelitis, contracting – Poliosophobia.
Politicians – Politicophobia.
Pope – Papaphobia.
Poverty – Peniaphobia.
Praise, receiving – doxophobia.
Precipices – Cremnophobia.
Prescribing medicine for patients by a doctor – Opiophobia.
Priests or sacred things – Hierophobia.
Progress – Prosophobia.
Property – Orthophobia.
Prostitutes or venereal disease – Cypridophobia, Cypriphobia, Cyprianophobia, or Cyprinophobia.

Punishment or flogging – Mastigophobia.
Punishment by a rod or other instrument, or of being severely criticised – Rhabdophobia.
Punishment – Poinephobia.
Puppets – Pupaphobia.
Purple, colour – Porphyrophobia.

Rabies – Cynophobia, Hydrophobophobia, Hydrophobia, Kynophobia, or Lyssophobia.
Radiation or X-rays – Radiophobia.
Railroads or train travel – Siderodromophobia.
Rain – Ombrophobia or Pluviophobia.
Rape – Virginitiphobia.
Razors – Xyrophobia.
Rat, great mole – Zemmiphobia.
Rectum or rectal diseases – Proctophobia or Rectophobia.
Red colour or blushing – Erythrophobia, Erytophobia or Ereuthophobia.
Relatives – Syngenesophobia.
Religion or gods – Theophobia.
Religious ceremonies – Teleophobia.
Reptiles – Herpetophobia.
Responsibility or duty, neglecting – Paralipophobia.
Responsibility – Hypengyophobia or Hypegiaphobia.
Ridiculed, being – Catagelophobia or Katagelophobia.
Riding in a car – Amaxophobia.
Right side, things on the right side of the body – Dextrophobia.
Rivers – Potamphobia or Potamophobia.
Road travel or travel – Hodophobia.
Robbers or being robbed – Harpaxophobia.
Rooms, empty – Cenophobia or Centophobia.
Rooms – Koinoniphobia.
Ruin – Atephobia.
Running water – Potamophobia.
Russians – Russophobia.

Sacred things or priests – Hierophobia.
Satan – Satanophobia.
Scabies – Scabiophobia.
School, going to school – Didaskaleinophobia.
School – Scolionophobia.
Scientific terminology, complex – Hellenologophobia.
Scratches or being scratched – Amychophobia.
Sea or ocean – Thalassophobia.
Self, seeing oneself in a mirror – Eisoptrophobia.

Self, personal odour – Bromidrosiphobia or Bromidrophobia.
Self, being alone – Autophobia, Eremophobia, Eremiphobia or Isolophobia.
Self, being dirty – Automysophobia.
Self, being oneself – Autophobia.
Self, being seen or looked at – Scopophobia or Scoptophobia.
Self, being touched – Aphenphosmphobia.
Self, that one has a vile odour – Autodysomophobia.
Semen – Spermatophobia or Spermophobia.
Sermons – Homilophobia.
Sex – Genophobia.
Sex, opposite – Heterophobia or Sexophobia.
Sexual abuse – Agraphobia or Contreltophobia.
Sexual intercourse – Coitophobia.
Sexual love or sexual questions – Erotophobia.
Sexual perversion – Paraphobia.
Shadows – Sciophobia or Sciaphobia.
Sharks – Selachophobia.
Shellfish – Ostraconophobia.
Shock – Hormephobia.
Sin or of having committted an unpardonable sin – Enosiophobia or Enissophobia.
Sin – Hamartophobia.
Single: staying single – Anuptaphobia.
Sinning – Peccatophobia.
Sitting down – Kathisophobia.
Sitting – Cathisophobia or Thaasophobia.
Situations, certain – Topophobia.
Skin disease – Dermatosiophobia.
Skin lesions – Dermatophobia.
Skin of animals, fur – Doraphobia.
Sleep – Somniphobia.
Sleep or being hypnotised – Hypnophobia.
Slime – Blennophobia or Myxophobia.
Slopes, steep – Bathmophobia.
Small things – Microphobia, Mycrophobia.
Smells or odours – Olfactophobia.
Smothered, being or choking – Pnigophobia or Pnigerophobia.
Snakes – Ophidiophobia or Snakephobia.
Snow – Chionophobia.
Social (fear of being evaluated negatively in social situations) – Social Phobia.
Society or people in general – Anthropophobia or Sociophobia.
Solitude – Monophobia.
Sounds – Acousticophobia.
Sourness – Acerophobia.

Space, closed or locked in an enclosed space – Cleithrophobia, Cleisiophobia, Clithrophobia.
Space, outer – Spacephobia.
Spaces, confined – Claustrophobia.
Spaces, empty – Cenophobia, Centophobia or Kenophobia.
Spaces, open – Agoraphobia.
Speak, trying to – Glossophobia.
Speaking – Laliophobia or Lalophobia.
Speaking aloud, voices or noises, or telephones – Phonophobia.
Speaking in public – Glossophobia.
Spectres or ghosts – Spectrophobia.
Speed – Tachophobia.
Spiders – Arachnephobia or Arachnophobia.
Spirits – Pneumatiphobia.
Stage fright – Topophobia.
Stairs or climbing stairs – Climacophobia.
Stairways – Bathmophobia.
Stand, inability to – Basiphobia or Basophobia.
Standing upright – Basistasiphobia or Basostasophobia.
Standing up – Stasiphobia.
Standing up and walking – Stasibasiphobia.
Stared at, being – Ophthalmophobia.
Stars – Siderophobia or Astrophobia.
Statements, false or myths or stories – Mythophobia.
Staying single – Anuptaphobia.
Stealing – Cleptophobia or Kleptophobia.
Step-father – Vitricophobia.
Steep slopes – Bathmophobia.
Step-mother – Novercaphobia.
Stings – Cnidophobia.
Stooping – Kyphophobia.
Stories or myths or false statements – Mythophobia.
Strangers or foreigners – Xenophobia.
Streets, crossing streets – Dromophobia.
Streets – Agyrophobia.
String – Linonophobia.
Storm, thunder – Brontophobia.
Stuttering – Psellismophobia.
Suffering and disease – Panthophobia.
Sun or sunlight – Heliophobia.
Sunshine or daylight – Phengophobia.
Surgeon's fear of operating: work or functioning – Ergasiophobia.
Surgical operations – Tomophobia.
Swallowing or eating – Phagophobia.
Symbolism – Symbolophobia.
Symmetry – Symmetrophobia.

Syphilis (lues) – Luiphobia or Syphilophobia

Tapeworms – Taeniophobia.

Taste – Geumaphobia or Geumophobia.

Technology – Technophobia.

Teenagers – Ephebiphobia.

Teeth – Odontophobia.

Telephones, noises or voices, or speaking aloud – Phonophobia.

Telephones – Telephonophobia.

Termites – Isopterophobia.

Tests, taking – Testophobia.

Tetanus or lockjaw – Tetanophobia.

Theatres – Theatrophobia.

Theology – Theologicophobia.

Things, many – Polyphobia.

Things, large – Megalophobia.

Things or places, narrow – Stenophobia.

Things, small – Microphobia or Mycrophobia.

Thinking – Phronemophobia.

Thunder – Ceraunophobia.

Thunder and lightning – Astraphobia, Astrapophobia, Brontophobia or Keraunophobia.

Tickled by feathers or feathers – Pteronophobia.

Tied or bound up – Merinthophobia.

Time or clocks – Chronophobia.

Toads – Bufonophobia.

Tombstones – Placophobia.

Tornadoes and hurricanes – Lilapsophobia.

Touched, being touched – Aphenphosmphobia, Haphephobia or Haptephobia or Chiraptophobia.

Trains, railroads or train travel – Siderodromophobia.

Tramps or beggars – Hobophobia.

Travel or road travel – Hodophobia.

Trees – Dendrophobia.

Trembling – Ttremophobia.

Trichinosis – Trichinophobia.

Tuberculosis – Phthisiophobia or Tuberculophobia.

Tyrants – Tyrannophobia.

Ugliness – Cacophobia.

Undressing in front of someone – Dishabillophobia.

Urine or urinating – Urophobia.

Vaccination – Vaccinophobia.

Vegetables – Lachanophobia.

Venereal disease or prostitutes – Cypridophobia, Cypriphobia, Cyprianophobia, or Cyprinophobia.

Ventriloquist's dummy – Automatonophobia.

Vertigo or dizziness when looking down – Illyngophobia.

Virginity, losing one's – Primeisodophobia.

Virgins or young girls – Parthenophobia.
Vision: double vision – Diplophobia.
Voices or noises, speaking aloud or telephones – Phonophobia.
Voids or empty spaces – Kenophobia.
Vomiting secondary to airsickness – Aeronausiphobia.
Vomiting – Emetophobia.

Waits, long – Macrophobia.
Walking, standing up and – Stasibasiphobia.
Walking – Ambulophobia, Basistasiphobia or Basostasophobia.
Washing – Ablutophobia.
Wasps – Spheksophobia.
Water – Hydrophobia.
Waves or wave-like motions – Cymophobia or Kymophobia.
Wax statues – Automatonophobia.
Weakness – Asthenophobia.
Wealth – Plutophobia.
Weapons, nuclear – Nucleomituphobia.
Weight, gaining – Obesophobia or Pocrescophobia.
Wet dreams – Oneirogmophobia.
Whirlpools or dizziness – Dinophobia.
White, the colour – Leukophobia.
Wild animals – Agrizoophobia.
Wind – Ancraophobia or Anemophobia.
Wine – Oenophobia.
Witches and Witchcraft – Wiccaphobia.
Women – Gynephobia or Gynophobia.
Women, beautiful – Caligynephobia or Venstraphobia.
Wooden objects or forests – Xylophobia.
Words – Logophobia or Verbophobia.
Words, long – Hippopotomonstrose-squipedaliophobia or Sesquipedalophobia.
Work or functioning; surgeon's fear of operating – Ergasiophobia.
Work – Ergophobia or Ponophobia.
Worms – Scoleciphobia.
Worms, being infested with – Helminthophobia.
Wrinkles, getting – Rhytiphobia.
Writing – Graphophobia.
Writing in public – Scriptophobia.

X-rays or radiation – Radiophobia.

Yellow colour – Xanthophobia.

Acknowledgements

I am extremely grateful to my family, Louise, Elizabeth and Alexander, for their patience during my months of work on this book. Also to Jill Firman for her diligence (and unique ability to decipher my handwriting), and for the ongoing support of Rupert Lancaster and his great team at Hodder & Stoughton, and to my good friend, adviser and literary agent, Ed Victor.

A great many individuals, some of whom have asked me not to reveal their name, have told me about their memories of fearful times, and for these I am very grateful. They include Sudesh Dahad, Caroline Fiennes (widow of James Fiennes), Caroline Fiennes (widow of Mark Fiennes), Paul and Sally Martin, Sarah Outen, John Peters, and Will Pooley. There are others who have helped in the gathering of information which has enabled me to write this book, and they include Michael Fox, Anna Kiernan, John Muir, Nicola Robey, Andrew Sewell, Dr Richard Sherry, Sandy Skilton, Keith Spiers, Dr John Stewart, John Tulloch, and Ralf Webb.

Picture Acknowledgements

Author's Collection: 1 below left, 4, 5 above, 7, 9 above and below right, 10 below. © Alamy: 3 above/Jenny Matthews, 3 below/Lee Karen Stow, 5 below/Royal Geographical Society, 6 above/Chris Howes/Wild Places Photography, 9 below left/Rick & Nora Bowers, 14 above right/ World History Archive, 15 below/Paul Doyle, 16 above/Anders Ryman. © AP/Press Association Images: 8 above, 8 below/Kerry Berrington. © Gary Caskey/Reuters: 11 below right. © Getty Images: 2 above/Bojan Brecelj, 2 below/Bettmann, 6 below/Karen Kasmauski/National Geographic, 10 above/Sobrevivientes de los Andes/CON, 11 above/Universal Images, 14 above left/Laski Diffusion, 14 below left/Pascal Guyot/AFP, 15 above/ Miguel Tovar/STF, 16 below/Joshua Lim/Orlando Sentinel/TNS. © Francois Guillot/AFP/ Getty Images: 1 above/ *Visage du Grand Masturbateur* 1929 by Salvador Dali, retrospective exhibition at the Centre Georges Pompidou Paris 2012-13, on loan from Museo Nacional Centro de Arte Reina Sofia Collection, Madrid. © Interfoto/Sammlung Rauch/ Mary Evans Picture Library:14 below right. © Ian Parnell: 13. © Marek R. Swadzba/Shutterstock.com: 1 centre left.© Stephen Venables: 12.

Bibliography

Birmingham, Lucy and McNeill, David, *Strong In the Rain: Surviving Japan's Earthquake, Tsunami and Fukushima Nuclear Disaster.* (New York, Palgrave Macmillan, 2012)

Brown, Brené, *Rising Strong.* (London, Vermilion, 2015)

Bullimore, Tony, *Saved*. (New York, Time Warner, 1998)

Carlo, Philip, *The Butcher: Anatomy of a Mafia Psycopath.* (Edinburgh, Mainstream Publishing, 2012)

Connolly, Cyril, *The Unquiet Grave.* (New York, Persea Books, 1981)

Davies, Nick, *Dark Heart*. (New York, Random House, 1997)

Figes, Orlando, *Crimea: The Last Crusade.* (London, Allen Lane, 2010)

Grant, Michael, *Fear.* (London, Electric Monkey, 2015)

Harkin, James, *Hunting Season: The Execution of James Foley, Islamic State and the Real Story of the Kidnapping Campaign that Started a War.* (London, Abacus, 2016)

Hayes, Sophie, *Trafficked*. (London, HarperCollins, 2012)

Hazell, Alastair, *The Last Slave Market*. (London, Constable, 2012)

Hillyard, Paul, *The Book of the Spider.* (New York, Random House, 1994)

Hillyard, Paul, *Book of the Spider: from Arachnophobia to the Love of Spiders.* (London, Hutchinson, 1994)

Humphrey, Derek, *Final Exit: The Practicalities of Self-Deliverance and Assisted Suicide for the Dying.* (New York, Dell, 1992)

Hunter, Gaz, *The Shooting Gallery.* (London, Orion, 1999)

Jeffers, Susan, *Feel the Fear ... and Beyond: The Essential Companion to the Worldwide Bestseller Feel the Fear and Do it Anyway.* (London, Vermilion, 2000)

Jeffers, Susan, *Feel the Fear and Do it Anyway: How to Turn Your Fear and Indecision into Confidence and Action.* (London, Vermilion, 2007)

Johnson, Douglas, *The Root Causes of Sudan's Civil Wars.* (Suffolk, James Currey, 2012)

Junger, Sebastian, *War.* (London, Fourth Estate, 2011)

Lockwood, Jeffrey, *The Infested Mind: Why Humans Fear, Loathe and Love Insects.* (New York, OUP USA, 2013)

Macfarlane, Robert, *Mountains of the Mind: A History of a Fascination.* (London, Granta, 2008)

Marlantes, Karl, *What It Is Like To Go To War.* (New York, Atlantic Monthly Press, 2011)

Peters, John and Nichol, John, *Tornado Down.* (London, Michael Joseph Ltd, 1992)

Pran, Dith, *Children of Cambodia's Killing Fields, Memoirs by Survivors.* (Connecticut, Yale University Press, 1997)

Rhodes, James, *Instrumental.* (London, Canongate books, 2015)

Russell, Alan, *Dresden: A City Reborn.* (London, Bloomsbury, 2013)

Simpson, Joe, *This Game of Ghosts.* (London, Jonathan Cape, 1993)

Smith, Alistair, *Carnage: The German Front in World War One (Images of War)*. (London, Pen & Sword Military, 2012)

Thomas, M.E., *Confessions of a Sociopath: A Life Spent Hiding in Plain Sight*. (London, Pan, 2014)

Van Emden, Richard, *The Somme: the Epic Battle in the Soldiers' Own words and Photographs*. (London, Pen & Sword Military, 2016)

Yogis, Jaimal, *The Fear Project: What Our Most Primal Emotion Taught Me about Survival, Success, Surfing... and Love*. (Pennsylvania, Rodale Books, 2013)

Index

Index

An invitation from the publisher

Join us at www.hodder.co.uk, or follow us on Twitter @hodderbooks to be a part of our community of people who love the very best in books and reading.

Whether you want to discover more about a book or an author, watch trailers and interviews, have the chance to win early limited editions, or simply browse our expert readers' selection of the very best books, we think you'll find what you're looking for.

And if you don't, that's the place to tell us what's missing.

We love what we do, and we'd love you to be a part of it.

www.hodder.co.uk

@hodderbooks

HodderBooks

HodderBooks